The Methodological Heritage of Newton

The
Methodological
Heritage of
NEWTON

Edited by
ROBERT E. BUTTS
JOHN W. DAVIS

University of Toronto Press

Copyright Canada 1970 by
University of Toronto Press
SBN 8020 1597 2

Published in Great Britain by
Basil Blackwell, Oxford
SBN 631 12200 1

Printed in Great Britain by
Western Printing Services Limited, Bristol

To N. R. Hanson
1924–1967

GIFTED ADVENTURER IN IDEAS AND IN LIFE

Acknowledgments

The editors, and the Department of Philosophy of which they are members, owe many debts incurred in the preparation of this volume. Professor John W. Davis conceived the original idea of the conference that provided the basis for the present volume. An idea needs substance. This came in the form of enthusiastic endorsement of the project by Dr. John Rowe, in 1966–67 Dean of Talbot College in the University of Western Ontario. Through him the department secured the funds necessary for a successful meeting. How can he be thanked? We realize that there is no way, and so does he. The grant-in-aid of publication of this volume came from the University of Western Ontario Committee on Publication in the Humanities and Social Sciences, and we here acknowledge this grant with thanks. The editors also thank Dr. Rowe for generous grants from the Talbot College research budget. Without this support the present volume could not have been readied for publication in any form.

The editors also owe much to friends and colleagues. The list cannot be complete, but among those who contributed in important ways to the project the following must be mentioned: Colin Burnett, who helped in tracking down references; Mrs. Pauline Campbell, Mrs. O. M. Hitchins, and Miss Judy Walsh, who expertly prepared the typescript; Professors F. E. L. Priestley and Edward Madden, who read and commented on the papers in this volume written by the editors; Professors W. K. Wilson, D. J. Hockney, and C. D. Rollins, who acted as silent co-editors with respect to some papers; Gerd Buchdahl, whose timely arrival as Visiting Professor of Philosophy in 1966–67 actually set the stage for a colloquium on Newton.

London, Canada   R.E.B.

March 1968   J.W.D.

Contents

The Methodological Heritage of Newton

I
Introduction

ROBERT E. BUTTS and JOHN W. DAVIS

A colloquium entitled "The Methodological Heritage of Newton" was held on 31 March and 1 April 1967, at the University of Western Ontario. The papers by Hanson, Priestley, and Buchdahl were delivered at the colloquium. The authors have revised the texts as they wish them to appear here.

The session on Buchdahl's paper was chaired by Professor Lewis W. Beck of the University of Rochester; the session on Priestley's paper by Professor Nicholas Rescher of the University of Pittsburgh; and the session on Hanson's paper by Professor E. H. Madden of State University of New York at Buffalo.

Because of the untimely death of Professor Hanson a few short weeks after the colloquium, the editors must take responsibility for the text of his paper as it appears. The paper is an outgrowth of an earlier paper delivered at the Boston Colloquium for the Philosophy of Science, so that by the time it was delivered at the University of Western Ontario it had reached a more or less final version. The revisions made are editorial only, having to do with the formal aspects of the paper.

A paper by P. K. Feyerabend was scheduled for presentation at the colloquium but the author's illness prevented its delivery. The paper here printed is a later version of the paper that was to be given. The other papers by Butts, Davis, and Laudan were especially prepared for this volume.

The purpose of this Introduction is to provide a summary of the papers, to make some suggestions about contexts which may prove helpful in reading the papers, and tentatively to suggest some of the relationships that may be found among the papers. It was a consensus of those at the colloquium that the papers of which this volume is an outgrowth had an unusual degree of unity. In the course of the discussion that occurred after the papers, both formally and informally, many of the same themes were struck.

The title of the colloquium was retained as the title of this volume because it seemed to the editors to be an apt rubric under which to group the seven parts. "Methodological Heritage" may seem unnecessarily narrow, especially since a number of the papers discuss more wide-ranging philosophical issues. Methodology, for most philosophers, is an enterprise that is not totally absorbed in giving *ex post facto* form to what might be taken as the steps actually followed by a given scientist in producing his theories or in making his experimental tests. There is methodology as the general attempt to formulate rules of scientific method (either rules of confirmation or of discovery), and there is methodology as the general philosophy of science (including concern for rules of confirmation, and the like). Only the papers by Laudan on Reid and by Butts on Whewell deal with methodology in the former sense – and that only sparingly. The other papers deal with those larger questions that touch upon all aspects of the conceptual background – historical, philosophical, and narrowly methodological – that developed in the wake of Newton's science. The papers show, both in their variety and in their inevitable attention to common themes, the richness of philosophical matter to be derived from a great scientific synthesis. Had Newton left only a set of directives for doing science, no alternative would be available except to discard it as uninteresting and unworkable. What he left – the papers in the present volume are illuminating proof of this – is a rich complexity of philosophical problems whose attempted resolution helps our understanding of both method and positive science.

Hanson's paper is a contribution to a standing problem in Newtonian studies, the interpretation to be put on the vexed phrase "Hypotheses non fingo," ("I feign no hypotheses") in the 1713 second edition "General Scholium" of the *Principia*. For a bibliography of some recent works dealing with the problem see Maurice Mandelbaum's *Philosophy, Science and Sense Perception: Historical and Critical Studies* (Baltimore, 1964), p. 72, footnote 12, as well as Mandelbaum's article "Newton and Boyle and 'Transdiction,' " in the same volume.

The key to Hanson's rewarding approach in the present volume lies in his recognition that a taxonomy of Newton's use of the word "hypothesis" is now bringing diminishing returns and that the time has come to offer semantical criticism of the various usages, suggesting some as valuable applications and others as lapses on Newton's part. The worth of such an approach depends upon the individual's ability as a conceptual critic, and Professor Hanson enjoyed eminent ability in this direction.

Hanson finds the propositional or assertoric content of empirical hypotheses to be summarized by the unpronounceable mnemonic scvapo, that is the idea that hypotheses are synthetic in sign design, have a contingent semantical status, are always vulnerable to counterevidence, and are epistemologically *a posteriori*. Intersecting with this array of distinctions a cross-classification is made in terms of a distinction of scientific statements into those that are observational and those that are theoretical. (Hanson allows that the distinction is a rough and ready one.) Both classes of statements, observational and theoretical, can be either confirmed or supposed, producing the matrix of possibilities for scientific hypotheses as O_c (observation confirmed), O_s (observation supposed), $\odot_c$ (theoretical confirmed), and finally $\odot_s$ (theoretical supposed). Each of these possibilities is a scvapo claim.

The next move is obvious: apply this apparatus to Newton's uses of the word "hypothesis," using the distinctions made as the basis for criticism. In the first place, can an O_c, a confirmed observation, be an hypothesis either for sound theory or for Newton? For theoretical purposes only, by those who maintain the dubious epistemology of the "fallibilist," says Hanson. A fallibilist in his usage says *all* scvapo claims are hypotheses! When an O_s is called an "hypothesis" it may simply be a statement of initial conditions. An $\odot_c$ when called an hypothesis indicates the scvapo quality of the laws of nature. An $\odot_s$ is called an "hypothesis" to stress its speculative character. But, contends Hanson, there is a fifth use of hypothesis, the one at issue in the expression "Hypotheses non fingo," an hypothesis in the pejorative sense of a metaphysical prejudice. Hanson has, with model clarity, shown not only that Newton uses hypothesis in this fifth sense, but also that, when his terms are properly understood, he uses the term in non-pejorative senses as well. He thus reconciles in an elegant manner a long-standing problem of what Newton could have meant by his famous phrase "Hypotheses non fingo."

In the paper by Davis, Berkeley's criticism of Newton in *The Principles of Human Knowledge* (1710), sections 110–17, provides the basis for discussion of Berkeley's critique of Newtonian doctrines of absolute space and Newton's putative reply to these criticisms in the General Scholium added to the *Principia* in the second edition of 1713. In the first section of this paper a commentary on sections 110–17 of the *Principles* is given in order to separate the dynamical from the theological considerations that Berkeley presents. In the second section the sources of Berkeley's critique are examined. There has been some difference of opinion as to whether Berkeley's Newton is the Newton of the *Principia* or the *Opticks*. Davis argues that the major Newtonian influence on Berkeley was the *Principia* through most of his career and that the *Opticks* with its important metaphysical "Queries" xxviii and xxxi although available to Berkeley in 1706, did not become influential until the *Siris* in 1744. It is also contended that the views of Newton and Raphson are but one element from which Berkeley recoiled in forming a view of space directed primarily against the belief that extension is an attribute of God. In the third and most controversial section of the paper the author argues (i) that Berkeley's attack in the *Principles*, so far as it was directed against Newton, had no influence at all in inducing Newton to publish the General Scholium, and (ii) that because there is no evidence to the contrary, the attack of Leibniz seems sufficient to account for the publication of the General Scholium, making public views about God which Newton had held for many years.

F. E. L. Priestley's paper, "The Leibniz-Clarke Controversy," surveys the main issues raised in the last phase of the titanic struggle between Leibniz and Newton which began in 1699 and ended with the death of Leibniz. The whole controversy, including the Correspondence discussed by Priestley, still smoulders; the issue involved will probably never be resolved to the point where consensus is reached.

Priestley's most general thesis, amply supported by the argument of the whole paper, is that the protagonists never really came to grips since real debate would have involved discussion of fundamental assumptions, a discussion which never took place. The infrequency with which original philosophers understand one another is common knowledge, but it is always interesting to see it worked out, as Priestley does, in the particular case. The comments in this summary will be directed only to discussion of the *Sensorium dei* passages, the most contentious aspect of Priestley's paper. It will be recalled that in his first paper Leibniz charged that Newton's views were destructive of natural religion, citing as an instance of irreligion Newton's alleged view that "Space is an organ, which God makes use of to perceive things by." Koyré and Cohen in a well-known paper in *Isis* (1961), "The Case of the Missing Tanquam," have discussed anew the question of the sensorium in the light of an interesting textual find. The textual discovery is that in the final paragraph of Query xx of the Latin edition of Newton's *Opticks* (1706) some copies contain a version of the sensorium passage not containing the *tanquam*. The inclusion of the *tanquam* passage weakens the formal identification of space with the sensorium of God. After examining a number of copies of the Latin edition of the *Opticks*, Koyré and Cohen conclude that some time after completion of printing, but before binding, Newton and Clarke introduced the *tanquam* passage as we now know it. The passage occurs on a cancelled page, but there are at least five copies of the edition in which the page in question (315) is the original page, without the disputed passage. Koyré and Cohen suggest that Leibniz could have encountered an original copy without the *tanquam*, and that the earlier passage in which space is identified with God's sensorium expresses Newton's real conviction. Newton's dynamical views are linked with his metaphysical and religious views in the discussion of space, despite Newton's efforts in general to keep his science and religion apart. The point thus is of considerable importance in understanding Newton's "methodology," in the extended sense of the term referred to earlier in this introduction.

Priestley challenges the inferences Koyré and Cohen draw. There is no proof that Leibniz read the original unrevised copy, and none of the five known copies of the *Opticks* containing the unrevised original is in a Continental library. Moreover, there are two sensorium passages in the 1706 queries, the passage in Query xx under discussion, and another near the end of the final query, which unequivocally assigns a sensorium to God. But more important Priestley argues that the *tanquam* is not as important in any case as Koyré and Cohen contend. Urging that Koyré and Cohen may have been misled by Clarke's English translation, Priestley argues that the disputed passage is not a counterfactual in the imperfect subjunctive but an exact comparison, a "just as" expression. Such a comparison, whether conveyed by *tanquam* or *comme* was unacceptable to Leibniz. Priestley develops this reading in an impressive and convincing manner.

Newton's view of space, as both the Priestley and Davis papers suggest, is a crux in Newtonian studies. Discussion of space provides the point of contact between Newton's scientific views and his philosophical and theological views. Despite Newton's efforts to keep these aspects of his thought apart they intersect over the question of space.

Gerd Buchdahl's paper, "Gravity and Intelligibility: Newton to Kant," appears in its position in the volume because of the editors' decision to arrange the five middle papers in roughly historical sequence depending upon the figures discussed. Actually, the paper might have stood first insofar as its far-reaching philosophical significance is concerned. Buchdahl only incidentally traces the history of a problem from Newton to Kant; more important, he offers Kant's treatment of the problem of the intelligibility of gravity as a case study in the field of much wider philosophical concerns. As such, his paper might stand as a conceptual prolegomenon to the other papers in the volume.

The problem Buchdahl concentrates attention on is basic to an understanding of Newton's philosophy of science (and to certain general features of all philosophies of science): the principle of gravitational attraction was taken as an explanatory hypothesis, yet Newton claimed also that it was derived from the phenomena, and that the warrant for its certainty is inductive. Part of the problem is that Newton's preferred physical model viewed all dynamical relations as forms of particle collision; gravity, to the contrary, appears to be a form of action at a distance. But Newton insisted that gravity actually exists (is a true cause) and that the law expressing it is inductively established. Is gravity, then, a *basic* cause (apparently in contradiction of the preferred physical paradigm), or can it also be accounted for by some other explanatory principle? Of deeper significance: what, after all, are the philosophical criteria for choosing hypotheses? The vitally important thing to note, and Buchdahl's account is masterful in bringing this out, is that the intelligibility of gravity became a much discussed and prestigious problem, *even though* the law of gravity was regarded as having been established inductively, once and for all.

Buchdahl's central contention is that debate on the issues just mentioned generated a much richer structure of distinctions connected with the basic methodological problem of selection of hypotheses. He distinguishes between (1) the "comprehensibility" of an hypothesis, which divides into (a) its "possibility," and (b) its "intelligibility"; (2) the "probative strength" of an hypothesis; and (3) the "reasonableness" or "rationality" of an hypothesis. Buchdahl intentionally leaves the meaning of comprehensibility vague, mainly because it is the development of this very concept that he wishes to trace in the essay. Rationality of an hypothesis has to do with its incorporation into a larger theoretical framework (see the discussion of Whewell's concept of "consilience of inductions" in the paper by Butts), and with certain "regulative principles" that determine an hypothesis' acceptability in a given conceptual framework. With respect to the probative strength of Newton's law of gravity, all persons involved take it as established inductively, that is, experientially. Newton's fourth Rule of Philosophizing in a sense gives the apparent guarantee of the probative strength of the law. (For alternative discussions of Newton's Rule IV, see the papers by Laudan, Butts, and Feyerabend; additional comparisons will be given in this Introduction, below.)

Phrased in Buchdahl's terms, the problem at issue becomes: given that all parties agree about the probative strength of the law, the only issue can be a disagreement about its comprehensibility or its rationality. This way of putting the problem is illuminating. As Buchdahl shows in his brief discussion of Locke and Hume, and in his extensive discussion of Kant, getting clear about the rationality or comprehensibility of a law (one can generalize from the present case of Newton's law of gravity) is equivalent to getting clear about both the "metaphysical" background of a scientific theory and the general methodology germane to the problem of the acceptability of hypotheses. It is in this important respect that Buchdahl's way of putting the question gives conceptual guidance for following the detailed discussions in all of the papers in this volume.

For example, Hanson's elaborate discussion of the semantics of "hypothesis" is in part a general methodological model for understanding both the probative force and the rationality of hypotheses. As the discussion in the papers by Priestley and Davis brings out, Leibniz, Clarke, and Berkeley were all concerned with getting a clear view (in the case of Leibniz and Berkeley, a view at variance with that of Newton) of the general metaphysics and theology that would have to obtain given Newton's physics as epistemically established. In the papers by Laudan and Butts, Reid and Whewell are presented as attempting to elaborate philosophies of science that will decide the rationality and comprehensibility of Newton's system, Reid attempting to undergird Newton's methodology with an empiricist epistemology, Whewell attempting to save Newton's rules of philosophizing as components in his (Whewell's) own more rationalistic theory of science. Finally, Feyerabend's treatment of Newton's methods and results (in optics) brings out forcefully what might be called the *ethical* dimensions involved in arguing for (or assuming) the rationality of a certain method and its resulting positive science.

A few words should be added about Buchdahl's treatment of Kant. Along with others, Kant regarded the law of gravity as an empirical (contingent) generalization. He also regarded gravity as a basic property. Thus, for Kant the problem of the intelligibility or comprehensibility of gravity cannot be reduced either to appeal to empirical scientific considerations, or to appeal to logical matters. After all, if the law is contingent, all that the mechanics of the day can do is to repeat the reasoning and experimentation; logically the law's opposite must be regarded as conceivable – there is nothing self-contradictory about the notion of gravity. Kant shifts the problem of comprehensibility on to new ground by urging us to see the concept of gravitational force as a theoretical construct operating at the level of "reason in its hypothetical employment." Concepts like force are basic ingredients giving systematization to the data of dynamics; they are imported into nature as part of the epistemological grammar by means of which the data will be organized, and thus made intelligible. The rationality of the concept of gravitational force is thus saved by viewing it as an *a priori* component in those general systems that generate the specific forms that sciences must take.

In addition, Kant argued that the real possibility of a concept could only be shown by means of what he calls a "construction," roughly, the provision of an analogy in applied mathematics that would increase the plausibility of a concept, thus rendering it intelligible. Kant hoped to be able to produce such a construction for the concept of matter generally, but failed in his attempt. But what Buchdahl brings to light in his discussion of Kant is that the problem of the rationality or comprehensibility of a concept is more complex and many-faceted than had earlier been supposed. Kant's main contribution was the spelling-out of these complexities, a task that directs our attention to broad-scale methodological concerns having to do with the general epistemological and metaphysical systems that given sciences may be taken as presupposing.

The papers by Laudan and Butts can be read as proposing two competing philosophies of science as partial interpretations of Newton's pronouncements on methodology. Laudan presents Reid as the first British philosopher who attempted to take Newton's methodology literally; thus he produced an empiricist (one might want to say "positivist") Newton. Whewell in part agreed with such a characterization; his discussion of Newton's rules of philosophizing was largely an attempt to assimilate the rules to his own philosophy of science, and to oppose an empiricist Newton by means of his own concepts of "consilience of inductions," "necessary truth," and the like, and by means of his own novel theory of induction. Nevertheless, Whewell's treatment of Newton is antagonistic to an interpretation like Reid's.

Laudan shows that Reid attempted to adopt Newton's methodology literally, and to look for the empiricist philosophical arguments needed to read it in what Reid took to be its own terms. Laudan displays at length Reid's generous inclination to agree with the letter of Newton's methodological *obiter dicta*. For example, Reid accepted Newton's "hypotheses non fingo," and elaborated no fewer than seven specific arguments against the hypothetical method and in favour of a strictly empiricist inductivism. He also accepted Newton's rules of philosophizing as the general axioms underwriting the legitimacy of induction, where induction was taken to be a method involving three steps: (1) observation and experimentation; (2) "reduction" of the facts to a general law; and (3) derivation of further facts from the general laws.

This is not to say that Reid added nothing new to the philosophy of Newton's methodology. Like Hume, he was concerned to find a philosophical reconstruction of the concept of cause, and to find a justified way of construing induction. He agreed with Hume that some principle of uniformity is required in order to justify inductive beliefs; he also agreed that our confidence in the uniformity of nature is non-rational. However, unlike Hume, he located the strength of our convictions in some inductions in an innate disposition of human nature – one might call it an instinct to generalize. This became an important idea in nineteenth-century philosophy, and was even found not wholly unacceptable to a great enemy of traditional empiricist philosophies of science like Whewell.

In the discussion of Whewell's critique of Newton's rules of philosophizing in the paper by Butts, one sees a very different approach to Newton's methodology. Whereas Reid tried to read Newton deferentially and literally, Whewell sought to take from Newton only what was needed to support his own philosophical views. Butts brings out two items in Whewell's critique that might profitably be compared with what Laudan says about Reid. Reid is presented as having sought an empiricist interpretation of Newton's *vera causa*. In the end, a true cause is to be viewed as an observable, an antecedent empirical event that takes the place of initial conditions needed to specify a law. Whewell found great difficulties with this inclination to locate true causes in an empirical (observational) context. Instead, he argued that we should take more seriously Newton's insistence in the first rule that true causes be regarded as functioning as *adequate explanations* of the data. The shift is important, because Whewell is here inviting us to attend to certain features of the methodology of scientific *systems*, and to raise questions about the acceptability of hypotheses as explanatory devices. He thus comes to regard true causes as constructs in hypothetical systems that explain more than one set of data; gravitational attraction is an acceptable hypothesis because inductions from motions of heavenly bodies, from motions of terrestrial bodies, from behaviour of the tides, and so on, all become consilient in the system in which gravitation is ingredient. (Compare this with Buchdahl's discussion of "rationality.")

A second major feature in the philosophical differences between systems like Reid's and Whewell's comes out clearly in the discussion of Newton's fourth rule in the papers by Laudan and Butts. The rule is: In experimental philosophy, propositions collected from phenomena by induction are to be held as true either accurately or approximately, notwithstanding contrary hypotheses; till other phenomena occur by which they may be rendered either more accurate or liable to exception. Laudan takes Newton as intending, and Reid as accepting, that this rule indicates the fallibility of any given induction. They thus read the final clause of the rule as suggesting that additional data might falsify an induction earlier taken to be valid. Whewell reads the rule (and suggests that Newton did also) as implying that some scientific conclusions are established conclusively by induction, although future thought about the law's place in a theoretical network of propositions might lead us to refine it, to "render it more accurate," to elaborate it in such a way that it can "handle" exceptions. Whewell's only quarrel with Newton was on the question of what it is that might lead us so to refine or adapt a law. He chides Newton with having thought that future *experience* might so constrain us, whereas in truth only conceptual considerations arising from trying to fit the law into a larger theoretical framework can force the refinement. As Butts brings out, the difference between Newton and Whewell (and in the comparison here at issue, between Reid and Whewell) is based largely upon competing theories of induction, with Whewell's own theory relying heavily on the imposition upon data of conceptual elements that are empirically irreducible.

The difference between regarding a law as falsifiable or as refinable but not falsifiable plays an important part in the paper by Feyerabend. He reads Rule IV in Whewell's way, and shows in some detail that the rule exerted a conservative force on the development of Newton's science, indeed, that it was one ingredient in what he calls the "rule of faith" that underwrote the empiricist philosophy that accompanied development of Newtonianism. Feyerabend's paper is part of a larger story that he has been telling in dramatic fashion in a number of papers. To supply additional perspective for the understanding of the present paper, a brief summary of his general attack upon traditional empiricism will be given.

Feyerabend variously identifies his target as "radical empiricism," "theoretical monism," or simply "empiricism." This philosophy moves historically from Newton to certain "orthodox" contemporary philosophers of science, among others, Carnap, Nagel, and Hempel. He objects to the hardened contemporary form of this empiricism because he thinks that it discourages metaphysics while entailing it, that if followed, it will impede the growth and development of science, that its general methodology is logically and philo-sophically defective, and that it leads to a kind of autocracy in ideas. In philosophy of science the form that this empiricism takes is well known. The central contention is that science consists of general theories that be-come more and more general with the introduction of more inclusive laws and hypotheses – growth in science is thus in the direction of greater inclu-siveness of theories. Coupled with this view of theoretical progress is the concept that all sciences of a certain kind deal with a preferred observation language, that, in other words, the theories of increasing degrees of inclu-siveness all deal with the same subject-matter, the same "given."

Feyerabend's objections to this philosophy of science are pointed and re-quire serious consideration. Central to his critical position is the proposition that science, viewed under this classical modern model, is a kind of mono-lithic "self-truth-generating" system. A theory that is not questioned, except in the sense that we look for more general statements of its laws, is self-guaranteeing as to truth. There is a peculiar circularity: the system specifies both the form and the matter of observation, yet the observations are sup-posed to establish the system. Of course, defenders of the position insist that if disconfirmations of the scientific system arise, it will be abandoned. Feyerabend's point, however, is that the view guarantees that falsifying cases will never arise. We can refine the laws in the system, but since the system generates its own observational material, no genuine falsification can ever result. Hence the system, on Feyerabend's view, is methodologically conservative and ideologically suspect.

Feyerabend seeks to bolster this set of claims by questioning two of the basic tenets of standard empiricist philosophy of science. He argues that no epistemological sense can be made of the claim that science has available to it a common observational material, and he contends that the test of theories of high levels of generality cannot be got by "consulting the facts." Feyera-bend is one of many contemporary philosophers who question the "myth of the given." Indeed, so compelling have the arguments of Feyerabend and others been that the burden of proof seems to have shifted to those who wish to continue to think that there is a common observational core. On the second point, Feyerabend's position is novel and striking. In brief, the point is that unless a whole new system is introduced as a competitor, no scientific theory will ever be questioned in the required fundamental ways. He reads progress in the history of science as resulting from the introduction of com-peting systems that are fundamentally incompatible with prevailing systems.

Since each system generates its own decisive observation language, it cannot fail unless challenged. We must thus replace "theoretical monism" with "theoretical pluralism." The unit of test is not a single theory confronted by the facts; it is one whole theory whose right to rule is challenged by a theory with which it is incompatible. In the end, the evaluation of theories of wide generality is not empirical (based on normal canons of confirmation in compliance with the common observation language), it is based upon non-evidential considerations connected with scientific ideologies and what Feyerabend calls, in the paper in this volume, "party lines."

It is against the background of Feyerabend's complex attack upon "empiricism" that his paper in this volume should be read. His contribution to this book can quite properly be regarded as an illustration of part of his general position supplied by means of consideration of one important histor-rical example – Newton's treatment of optical phenomena. In this connec-tion the analogy between what Feyerabend identifies as the Protestant Rule of Faith and Newton's underlying confidence in the inductive methods that he thought crucial to the establishment of his own physics is illuminating and novel. Coming to regard scripture as the basis of religion is equivalent to adopting a rule of faith that *ornaments* actual religious beliefs and practices. Similarly, Newton's rules of philosophizing are to be regarded as ornaments of preferred method. The point can be put in terms supplied by Whewell and Buchdahl: the probative strength of a theory cannot be seriously questioned when we have a rule (Newton's Rule IV) that allows refinement of a theory, but does not assume willingness to pit it against contenders. Feyerabend develops the point by showing that what might have been taken as *crucial tests* of Newton's optical hypotheses were in fact construed by Newton as *illustrations* of his hypotheses, and were so construed on the basis of New-ton's unwavering confidence in the efficacy of his "methods." Thus both Protestantism and modern science are based upon rules of faith, and follow certain party lines. It is probably fair to say that on Feyerabend's view the natural next step after methodology is in the direction of the politics of science, or the ethics of science. What he invites us to do, after all, is to con-sider and question the *ideologies* that apparently lie beneath the surface of positive science.

In sum, then, the papers in this volume do indeed illustrate important features of the methodological heritage of Newton. Some show the lasting importance of concern for the basic metaphysical and theological accompa-niments of science. Some show the enormous complexities involved in trying to be clear about apparently simple matters: what is an hypothesis? when is a scientific hypothesis satisfactory? what is the method involved in a great scientific discovery? Some give witness to the fact that methodologies are not philosophically neutral, that they imply many different general philosophies of science. And some show that beyond questions of method lie deeper questions concerned with the terms on which we would be warranted in accepting a given science as true, no matter what. Finally, the papers, taken as a group, exhibit the value of Newton's work in science for suggesting an understanding of what science is all about. Newton's theories may be ranked as one of the two greatest achievements in physics; they should also be ranked among the most important cases to be studied by those interested in grasping the methodological and broadly philosophical basis of science.

II
Hypotheses Fingo

N. R. HANSON

"Hypotheses non fingo" has meant different things to different people, for different reasons. For example, when Ernst Mach addressed this slogan he wrote as follows: "Newton's reiterated and emphatic protestations that he is not concerned with hypotheses as to the causes of phenomena, but as simply to do with the investigation and transformed statement of *actual facts* – a direction of thought that is distinctly and tersely uttered in his words 'Hypotheses non Fingo' ('I do not frame hypotheses') – stamps him as a philosopher of the highest rank."[1] Thus did Mach acknowledge the intellectual existence of Sir Isaac Newton within the history of philosophical thought, indicating that, by this pronouncement, Newton had distinguished himself as perhaps the first of the positivistic philosophers.

One of the things historians of science have been doing recently is this: they have been subjecting this "Machian" response to searching analysis. As it turns out, it isn't true of Newton that the term (or the concept) "hypothesis" meant one and the same thing for him at all times during his career; nor did it signify the same thing in all places within the *Principia Mathematica Philosophiae Naturalis*, in any one of the editions. That is the primary thing historians have concerned themselves with in this connection, such men as Alexandre Koyré, Rupert Hall, Richard S. Westfall, Edward Strong, and especially I. Bernard Cohen – all of whom have dazzled us with displays of versatility and variability in Newton's use of this "hypothetical" terminology. One of the things Professor Cohen unearthed during his researches has particular application vis-à-vis this first point. He has shown[2] that in the first edition of the *Principia* (1687), there are two pronouncements which not only serve as hypotheses, but are actually labelled as such – Hypothesis v and Hypothesis vi. These expressions are then simply transformed, word for word, such that in the second edition (1713), the same sentences appear

1 Ernst Mach, *The Science of Mechanics* (Chicago, 1919), ch. i, pt. 3, sec. 6, p. 193.
2 In the Wiles Lectures, given in 1966 at the Queen's University, Belfast; to be published by the Cambridge University Press.

ipsissima verba; but now they are not called hypotheses at all. They are called "Phaenomena." This is acutely interesting because in several places Newton answers the question "what is an hypothesis?" by saying that an hypothesis "is whatever *is not* deduced from the phenomena."[3] Again, he observes: "an hypothesis is any proposition [*sic*] which is not phenomenologically based; one which is neither a phenomenon [*sic*] nor deduced from phenomena."[4] Yet, in the face of this stressed opposition between hypotheses and phenomena, Newton takes two pronouncements which began as hypotheses and reproduces them identically within the second edition, at which time they are called phenomena. A man as sensitive to conceptual tensions as Newton might have acknowledged that these strikingly different uses signalled *some* change in his concept of hypothesis! For us it must be a signal of semantical slidings and glidings in Newton's notion of the hypothetical.

A further thing these historians of science have been doing: they have been focusing upon particular uses of the word hypothesis in Newton's writings, uses which italicize the fact that he even knew what it was for an hypothesis to serve within *explanations* – he knew how to give an explanation of a phenomenal state of affairs *via* an hypothesis. Thus, for example, Newton writes in a projected Fourth Book for *The Opticks*: ' ... the truth of this hypothesis I assert not, because I cannot prove it, but I think it very probable because a great part of the phenomena of nature do easily flow from it, [phenomena] which seem otherwise inexplicable."[5]

So here one possible function of an hypothesis for Newton is that it might explain something. He says again in *The Opticks*: "My design in this Book is not to *explain* the Properties of Light *by Hypotheses*, but to propose and prove them by Reason and Experiments."[6] Thus Newton is acknowledging that it makes sense for the properties of light to be *explained by hypotheses*, although he disavows that such is his objective in this place. Early in his career he wrote a paper entitled "An Hypothesis To Explain The Properties Of Light, Discoursed Of In My Several Papers."[7] Again, explanation by hypothesis. It is this explanatory function of hypothesis which is of signal importance in understanding Newton's natural philosophy; it has surely

3 Cf. Isaac Newton, *Sir Isaac Newton's Mathematical Principles*, ed. Florian Cajori (Berkeley, 1946), General Scholium, penultimate paragraph, p. 547.
4 Newton to Roger Cotes, 28 March 1713, quoted in J. Edleston (ed.), *Correspondence of Sir Isaac Newton and Prof. Cotes* (London, 1850), p. 155.
5 University Library Cambridge, MS. add. 3970.
6 Isaac Newton, *Opticks* (London, 1704), Book One, Part I, p. 1, my italics.
7 *Isaac Newton's Papers and Letters on Natural Philosophy*, ed. I. Bernard Cohen (Cambridge, Mass., 1958), pp. 177ff.

made a great difference within the writings of historians of science in our time. We shall, of course, return to this.

The serious concern of historians for the term hypothesis in the printed Newton has manifested itself in their exegetical explorations; no Newtonian use of the word has escaped the modern scholar's search. These uses are usually laid out and tabulated one after the other; indeed I shall be doing this myself in a trice. But there is something uncritical about such an undertaking. In 1966 I was honoured to serve as commentator on a paper by I. Bernard Cohen wherein he proceeded in just this way. Every use of hypothesis in the Newtonian corpus has a place somewhere in Professor Cohen's searching study. My move was as follows: I noted that if in some as yet undiscovered document it turned out that Newton had used hypothesis to mean a can of beans, or even to mean Gluteus Maximus – or any other apparently unrelated designatum – Dr. Cohen, along with most other historians, might simply *record* this as Use$_n$ and then taxonomize it along with all the others – as no better, no worse. In short, there is too little semantical criticism undertaken by historians, in virtue of which one might argue "Yes, on this occasion Newton chose his words carefully and *did* succeed in communicating effectively with his reader, whereas in this other place what he says seems absurdly unclear; a momentary lapse in exposition perhaps – or even in his thought?" Why should this suggestion strike so many Newton scholars as the next thing to sacrilege? After all, pointing out mathematical slips and blunders in Newton's work has become almost a professional specialization; I have even made a tiny play within that interminable game myself.[8] Why not the same possibility for Newton's uses of words? Nothing like this, a linguistic blunder, may ever be disclosed, of course, but that possibility should be left open to the careful scholar. This is especially the case when "philosophical terms" like *true, cause, prove, phenomena* and *hypothesis* are at issue. (Newton was no Austin!) The only way to come to grips with Newtonian discourse is to sustain one's capacities as a conceptual critic, and not slavishly to record as gospel every off-hand thing the great man actually said and scribbled. We must be sure of our own ground vis-à-vis conceptual analysis; we must be ready to assert what hypotheses are, if we are ever to position certain uses of hypothesis by Newton as being marginal uses, while his other employments are "in centre of the page" (i.e. clear and not problematic). This is part of what I wish to discuss here.

8 N. R. Hanson, "Another Mistake in the Principia," *Scripta Mathematica*, XXVI (1961), 83–85.

Look at the term itself: hypo-thesis. A dictionary would state its literal meaning as "beneath an assertion". An hypothesis falls short of being an assertion; it is less than a claim, not up to being a thesis advanced.[9] So just staring at the term itself suggests that an hypothesis (hypo-thesis) consists in an expression which is *less* than an actual assertion of, short of a commitment to, a thesis. Such a thesis would itself be propositional, true or false. Not the hypo-thesis, however. The hypothesis will articulate something *not yet known* to be true or false. It will consist not in something actually asserted – not in a proposition – but something (perhaps) just assumed for the purposes of argument – an "entailment tracer." An hypothesis would therefore be a supposition, or a conjecture; it might be a condition for inquiry, a condition required for some possible state of affairs actually to obtain. This last use, of course, has influenced logicians in our century. When they dub a proposition hypothetical in form, they mean that it is conditional; it is of the "if-then" structure.[10] It is hypothetical in its sign-design. It has the "syn-categorematic" terms "if-then" operating essentially within it. Such a pro-position might well be adopted as if it were true *because* of its multiform con-sequences' being realized in fact – always an excellent reason. That would mesh with the quotation from Newton just cited – where he urged that he was not asserting the truth of an hypothesis because he could not prove it. He thinks it very probably true, however, because many "phenomena of nature do easily flow from it which seem otherwise inexplicable."[11]

So far I have too thinly spread the notion of hypothesis before you and raised some small questions concerning what force(s) it had in Newton's diverse expositions. He makes the term range all the way from meaning "explanation"[12] through meaning "a foundation for all philosophy,"[13] to

---

9 Consider how "hypodermic" means "beneath the skin", or "hypochondria" means "below spirits" and "hypocrite" means "less than truth," and so on.

10 If conditions are instantiated, then state of affairs obtains.

11 This virtually encapsulates the spirit of "hypothetico-deductive" philosophies of science. Cf. Braithwaite, *Scientific Explanation* (CUP 1953), chs. I–III. Nonetheless, the role of hypotheticals as hypotheses has been sparse in the history of empirical science. As we will note when discussing hypotheses in mediaeval science (which were conditional in form), the usual scientific hypothesis embraces the categorical – what it enter-tains would be accepted as true were the available evidence but sufficient to warrant that. Hypotheticals are arguments; hypotheses are "as if" premises within arguments. What Newton entertains as hypotheses are thought to embody *probably true categori-cals*, never hypotheticals.

12 *Opticks*, Book One, Part I; and see also the Conclusion to his projected Book Four, within which five "explanatory" hypotheses are exfoliated. Univ. Lib. Cambridge, MS. add. 3970.

13 Univ. Lib. Cambridge, MS. add. 3965.

meaning "prejudice,"[14] and finally to meaning "unsupported speculation."[15]

Henceforth, I shall play the mediaeval logic-chopper – exploiting the method of exposition found within the Old Testament book *Deuteronomy*, the method sometimes dubbed "division." Thus with respect to any conceptual possibility one presents a pair of alternatives, and then seeks to determine under which of these two the concept in question falls. One proceeds thus until complete analysis results.[16] It is assumed that the alternatives initially entertained exhaust all possibilities. Let us proceed:

Of propositions it may be said either that they are *synthetic* or that they are *analytic*. This contrast concerns the "sign-design" characteristics of assertions.[17] Assertion P will then be designated analytic when its sign-design, its formal syntax, is such that P is consistent (within a language L) and entails only other consistent assertions, *while at the same time* P's negation, not-P, is inconsistent and entails inconsistencies.

P will be designated synthetic on the other hand, for obverse reasons – when its sign-design is such that P is consistent (within L) and entails only other consistencies *while at the same time* P's negation, not-P, is also consistent and entails only other consistent assertions.

It seems clear that the putative proposition which is going to count as constituting an hypothesis within the history of the empirical sciences will be *synthetic* in its syntactical form. It will be an entertained claim whose negation is an equally consistent claim. One could not simply reject such a negation (as self-contradictory) on the basis of inspection and reflection alone, because both the hypothesis and its negation are consistent in their sign-design. So the first thing about all hypotheses is that the claims they embody-by-supposing are synthetic in form (s).[18]

14 *Ibid.*, MS. add. 2667.
15 *Principia*, General Scholium.
16 Thus any material substance either will, or will not, offer resistance to a shearing force. If the substance does offer such resistance, it is a solid. If it does not, it is a fluid. Now any fluid substance either will, or will not, manifest a surface. If the substance does manifest a surface it is a liquid; in terrestrial space this surface will be the "uppermost" molecular sheath of the liquid as contained in, e.g., a beaker. (In outer space the surface will be that of a spheroidal droplet of the liquid in question.) If the substance does not display a surface, it is a gas. Now any gaseous substance will either ... and so on, *ad indefinitum.*
17 That is, assertions are claims couched in indicative sentences, of a declarative mood, such that they are either true or false.
18 One nagging qualification obtrudes here: it was signalled five paragraphs above. Hypotheses cited in mediaeval science, even up through the sixteenth century, are subjunctive and conditional in mood and sentence structure: "If the earth were to move, no stars could appear to us as fixed"; "Were the stars infinitely distant, they could not circle 'round the earth in a finite time," ... etc. This historically specialized employ-

The second thing that obtains for all hypotheses is that the propositions they encapsulate can be either *contingently* true or *necessarily* true. We have now moved over from syntax to semantics; from sign-design to meaning. The possibilities again: (1) Hypotheses might ultimately turn out to be true in virtue of the empirical facts they accurately describe; they would thus be discovered to be true *contingent* upon those facts' being what they turn out to be. Or hypotheses might ultimately turn out to be true in a way that "All fathers are parents" and "Bicycles have two wheels" are true – that is, the propositions they express may be necessarily true. Here the ultimate truth of hypotheses would be a function of the meanings of the term through which they are articulated. Given those meanings the hypothesis will (ultimately) turn out once and for all as indefeasibly true (or false). No mere experiential happening could force a re-evaluation of the thus hypothetically expressed proposition's truth-status. (2) If hypotheses are adjudged to express propositions which are (ultimately discovered to be) *contingently* true, however, then their truth assignment is forever reviewable (e.g. "are the facts *really* as described?").

Again, indubitably, empirical hypotheses, if ultimately disclosed as true at all, must be contingently true. They will be *discovered* true in virtue of the degree to which their subject-matter factually supports what is asserted in the proposition expressed within the hypothetical utterance. That is the situation in empirical science. Indeed, whenever what purports to be an empirical hypothesis can ultimately be disclosed by analysis alone to have been necessarily true, it is promptly retitled a "definition" and construed thenceforth as telling us only about the logical and linguistic locutions which the scientist has legislated into existence. They tell us nothing true about that scientist's factual subject-matter, for that subject-matter will be described only in synthetic propositions possessed of equally synthetic negations – to decide between which requires not just reflective analysis, but experience.

So that is our second alternative, and the second thing that can be said about empirical hypotheses: they articulate and embody claims which are contingently true, if true at all (c).

ment of hypothesis brackets in one conditional both what we would customarily designate "the hypothesis" and the conclusion which follows therefrom. Mediaeval hypotheses are subjunctive *arguments*. Our hypotheses, and Newton's, correspond only to the *protasis* of the Schoolmen's subjunctive-conditional hypotheses (which are hypothetical in logical form). That protasis, when freed of its intra-inferential hooks and links embodies an indicative sentence in the declarative mood – entertained hypothetically and not assertorically. It is the hooks and links that are subjunctive and conditional.

The third thing we can say of hypotheses has already been said. Again, the possibilities: (1) Could hypothetical claims be invulnerable? (2) Or *must* they be vulnerable to possible disconfirmation? Either it makes sense to conceive of evidence as counting against what the hypothesis entertains, or it makes no sense at all. What possible evidence *could* count against "All Euclidean, plane, equilateral triangles are equiangular"? Surely if one understands the geometrical frame of reference within which such discourse would be articulated at all, it would not make any sense to suppose it could be false. The claim is invulnerable in L (i.e. Euclidean geometry). Hence it is not, and never could be, entertained as an empirical hypothesis such as might punctuate the history of natural science – all of which hypotheses entertain claims that are vulnerable to the facts (and the possible facts), of experience, experiment and observation. Of a genuine scientific factual hypothesis, for example, "There are no canals on Mars," it might turn out that, even after all of us had accepted the claim, thus entertained, as true, we were completely wrong. The planetary investigator may have made some mistake in calculation or calibration; the instrumentation may have been covered with jam (or the computer-technician imbued with drink). All sorts of reasons could be pondered that might force our reappraisal of the claim in question. Mars *may* have canals, all present evidence to the contrary notwithstanding. Further observations are always to the point with genuine scientific hypotheses; future observations as well. Empirical hypotheses thus entertain, as a matter of principle, claims vulnerable to possible disconfirmation (v).

Our next dichotomy concerns whether empirical hypotheses express propositions which come to be known to us *a priori* or *a posteriori* – through pure cerebration alone, or through observational and experimental experience. Our earlier contrasts concerned syntax, semantics, and defeasibility, respectively; this one turns on *epistemological* issues. Again the way is clear; the hypotheses of empirical science posit propositions which are known to us through experience and only through experience. Reflection alone cannot ever be sufficient to give us certitude with respect to the kind of non-formal knowledge that typifies the assertoric content of empirical hypotheses. So *a posteriori* it is! (APO)

To recapitulate:

As between S(ynthetic) and A(nalytic) sign-designs, hypotheses are suppositions of claims which are always S.

As between the C(ontingent) and N(ecessary) semantical status, what hypotheses entertain are always C.

As between v(ulnerable) and ɪ(nvulnerable) postures towards counter-evidence, hypotheses posit propositions which are always v.

As between APO(steriori) and APR(iori) epistemic strata, what hypotheses hold up for deductive development and decomposition is always APO.

S-C-V-APO: there is the logico-conceptual key to th e status of the propositional content of the scientific hypotheses as we know them. That gives us the virtually unpronounceable mnemonic SCVAPO.

Scientific hypotheses are thus suppositions of claims which are fundamentally SCVAPO in all conceptual and logical respects. Scientific hypotheses embody what are thus sharply to be contrasted with expressions of a totally different kind – those which, by "reverse-mnemonics," may be identified as ANIAPR claims. These assertions are analytic syntactically, necessary semantically, invulnerable as regards their possible defeasibility, and *a priori* with respect to their epistemological status. Such statements are, tersely, degenerate tautologies – something never to be said of what is entertained as a basis for inference by a genuine scientific hypothesis.[19]

Another cluster of distinctions will now be made to intersect with the first conclusion we have already reached; to wit, that hypotheses are non-assertoric positings of propositions which are SCVAPO. I now make a distinction which will not survive long under the analysis of today's "tough-minded" philosophers of science.[20] Indeed, it is a distinction which I have often challenged in print myself.[21]

Distinguish between "observational propositions" or "observation statements," and others which are usually dubbed "theoretical statements." I mean by this cosmic-comic language nothing so sweeping as is at first suggested. Nothing more is intended than that the *relationship* of an observation statement to its subject-matter is intimate and very direct. That is all. The terms in an observation statement *seem* directly to designate objects, events, and processes in the subject-matter itself. They do not actually, of course.

19 The unavoidable indirectness of locutions appropriate to hypotheses and the "proto-propositions" they embody derives from one analytical fact. Propositions (i.e. statements, assertions, claims) can be SCVAPO. Hypotheses cannot. Hypotheses are not propositions; they are "less than" assertions – "beneath" claims. They are entertainings or suppositions of assertions, and hence of the wrong logical type to be true or false or SCVAPO. Newton is too often not alert to this distinction (see his letter to Cotes, cited above), and modern Newton scholars are not noticeably different.
20 Yesterday's "tough-minded" would have staked everything on preserving this distinction; only the then "tender-minded" opposed them. The roles are now quite reversed.
21 At first *I* appeared to be "tender-minded" for doing so. But with Hempel, Feyerabend, Sellars, and Hesse now urging the same point, the *dramatis personae* seem cast very differently in 1967 from ten years before.

Much recent philosophy of science has been dedicated to disclosing that a "given," or a "pure" observation language is a myth-eaten fabric of philosophical fiction. But permit the issue to float thus *pro tem*.

The relationship between a theoretical statement and its subject-matter, on the other hand, is rather indirect, perhaps it is not even a clear and unambiguous relationship in all respects. (What theoretical terms "designate," and what theoretical statements "describe," are vexed questions in contemporary logic of science.)

So that if I say that there are fifteen books in this room, that claim will be true or false in virtue of certain uncontroversial data.[22] We can look, and we can identify, and we can count – and we can find out *directly* whether such a claim is true or false (especially when no photograph albums obtrude). Hence, "There are fifteen books in this room" is an observation statement. If I say "There is a twin-trunked elephant under my table," that also is an observation statement *if* it is agreed in advance that certain uncontroversial experiences will count either to support or to disconfirm this claim. (When is a trunk "twinned"?) We see nothing. No elephant at all. The observation claim is therefore false.

Whereas, if I make a claim of a different kind, for example, "All bodies free of unbalanced, impressed forces will either remain at rest or move uniformly in a straight line *ad indefinitum*" – that is a theoretical claim. Nothing directly open to our sensory inspection will either clearly confirm or definitely disconfirm such a statement. Or one may make comparable remarks about, for example, the properties of an ideal fluid, a fluid which is incompressible, inviscid and irrotational, and obeys Newton's infamous "sine-square" law. Of such a fluid one could say "No resistance is generable therein" – a surprising, paradoxical property for any fluid! That again would be a theoretical claim, for an issue would arise concerning whether there is any proper subject-matter which relates to that assertion. Is the assertion at least possibly false? That must be so; yet what falsifies it? What, indeed, would incline one even to make statements about ideal fluids, perfectly rigid levers, completely elastic bodies, absolutely frictionless surfaces and *perpetua mobilia*, when it is so easy to show that there are no such things?

There is an enormous penumbral area between "straightforward" observation claims and "straightforward" theoretical claims. The challenge is to find a pure observation claim wholly unformed by any theory, or to find a pure theoretical claim wholly neutral vis-à-vis any possible experience.

22 Is a photograph album a book? Suppress such queries temporarily.

Granted, the problem is formidable. I concede also that twilight is a perplexingly unclear time of day, and it sometimes confuses us when we undertake to identify a distant shadow as that of a friend, or of an enemy. Even so, midnight is still very different from noon, however irritatingly indefinite may be the interim states. Similarly, observation statements (in their "purest" form) are different from theoretical statements. Even allowing that in any observation statement the cloven hoofprint of theory can readily be detected, and allowing further that in any theoretical statement proto-observations will obtrude sooner or later – even allowing all this (indeed *Patterns of Discovery* demands all this), the primary distinction between observation statements and theoretical statements is still required in order to detect the presence of both within either.[23] So, observation statements relate closely to their subject-matters (how else could philosophers have for so long made so much of the importance of ostensive definition?); and theoretical statements are considerably more distant (semantically) from *their* subject-matters.

Alongside this contrast between O(bservation) statements and ⊙(theoretical) statements, distinguish further O-statements which are highly confirmed, from O-statements which are not as yet confirmed. By this last I do not mean disconfirmed; I mean simply not as yet put to the test. The evidence is not yet fully in. An O-claim is confirmed when, on counting the books in my room, I report my findings in the very words of that O-claim. The O-claim is: "There are fifteen books in this room." The report of my research is that "There are fifteen books in this room." Thus the O-claim is confirmed (*c*). If, on the other hand, I were to spout the words "There are 4080 undergraduates at Yale University," this would be a claim not yet confirmed (for me, at least), and I should have yet to put it to the test (as you would have to do too if you did not know the facts and sought to determine whether my O-claim were true). Other assertions have this same status because they are observational claims-in-principle, that is, falsifiable. We know what it would be like to test them, but we have not yet been in a technological position to put them to the test: for example, "There is a purple, twin-peaked mountain on the surface of Venus." So these are also observation claims, but not yet confirmed nor disconfirmed. The symbol *s* will signify these as yet unconfirmed claims and could be understood to designate "supposed." To be supposed, then, will be the most positive assignment open to such unconfirmed

---

23 I must be able to distinguish men from women in order to remark one man as effeminate; I must be able to do this even if, for some zany theoretical reason, I would urge that *all* men are effeminate.

propositions. And since we cannot assert o as true, we therefore *suppose* O. Hence we write O_s.

So, similarly, with theoretical claims: distinguish those which have been confirmed (*c*), at least to some extent – for example, within analytical lunar theory – from those which are only supposed to obtain (*s*) for the purpose of generating certain conclusions therefrom. Newton's remarks concerning "hypotheses which explain"[24] are probably $\odot \hat{s}$ in just this sense.

Consider: Every two particles in the universe are such that they attract each other directly as their masses and inversely as the square of the distance between them. That is surely $\odot_c$. It is confirmed in some sense; an immense amount of conceptual order and inferential machinery to which we are now irrevocably committed *depends* on this particular $\odot$ claim's subsisting in itself in some form. Granted, the ancient "Law-form" of Newton, with its suggestion of archaic notions such as attraction or gravitational force, need not be defended. A more cautious exposition might simply record it as a kinematical fact that pairs of objects *do* move in this way with respect to each other – that is, towards each other directly as their masses and inversely as the square of the distance between them.[25] Myriad other ways of formulating this commitment are known. It is not extravagant, then, to speak of any such claim as being confirmed ($\odot_c$). So laws of nature, such as $F = ma$, have been confirmed, despite their being "theoretical" in a manner which makes it impossible for us to put them immediately or directly to a test.

This is to be contrasted with a theoretical claim which is not as yet confirmed, but just supposed: $\odot_s$. Imagine, for example, a cosmologist who argues for a creation *ex nihilo* of H-atoms throughout the universe, where he reasons thus because of philosophical commitments, for instance, the conservation of energy (Hoyle's once standard posture), his would be an $\odot_s$ claim. This energy theory was for years neither confirmed nor disconfirmed. Present exercises in quasar astronomy, however, are conspicuously not "according to Hoyle." They reflect quite negatively on the *steady state theory* and on the *perfect cosmological principle* – that the universe will appear the same in all directions from any point in space and from any point in time – things do not look very good for the 'New Cosmologies', for there do definitely appear to be preferred axes within the universe's past and bulk. Concerning *our* philosophical issue, however, the "big bang" cosmology will

---

24 In *Opticks*, Book One, Part i.
25 Within such a rendering the provision of values for these latter parameters (m_1, m_2, r^2), will not be a measure of the magnitude or intensity of F (in $F = G\,[m_1\,m_2/r^2]$), as in the 1687 version, but rather a delineation of the *rate of closing* between m_1 and m_2.

serve us just as well. It also is replete with claims as yet not fully confirmed to the effect that our universe is at the moment in a state of expansion from an initial explosion out of a "primal atom of infinite energy." That also must be an O_s.

We have thus constructed two arrays of distinctions which may be made to intersect obliquely. As a first approximation, scientific hypotheses were adjudged to be SCVAPO, that is, synthetic in their sign-design, contingent in their semantical status, forever vulnerable to possible disconfirmation, and epistemologically such that they cannot be otherwise known than *a posteriori*. Now just above we have also divided, very roughly it is granted, all scientific statements into (1) observational (O) or theoretical ($\odot$), and (2) those that are confirmed (*c*), or only supposed (*s*). That produces a matrix of

$$O_c \qquad O_s$$
$$\odot_c \qquad \odot_s$$

possibilities which will recast scientific hypotheses into a quadrupartite

those which are O_c
those which are O_s
those which are $\odot_c$, and
those which are $\odot_s$ –

classification – *all* of these being understood to be SCVAPO claims.

Consider as a confirmed observation claim something of this kind: "The sun rose this morning." Were a person to dub *that* "an hypothesis" – despite our long history of relevant confirming testimony, reams of appropriate astronomical theory, a squadron of eye-witnesses, and even his own visual encounter with the dawn – were he still to express doubt about such a claim (as he *would* do by calling it an hypothesis), he would only be signalling his agreement with, and support for, the extreme philosophical position identified as *fallibilism*. That is, to the extent that "The sun rose this morning" is stressed as being an hypothesis, to that same extent the *negation* of that claim constitutes a logical possibility and a viable option. Such a philosopher might urge also that it is merely an hypothesis that the world exists, or that anything exists, or that you are here now confronting these words. Indeed, through this lens, all non-formal claims – all SCVAPO claims – harbour within them the logical possibility of being false, of being defeasible. More than this conceded truth, however, some active and practical doubt seems to obsess the Fallibilist. Ordinarily embraced truths like "Animals need food" are stressed as being but contingently true; against them one might still entertain a consistent dubiety. Early members of the Vienna Circle, apparently following Wittgenstein, somehow found it informative to refer to all observation statements whatsoever as hypotheses in precisely this sense. Further observations would always be to the point, and relevant, and conceivably disconfirmatory therefore. It was never "L-false" to deny such a claim, and to that extent it served as nothing more than an hypothesis, a dubitable guess about what is the case. That would be the effect on an O_c of calling it an hypothesis.

Now contrast this with so dubbing (as hypothetical) an observation claim which is merely supposed, O_s – one *not* fully confirmed at the time of consideration. Imagine that during an undergraduate physics course the Professor asks his students to undertake a calculation in the following terms: "Our hypothesis in this problem is that we have two masses within an infinite vacuum, one of 10 tons and the other of 1000 tons; they are one mile apart. Of course, they're related as in $F = G\ (m_1m_2/r^2)$. Compute F."

To call O_s an hypothesis here simply indicates that it is serving as an *initial condition*. In the same spirit the Professor might ask: "Allow that the Gemini Capsule were to pass within 100 miles of the lunar surface, parallel to the tangent from the point directly 'below' it. What would its velocity have to be (relative to the moon's centre of mass), to *prevent* gravitational capture?" This could even be a genuine question for a NASA team; they would have to establish their skill with respect to a set of hypothetical conditions in order to generate answers required during the real test.

This reference to an O_s as an hypothesis (i.e. as an initial condition), is to be contrasted with our first, where an O_c was termed "hypothetical" – this latter being only an indication of fallibilism, from which philosophical stance *all* observation claims appear to be permanently vulnerable to exposure as *false* (– most unrealistic, practically speaking). Here we are supposing certain observation statements to be invulnerable in order to get a computational problem "off the ground."

Now contrast both of these uses of hypothesis with its application to a $\odot c$, a confirmed theoretical claim. It might be an hypothesis of celestial mechanics that the energy of a physical system (e.g. our circumsolar array) is always conserved.[26] An intimately related hypothesis of analytical mechanics is that *perpetua mobilia* (first kind) are physically impossible, and hence inconstructable. And it is an hypothesis of particle dynamics that unperturbed bodies

26 Perhaps, however, that is a *definition* of a physical system? Would an object-constellation with respect to which there is an "energy-leak" qualify as a physical system?

either remain at rest or move *sans* accelerations.[27] Such hypotheses might be imagined inscribed in Gothic letters and purple ink at the top of a page of scientific theory. Clusters of such expressions are what "make the theory go" (to use Clerk Maxwell's happy phrase). Now in this context, to term an $\odot_c$ an hypothesis means only that logically consistent alternatives are imaginable. It is logically conceivable that Leonardo built a perpetual motion machine (of the first type); there may be many things wrong with that claim, but *not* that it is demonstrably inconsistent. One cannot unpack anything of the form (Q-and-not-Q) from it, as one might from the remark that Leonardo built a three-wheeled bicycle, or a square wheel. That is all that one would usually mean by terming such an $\odot_c$ an hypothesis. For specialized conceptual motives one might so term an $\odot_c$ (i.e. as an hypothesis), even where there would be no good observational, or theoretical, or scientific reason for having any genuine (practical) doubts about the claim itself. An individual might purport to doubt the *principle of conservation of energy*, as when he vaguely speculates about constructing a perpetual motion machine. He may possess no genuine reason for doubt of that kind, other than his benighted aspiration to build a *perpetuum mobile*, and yet still insist on calling the principle an hypothesis – just because logically consistent alternatives to it are generable. The denial of the principle of the conservation of energy is not of the same logical form as "This is a three-wheeled bicycle," or "John is a married bachelor," or "ABC is an equiangular, Euclidean, plane triangle, but it is not equilateral." These latter are syntactically inconsistent, or semantically untenable; a denial of the principle may be neither.

Contrast all this now with an $\odot_s$, a theoretical claim (however unfamiliar and perhaps even counter-intuitive), which is nonetheless entertained as a basis for theory construction. The hypothesis of the continuous creation of H-atoms did certainly seem so to function within the "new" cosmology of Hoyle and his associates. It was a SCVAPO claim which could not be directly or immediately tested, as a matter of principle. Yet it had to anchor the entire conceptual framework of a most provocative, controversial, and influential cosmological theory; it was a *supposed* commitment, therefore. It was an $\odot_s$ treated as an hypothesis.

Consider now the multiform analogues of these SCVAPO claim-types as they figure within Newton's *Principia* – being designated hypotheses there in exactly these senses already explored. Requesting you to do so constitutes the denouement of this paper. Without question *all* things hypothetical for

27 Perhaps *that is* a definition too?

Newton are scvapo-related. All his hypotheses, *pro* and *contra*, embody assertions that are synthetic in their sign-design. They contain claims that are all contingently true, or contingently false, vis-à-vis their semantical status. They posit vulnerable claims for our attention as hypotheses. What they express *could* have been false. And the way in which we come ultimately to know what they express is always by way of experience. Knowledge of the assertoric content of Newton's hypotheses is forever *a posteriori*.

Remember our earlier analysis of the remark that it is an hypothesis that there are fifteen books in this room (when it is already certified observationally that there *are* fifteen books in this room). We suggested this to be but an expression of the near-pathological philosophical position called fallibilism. Is there anything in Newton like that? Not conspicuously, surely. But there is an aside made through Newton's mouthpiece Roger Cotes, the writer of the Preface to the second edition of the *Principia*. There "Newton-Cotes" argues that, with respect to the so-called axioms of motion, "there is no necessity whatsoever," – "... no tincture of necessity." This *might* be a mild expression of fallibilism for one who wished to stress, as did Newton, that every substantive proposition in classical mechanics had to be an empirical and contingent proposition.[28] That would distinguish natural philosophy from Euclidean geometry. It would demarcate it from mediaeval logic – contrasts both Newton and Cotes did often seek to draw. *Principia* systematizes propositions whose negations are consistent. So that *might* constitute a Newtonian locus for the use of hypothesis in our first sense – as a mild expression of fallibilism.

What of O_s as initial condition? In one place Newton's reasoning may be paraphrased as follows: "Let us suppose the moon to slow in its course. Since all bodies about the earth are 'heavy toward the earth'[29] at what rate would the moon then fall to earth?" College textbooks in astronomy challenge the student in much this same way. Newton's language is quite often exploited to this end: for example, "Our hypothesis is that body A is at rest." That is the occasion for one of his calculations to get under way. Thus there is no special conceptual problem in Newton about the uses of hypotheses to express initial conditions. He uses them thus very often, and regularly designates scvapo, O_s claims as conveyed by hypotheses.

How would he manage the highly confirmed theoretical claim? "Sun and

28 Indeed, I have witnessed the exploitation of these very same Newtonian words in defence of fallibilism.
29 Corollary 2, Hypothesis III; and see also Univ. Lib. Cambridge, MS. add. 3965: 2667.

earth move towards each other directly as their masses and inversely as the square of the distance between them – that is the measure of the central force 'bending' Earth from the inertial, tangential path it would otherwise pursue." Although a very highly confirmed hypothesis within most solar-astronomical contexts of inquiry, this is nonetheless an expression of a putative state of affairs alternatives to which have been seriously entertained.[30] Even in Newton's writings there are a couple of examples which bring this out. He argues that if the earth were replaced by a rotating ring of matter – that ring possessing the same axis and period of rotation, revolution, and orbit of the earth itself – the axis of that ring would precess precisely as the axis of the earth is found to do. This constitutes an hypothesis in this "O_c" sense. A very great deal depends on the context of Newton's attitude here. Within the late seventeenth century there was no proof whatsoever for this particular assertion three sentences above.[31] It was not something Newton himself was capable of proving, any more than he could then have found a general analytical solution to the n body problem. Nonetheless he did entertain certain such theoretical claims as being both sound and necessary as "conceptual anchors" for his further work; because he had no proof for them he styled them hypotheses – in this sense of theoretical claims as yet unconfirmed. So this is, for Newton, an hypothesis not in the fallibilistic sense (O_c), not in the "initial condition" sense (O_s), and not in the "there *are* logical alternatives" sense ($\odot_c$). This $\odot_s$ is hypothetical just because Newton cannot *prove* it!

In other places Newton concerns himself with similar for-now-unprovable hypotheses simply as a basis for explanation: the language he uses is significant. He seeks[32] to set out what in effect we should recognize as a version of the particulate hypothesis: to wit, that "all the great motions in the world depend on a certain kind of force (which in this earth we call gravity) whereby great bodies attract one another at great distances: so all the little motions in the world depend upon certain kinds of forces whereby minute bodies attract or dispel one another at little distances."[33] This is a breathtaking hypothesis in Newton's own hand; it is called and flourished as

---

30 Thus in 1743 Kant mused that the law of gravitation *might* have had an inverse three-fold form ($1/r^3$). And Clairault, perturbed by his own problems in lunar theory, once speculated concerning a law of gravitation of an inverse fourth-power form ($1/r^4$).

31 It was later supplied by Laplace, see W. W. Rouse Ball, *An Essay on Newton's "Principia"* (London, 1893), p. 110.

32 In a projected "Conclusion" to a Book Four of the *Opticks*: Univ. Lib. Cambridge MS. add. 3970, Hypothesis II.

33 *Ibid.*

an hypothesis in the bold style of contemporary theoretical physics. As we look back over the spectacular intellectual history of natural philosophy, or through our contemporary exercises in cosmology and elementary particle theory, Newton's Hypothesis II seems to be part of a familiar tradition. This is a sweeping explanatory hypothesis, synthetic in sign-design, contingent semantically, vulnerable and known *a posteriori*. Future observations could make us abandon such an O_s, just as Hoyle has abandoned his. Still, an O_s is founded only indirectly on experiential considerations – and future experiences may be acutely relevant to whether or not we continue to cleave to such a claim. Such hypotheses are as yet neither confirmed, nor disconfirmed. They serve as higher-order speculative claims which ground much of one's theoretical inquiries into a given subject-matter. They can serve to explain aspects of that subject-matter, as Newton mused in *The Opticks* (Book One, Part I). But more, $\odot_s$ often serve within hypotheses that reticulate and subsume within an inferential system volumes of otherwise unrelated observation-statements.

At the possible risk of boring the patient reader with reiterated summary, we can now distinguish *four* meanings of "hypothesis" within the Newtonian corpus.

1   When an O_c is called an hypothesis the gesture is that of the Fallibilist – i.e., *all* SCVAPO claims are hypotheses, even an obvious O_c like "I am awake." In this frame of mind the entire *Principia* might be viewed as one enormous conjunctive hypothesis.

2   When an O_s is called an hypothesis Newton may just be setting out initial conditions for a particular computation. Even an O_s like Holmes' "suppose that the gamekeeper did it" might well serve in this way, as a data-springboard from which the form of an argument therefrom may be tested.

3   When a $\odot_c$ is called an hypothesis Newton may only be noting the SCVAPO nature of even the most established laws of nature: "There is not the least hint of necessity about them." Logically possible alternatives are possible – which is no good reason in itself for thinking said law to be false; but it is vulnerable, in principle defeasible!

4   When an $\odot_s$ is called an hypothesis Newton may indeed intend to stress its speculative, unprovable, dubitable character. These are the potentially explanatory hypotheses which have made natural philosophy one of the boldest contributors to the history of human thought. Newton's Hypothesis II is surely such a bold contribution! His *theory of fits* is another.

In addition to these four distinguishable uses of "hypothesis" in Newton's works there is a fifth, and *this* (at long last!) is the one at issue in the expression "Hypotheses non fingo." He uses the expression for the first time in 1712(!), when writing out the General Scholium for the *Principia* (second edition). Until then, and in all his major work before and even after 1713, Newton's motto ought really to have been "Hypotheses fingo." He *did* frame hypotheses, in all of our examined senses above – and he did so as few other men of science have ever been able to do. He is one of the towering giants within the small society of creative hypothesis-designers. But he did not *feign* hypotheses (i.e. idle speculations and untestable opinions). After decades of depressing cavil with Cartesians and Schoolmen, and cut by starchy critics like the Bernoullis and Poleni – all of them tireless in their opposition to Newtonian theory – Sir Isaac moved to hit back. They always taunted him with the query: But "what is the cause of gravity?" And Newton always wisely declined to play their prose games, saying, as he does in the General Scholium: "it is enough that gravity does really exist, and act according to the laws which we have explained. ..." But his detractors were unsilenced, arguing that all that the *Principia* provided was a kind of *mathematical formalism*, a computation-recipe, in virtue of which one might succeed in grinding out numerical answers – but "that's not natural philosophy!" they would say. His patience now worn thin, Newton responds to such carping, cramped postures with his resounding "Hypotheses non fingo" – indicating thereby that numerical answers are infinitely preferable to irresponsible guesswork, however profound and multisyllabic the linguistic embodiments thereof. "... I have not been able to discover the cause of those properties of gravity from phenomena. And *I frame no hypotheses*; [or better, *I feign no guesswork*] for whatever is not deduced from the phenomena is to be called 'an hypothesis'; and hypotheses, whether metaphysical or physical, whether of occult qualities or mechanical, have no place in experimental philosophy."[34]

By 1712, for all sorts of reasons, sociological and professional, Newton *had* to respond to these Cartesian, and Aristotelian, and woolly "metaphysical" doubts about the worthwhileness of his theory. In order to stand up staunchly to all this strife Newton assumes in the General Scholium an unnecessarily rigid and haughty posture: "to the devil with all hypotheses," he says. But we must be careful to read him aright. For his meaning is, surely "to the devil with all this woolly, purple, capital-lettered, philosophical navel-contemplation. Essences, influences, effluvia, and virtues be damned;

34 Newton, *Principia*, General Scholium, p. 547.

I'm giving you here a quantitative account of matter in motion – indifferently applicable to stars, planets, satellites, tides, arrows, and point particles. Why churlishly reject these real descriptive achievements just because nothing like an Aristotelian explanation of such motions is gratuitously attached thereunto? And why speculate idly about these latter when there's no testing such pancreatic guesswork either way? Numbers rather than nothing; I describe phenomena rather than feign vain hypotheses!"

That is the bounded, but bruising force of Newton's "Hypotheses non fingo," and of it Newton let the Peripatetics and Cartesians have a tart taste.

Newton develops further this pejorative employment of "hypothesis" in a trying passage within the second edition of the *Principia* (1712): "Hypoth. IV. Every body can be transformed into a body of any other kind, and take on successively all intermediate degrees of qualities."[35]

In the printed editions this hypothesis appears without further comment, a fact which has perplexed Newton scholars, because this Hypothesis IV embodies a statement which Newton clearly *disbelieved*![36] (Contrast Rule III, which contradicts Hypothesis IV; pp. 398–99 in the Motte-Cajori version.) We owe to Professor I. B. Cohen the discovery of a projected revision of this passage which makes it at last clear what Newton had originally intended. In the revised manuscript Newton adds the explanatory sentence: "This is an Hypothesis of the Peripatetics and Cartesians and is directed only against their prejudices." Thus Newton cites Hypothesis IV originally only in the sense of "hypothesis" as it obtains in "Hypotheses non fingo" – it is a prejudice, an unfounded metaphysical posture to be despised, and never to be feigned by a serious natural philosopher. Alas, the printed Newton gives his guileless reader no guide concerning the real differences between *this* use of "hypothesis" (here in Hypothesis IV), and the superficially quite similar uses of the same term in Hypothesis III, and indeed in almost all of the other cited hypotheses in the *Principia* (e.g. in the eight hypotheses at the beginning of Book Three, first edition). Had I. B. Cohen not patiently untied this Gordian knot, we should still be cutting ourselves short of any full meaning of Newton's intentions.

That, then, is Newton's fifth major use of "hypothesis." An hypothesis, here, is simply an expression of some philosophical or metaphysical prejudice. This, of course, has no place in the assertive body of the *Principia*. Newton only cites it as indicating what others (who have gone wrong in

---

35 This is identical to Hypothesis III of the first edition (1687) as it appears on p. 402 of Dawson's facsimile.   36 In Univ. Lib. Cambridge, MS. add. 3965: 2667.

natural philosophy) still committed themselves to in 1712. His own oft be-clouded exposition has obscured for centuries this fifth use of "hypothesis" as it occurs in these dark passages. It *is* a genuine Newtonian use of the word. But alas, people like Mach and Kneale and Russell have seized upon this one pejorative use as constituting the major meaning of hypothesis in the writing of Newton – for which these philosophers then praise him, or berate his narrowness. We now know that there are *many* more signal uses of this idea within Newton, uses which are valuable and must be studied seriously by philosophers and historians.

Newton is a great natural philosopher, and hence a great hypothesis-framer. He conjectures responsibly. He introduces initial conditions. But he does not trade in unfounded metaphysical speculation. He will not put a scientific problem to sleep with any philosophical opium.

This is the terminus of my mission here, which has been to add my mite to the long history of discussion concerned with the function of hypotheses in the natural philosophy of Isaac Newton. My strategy has been to begin by erecting a logical framework for hypotheses – one which, through analysis, would exhaustively cite all possible candidates for that title. This approach seems preferable to the historians' more usual entry into the "Newtonian mysteries," where all Newton's actual employments of hypothesis are quoted, collected, collated, and classified – the result being an untidy logical array, however much learned and uplifting in other respects.

From both approaches, however, one thing emerges clearly. The concept of hypothesis in "Hypotheses non fingo" no more exhausts the fertile and creative facility for framing hypotheses in Newton's work than it does in all subsequent science. The empiricist in Newton had to note that, in a way, all non-mathematical propositions were to some degree hypothetical. The cal-culator in Newton had to begin his computations from initial conditions; putative matters of fact were granted as hypotheses. The modest theoretician in Newton saw the genuine possibilities of alternatives to his *axioms of motion* and his *law of universal gravitation*. And the creative natural philo-sopher in him perceived with startling clarity how the most comprehensive attempts at explaining phenomena had to proceed by hypothesizing univer-sal processes, supposing them to be fundamental to the entire inquiry at hand. This quadrupartite Newton did indeed *hypothesim fingere* – as well as, or better than, almost any man of science before or since. He did not feign fictions in his physics, however. That, and only that, was the burden of his pronouncement in "Hypotheses non fingo."

III
The Clarke-Leibniz Controversy

F. E. L. PRIESTLEY

The conflict between Newton and Leibniz was for some years confined almost exclusively within the circle of the learned, and was fought with some suggestion of reluctance and avoidance of open provocation on Newton's part. In the 1706 edition of the *Opticks*, obviously designed for Continental consumption, Descartes is attacked by name, but not Leibniz, and the attacks are directed against physical theories, not against philosophical and theological positions. The first break in this relative reticence seems to come with Cotes' preface to the 1713 *Principia*, and there are good grounds for believing that the more aggressive passages were introduced without Newton's connivance. In the last four paragraphs of his preface (p. xx), Cotes suggests that the supporters of a plenum are likely to be driven to seeing the world as caused, not by the will of God, but by some necessity of its own nature. "Therefore they will at last sink into the filthy mire of that most infamous herd who dream that all things are governed by Fate and not by Providence, and that Matter has existed always and everywhere by its own necessity, being infinite and eternal." (Tandem igitur delabi oportet in faeces sordidas Gregis impurissimi. Hi sunt qui somniant Fato universa regi, non Providentia ; Materiam ex necessitate sua semper et ubique extitisse, infinitam esse et aeternam.) Against these godless tendencies the surest protection is the Newtonian philosophy (*ibid.*): "For nowhere more surely than from this quiver could one draw forth missiles against the band of godless men." (Neque enim alicunde felicius, quam ex hac pharetra, contra impiam Catervam tela deprompseris.)

In the circumstances of the time, nothing could be much more provocative, more like a declaration of war, than Cotes' remarks. It was one thing to suggest or assert that the opponents were totally in error in their physical theories, that their hypotheses were figments of the imagination, romantic chimeras – this, though annoying, could still be part of a purely intellectual dispute. It was another thing altogether to assert that their doctrines led to and fostered atheism – this brings the whole argument into a much more serious, even dangerous area. To claim that one's own system supports religion is again one thing: Newton himself makes this claim. This need not entail the charge that the opponent's system subverts religion. Newton had in the 1706 *Opticks* attacked the Cartesian system as a physical theory; now Cotes had attacked it as a philosophy and theology. It is hard to believe that Newton himself, if he had properly supervised Cotes' preface, would have encouraged this unnecessary provocation. In fact it seems likely that he had not seen this part of the preface before publication. He had written to Cotes on 31 March 1713: "If you write any further Preface, I must not see it, for I find that I shall be examined about it."[1] If, as Edleston believes, Newton was still nervous about the row with Leibniz over the fluxions, he could hardly have wanted Cotes to write so provocative a passage involving views held by Leibniz. Whatever the case, Cotes' charge set a precedent for the resounding *tu quoque* from Leibniz which in 1715 turned the controversy into direct and open warfare ended only by Leibniz' death. The publication of the controversy in England in 1717 threw the dispute open to the public and lent it some of the special force of a national issue. Samuel Clarke, who was chosen to reply to Leibniz (Newton himself, as usual, seeking to avoid direct involvement), became not only the champion of Newton against Leibniz, but the champion of English philosophy against the Continental.

Leibniz had begun this battle with what was, indeed, to him a normal mode of opening a discussion. To Newton it must have seemed an act suggestive of extreme and calculated aggression. Instead of addressing a letter to Newton, or publishing an open letter, he had written to the Princess of Wales, ascribing what he took to be the decay in England not only of revealed religion, but even of natural religion, to the influence of Locke and Newton:

Mr. Locke, and his Followers, are *uncertain* at least, whether the Soul be not Material and naturally perishable.

Sir Isaac Newton says, that Space is an Organ which God makes use of to perceive Things by. But if God stands in need of any Organ to perceive Things by, it will follow, that they do not depend altogether upon him, nor were produced by him.

Sir Isaac Newton, and his Followers, have also a very odd Opinion concerning the Work of God. According to their Doctrine, God Almighty wants to wind up his Watch from Time to Time: Otherwise it would cease to move. He had not, it seems, sufficient Foresight to make it a perpetual Motion. Nay, the Machine of

---

1 J. Edleston, *Correspondence of Sir Isaac Newton and Professor Cotes* (London, 1850), pp. 156–57.

God's making, is so imperfect, ... that he is obliged to clean it now and then by an extraordinary Concourse, and even to mend it. ...[2]

It is hardly necessary to emphasize that to the seriousness of the charge of being a subverter of religion must be added the possible effect of making the charge, not as part of a public controversy, but in a private letter to a person of such power and importance as the princess. The princess was, indeed, in a peculiar position. An amateur of philosophy, she had known Leibniz well in Hanover. But since the death of Queen Anne and the consequent Hanoverian succession, she had become friendly with Clarke, with whom she now had philosophical discussions. Her obvious course was to let her two philosophical courts fight it out. She accordingly showed Leibniz' letter to Clarke and invited him to reply to it, and thenceforth acted as a sort of clearing-house for the correspondence.

This was by no means the first time, of course, that Clarke had been spokesman for Newton, and he was undoubtedly familiar with all Newton's views. It is also virtually certain, as Professor Koyré pointed out, and as recently published manuscript material tends to prove,[3] that Newton himself gave active assistance to Clarke in preparing the replies; indeed, Princess Caroline confirmed this in a letter to Leibniz. We can, then, take what Clarke says as an exact representation of Newton's own thought.

The dialogue established by the series of Leibniz' original letter and four further papers, with replies to each by Clarke, conveys to the ordinary reader a somewhat peculiar impression. There is much restatement of first positions and little development of new argument. What becomes clear is that each antagonist is arguing from his own set of premises, from his own philosophical context, which he takes as established. The real debate, which never takes place, would have had to be about the sets of assumptions underlying the positions of each. As it is, the vast gap between the two philosophers

---

2 The standard edition of Clarke's correspondence in English, now unfortunately out of print, is that of H. G. Alexander, *The Leibniz-Clarke Correspondence* (Manchester, 1956). The edition by André Robinet (Paris, 1957), follows the original manuscript text. Since my concern here is primarily historical, I use throughout the text of Clarke's original English edition of 1717, *A Collection of Papers which passed between the late Mr. Leibnitz, and Dr. Clarke, in the Years 1715 and 1716.* Unless otherwise stated, page numbers in parentheses refer to this edition.
     Clarke, p. 3. It must be remembered that at this time the Deist controversy was still raging, that Whiston had been deprived of his chair at Cambridge, and both Clarke and Newton had come under some suspicion of Arianism.

3 A. Koyré, *From the Closed World to the Infinite Universe* (New York, 1958), p. 301. For further evidence, see Koyré and I. B. Cohen, in *Archives Internationales d'Histoire des Sciences*, xv (1962), 63–126.

in their fundamental structures makes a real dialogue or debate impossible. This is illustrated in each of the main points of contention, as much as in what were in effect the rival conclusions: that Newton's philosophy is, from Leibniz' view, destructive of natural religion, and from Clarke's and Newton's, a main support of it.

Leibniz' first charge against Newton concerns the famous *sensorium* passage: "Sir Isaac Newton says, that Space is an Organ, which God makes use of to perceive things by." In an interesting article[4] based on the discovery of the original version of the first sensorium passage in the 1706 *Opticks*, Professors Koyré and Cohen have argued the probability that Leibniz had seen a copy containing the unrevised original text, which read:

Is not the whole of Space the Sensorium of a Being incorporeal, living, and intelligent; in that he sees distinctly and closely comprehends the most inward things themselves, and observes them wholly and thoroughly by their being present in him; of which [things], certainly, that which in us senses and reflects, surveys merely the Images in the Brain?

(Annon Spatium Universum, Sensorium est Entis Incorporei, Viventis, et Intelligentis; quod Res Ipsas cernat et complectatur intimas, totasque penitus et in se praesentes perspiciat; quarum id quidem, quod in Nobis sentit et cogitat, Imagines tantum in Cerebro contuctur?)

The revised version, substituted for the cancelled original in the majority of extant copies, and quoted by Clarke in reply to Leibniz, reads:

Does it not appear from Phaenomena that there is a Being, incorporeal, living, intelligent, omnipresent, who in infinite Space, as in his Sensory, sees the things themselves intimately, and thoroughly perceives them, and comprehends them wholly as present within his own presence; of which things indeed, that which in us senses and reflects grasps and considers in its little Sensorium merely the Images brought to it through the Organs of Sense? (My translation).

(Annon ex phaenomenis constat, esse Entem Incorporeum, Viventem, Intelligentem, Omnipraesentem, qui in Spatio infinito, tanquam Sensorio suo, res Ipsas intime cernat, penitusque perspiciat, totasque intra se praesens praesentes complectatur; quarum quidem rerum Id quod in nobis sentit et cogitat, Imagines tantum ad se per Organa Sensuum delatas, in Sensoriolo suo percipit et contuetur?)[5]

Koyré and Cohen rest their case mainly on the bluntness of Leibniz' own statement, which they feel would be a distortion on Leibniz' part of the later text with its *tanquam*. As they point out, there is no direct evidence that Leibniz had seen the original version, and of the five copies containing the

4 "The Case of the Missing *Tanquam*," *Isis*, LII (Dec. 1961), 555–66.
5 *Optice* (1706), p. 315 (Query xx).

unrevised sheet, none is in a Continental library. Until direct evidence is found, there are reasons to reject their theory. One is that Leibniz does not specify the passage he has in mind – he simply says that the assertion that space *is* the sensorium of God is to be found "expressly in the Appendix to M. Newton's *Opticks*," that is, in the queries. But there are two sensorium passages in the 1706 queries, the second of which remains unrevised, as Koyré and Cohen note, and which is certainly "express" enough to justify Leibniz' remark. It comes near the end of the last query, and speaks of God, "the powerful and ever-living Being, who is certainly everywhere present, and much more able by his Will to move all Bodies in his infinite *Sensorium*, and to fashion and re-fashion all the parts of the entire World at his bidding, than our Soul, which is the Image of God in us, is capable by its will of moving the members of our body."[6] Although this passage is not concerned with divine modes of perception, as the earlier passage is, it does unequivocally ascribe a sensorium to God, and would certainly allow Leibniz to make his comment fairly. Secondly, it seems difficult to believe that a controversialist like Leibniz, basing an attack on his opponent's words, would allow a reply which quoted a revised version without challenging the text. Yet when Clarke, in his first reply, quotes the Latin text in its revised *tanquam* form, Leibniz does not make any objection, does not say, as we should expect, "This is not Newton's statement as I read it."

But is the *tanquam* as important as Professors Koyré and Cohen suppose? Are they not perhaps led slightly astray by Clarke's (or Newton's) English version? Clarke translates *tanquam sensorio suo*, "as it were in his sensorium." The English, "as it were," with its use of the imperfect subjunctive, at once suggests a supposition contrary to fact – that God has in fact no such thing as a sensorium, but that we are supposing so by way of analogy. In Latin this would be conveyed by the use of *quasi* or *tanquam si*; it is not conveyed by *tanquam* nor by the French translation (*comme*) supplied to Leibniz. *Tanquam* suggests rather an exact comparison – "*just as* in his sensorium." One understands why Leibniz sees so little difference whether a *tanquam* or *comme* is there or not: "On s'excuse de n'avoir point dit que l'Espace est le *sensorium* de Dieu, mais seulement *comme* son *sensorium*. Il

---

6 *Optice*, p. 346 (Query XXIII): ... Nulli rei tribui potest, nisi Intelligentiae et Sapientiae Entis Potentis semperque Viventis; quod sit ubique scilicet praesens, possitque Voluntate sua corpora omnia in infinito suo *Sensorio* movere, adeoque cunctas Mundi universi partes ad arbitrium suum fingere et refingere, multo magis quam Anima nostra, quae est in Nobis Imago Dei, voluntate sua ad corporis nostri membra movenda valet.

semble que l'un est aussi peu convenable, et aussi peu intelligible que l'autre."
(P. 235) Clarke's further defence, that the word sensorium here does not mean
what Leibniz and Goclenius (author of the Philosophical Dictionary
Leibniz quotes), and indeed what all ordinary users of the term mean by it, is
essentially like a Lawyer's alternative defence. It says, in effect, "Granted
that Newton *did* say Space was God's sensorium, he did not mean by sensorium what you think." Professors Koyré and Cohen applaud this move of
Clarke's; they agree that "the Question is not what *Goclenius*, but what *Sir
Isaac Newton* means by the word."[7] But this is to side with Humpty Dumpty.
To use a term and then deny that it carries any of its root and usual meaning,
to assert that sensorium has nothing whatever to do with senses and sensation, is mere verbal anarchy.

But Leibniz' objections actually go much deeper than this. To start with,
even if Newton were speaking by way of analogy, Leibniz would deny the
validity of the analogy. God not only has no sensorium; he has nothing
analogous to a sensorium, nothing that can properly be compared with
one. To offer an analogy is to insist on a likeness, on a basis of comparison,
to say that even if God has not an actual sensorium, he has something corresponding or comparable with one.[8] As Leibniz makes clear, this is to ascribe to
God a mode of perception in some sense passive: "It supposes God to perceive Things ... by a kind of Perception, such as that by which Men fancy our
Soul perceives what passes in the Body. This is a degrading of God's knowledge very much. ..." (P. 239) The word "fancy" here indicates a second objection. Leibniz not only rejects the divine sensorium; he also rejects the
human. The analogy is unsound, he insists, in both its elements: it is unsound
in its attempt to compare divine perception with human, and doubly unsound in that its account even of human perception is false. "This way of
Perception is wholly Chimerical, and has no place even in *Human Souls*"
(*ibid.*). The theory of perception underlying Newton's analogy is, as we have
seen, that in the human body is a locality called the sensorium to which the
"images" of external objects of sensation are conveyed from the sense organs by the nerves, and where, by being co-present with the soul, the images
become perceived. (One notes in passing what an old-fashioned theory this
is to be offered in 1706.) Newton makes the point, in his elaboration of the

7 Clarke, p. 83. Koyré & Cohen, p. 562. It is interesting to note that Dr. Johnson
   erroneously remembered Newton's words as QUASI *sensorium numinis*, unconsciously supplying the correct Latin equivalent of Clarke's English version (Boswell, *Tour
   to the Hebrides*, 5 October).
8 For Newton's views on analogy between the human and divine, see R. and M. B.
   Hall, *Unpublished Scientific Papers of Isaac Newton* (Cambridge, 1962), pp. 108, 141.

sensorium passage, that God has no need of organs of sense, and perceives, not images of things, but the things themselves, by being present to them in infinite space. Leibniz' objection to this sort of theory is twofold. In the first place, it suggests that the physical can act upon the spiritual. This he denies. How, then, does Leibniz explain the "correspondence" between events in our perceptions and events in the physical world? Those followers of Descartes known as Occasionalists had made the physical event not the cause, but the "occasion" of the mental event, a theory ridiculed by Berkeley. Leibniz in effect severs also this sort of connection; the correspondence is there because of a pre-established harmony (*harmonia praestabilita*) between the sets of events, or, perhaps more exactly, between the two patterns of events. This harmony is of course divinely pre-established. The one set of events is then neither the cause nor the occasion of the other; both have been divinely ordained and ordered as concurrent series. Human beings perceive, consequently, not by having a particular location at which their soul can be influenced by the presence of physical images of objects, nor indeed by "being present" to anything, but because they have patterns and sequences placed in their minds. "The Soul knows things, because God has put into it a Principle Representative of Things without" (p. 107). God's mode of knowing, as creator of things and of minds, and of the harmony between them, is of a different character and order: "God cannot perceive Things by the same Means whereby he makes other Beings perceive them. He perceives them because he is able to produce that Means [the pre-established harmony]....And other Beings would not be caused to perceive them, if he himself did not produce them all *harmonious*, and had not therefore in himself a Representation of them; Not as if that Representation came from the Things, but because the Things proceed from Him, and because he is the Efficient and Exemplary Cause of Them." (P. 241) No matter how Newton explains his divine sensorium, or how many *tanquams* he inserts, his passage is still objectionable to Leibniz as suggesting that God derives knowledge from objects. We should not, Leibniz points out, really use the term "perception" in relation to God, since it implies things acting on him; he understands and wills things, and what he wills is the same as what exists (*ibid.*). God understands what "passes" in the World, not "because he is *present* to the Things," but because of their dependence upon him, "that is, by a continual Production of them, ... of what is good and perfect in them" (p. 239).

In the second place, the doctrine of the sensorium, whatever Newton means by the word, attaches special importance to locality. As Leibniz points out, the word has always signified "the Organ of Sensation," but if Newton and his friends now think fit "to explain themselves quite otherwise," he will not be against it. His other objections will remain. "More is requisite besides bare presence, to enable One thing to perceive what passes in another" (p. 25), and to reduce the sensorium merely to the locus of God, where he perceives merely by the fact of his presence to things,[9] is for Leibniz unintelligible. (He agrees with the Cartesians and with Malebranche in denying that the mere presence of the soul is enough for perception of what passes in the brain.) Presence in itself is not an activity. Space, after all, according to Newton, is intimately present to the body contained in it; does then Space, Leibniz asks, perceive what passes in a body, and remember it when that body is gone away? (p. 25) "A mere *Presence* or Proximity of Co-existence is not sufficient to make us understand how that which passes in One Being should answer to what passes in another" (p. 239). To this, Clarke's reply is based on the axiom, "Nothing can any more *Act*, or be *Acted upon*, where it is not present; than it can *Be*, where it is not" (pp. 42–43). This is for the Newtonians an important axiom; in its denial of the possibility of action at a distance it provides the most important proof of the constant, and immediate activity of God in the vast "extramundane space." But, says Clarke, the "Presence of the Soul is *necessary* (but not *sufficient*) to Perception." Presence in itself does not constitute perception, but there can be no perception without presence. This reply does not satisfy Leibniz, since it leaves unstated what else is necessary to perception, and still talks as if God, in perceiving, were acted on, that is, *passive*. Leibniz, firmly based in his own theory of pre-established harmony, is trying to force a debate on epistemology, which Clarke declines.

Another fundamental difference between Leibniz and the Newtonians concerns the nature of space. For Leibniz, "Space is the Place of *things*, and not the Place of God's Ideas: Unless we look upon Space as something that makes an Union between God and Things, in imitation of the imagined Union between the Soul and the Body" (p. 107). But this indeed is what the Newtonian analogy seems to be doing, and it might, as Leibniz points out, suggest the further analogy of God as the soul of the world. For Leibniz, space is merely the relations of bodies; it is "an *Order of Co-existences*, as Time is an *Order of Successions*" (pp. 54–59, 223). Where there are no bodies,

---

9 Clarke, p. 323: "God perceives every Thing, not by means of any Organ, but by being himself actually present everywhere. This everywhere therefore, or universal Space, is the Place of his Perception."

there can be no relations, so where there is no matter, there is no space. For Leibniz extension is a property of matter; all created substances, including angels, are bodies, and can, by their spatial relations to other bodies, be said to be in space, but such terms are inapplicable to God, who is not material, and not extended, and hence not in any spatial relation (p. 221). God is present to things, not "by Situation, but by Essence" (p. 65). The "real Space" (of Raphson), or the "absolute Space" of Newton, are figments of the imagination; "Mere Mathematicians, who are only taken up with the Conceits of Imagination, are apt to forge such Notions; but they are destroyed by superior Reasons" (p. 181). If there were such a thing as real space, it would "have a greater reality than Substances themselves"; God would not be able to destroy it, or even to change it (p. 97). Clarke, of course, repeats the doctrine of the General Scholium; "Space is a Property, or a consequence of the Existence of a Being infinite and eternal. Infinite Space is Immensity: But Immensity is not God. Infinite Space is *One* and *indivisible*. God, being Omnipresent, is really present to everything *Essentially* and *Substantially*. God does not exist *in* Space and *in* Time, but his Existence *causes* Space and Time. He himself suffers no Change at all, by the Variety and Changeableness of Things which live and move and have their Being in him." This strange doctrine [as Leibniz seems to find it] is the "express Assertion of St. Paul ... (Acts, xvii, 27, 28)." "God is neither a *Mundane* Intelligence, nor a *Supra-Mundane* Intelligence [the latter being Leibniz' term]; but an *Omnipresent* Intelligence, both *In* and *Without* the World. He is *In* all, and *Through* all, as well as *Above* all. ..." (Pp. 77, 85, 303, 29, 47)

Leibniz' treatment of this General Scholium doctrine shows how far apart the two disputants are in their metaphysical contexts. He makes a leap from Clarke's definition of space as a property which *belongs to*, or is *caused by* "the essence of God" (although Clarke says by his "Existence") to an equation of space *with* the divine essence, or, alternatively, to making space a property of God. The phrasing of the General Scholium, which Clarke quotes, in saying that God is *not* space or time, is *not* infinity or duration, but being infinite and everlasting "constitutes" space and time, seems intended, however obscurely, to guard against Leibniz' interpretation. It is perhaps significant that in this case Leibniz does not, as he often does elsewhere, sweep away the guard – he simply does not seem to recognize that it is there. If space is part of God's essence, he says, bodies in space would fill up part of God's essence (and, presumably, diminish it). Or again, if space is a property of God, how can he be *in* it? He can obviously think of Clarke's space only in terms of parts occupied by extended beings. Thus he also argues that space, having parts, being sometimes full, at others empty, hence changes; but God does not change, so space cannot be part of his essence (pp. 193–95).

To each disputant the system of the other is not only unacceptable but virtually inconceivable. To Leibniz the Newtonian philosophy is a wild figment of the imagination:

In the time of Mr. Boyle, ... no Body would have ventured to publish such chimerical Notions. ... Mr. Boyle made it his chief Business to inculcate, that every thing was done *mechanically* in natural Philosophy. ... What has happened in Poetry, happens also in the Philosophical World. People are grown weary of rational Romances, such as were the French Clelia, or the German Aramene; and they are become fond again of the Tales of Fairies. (*Ibid.*, p. 267)

And again, "All those who maintain a *Vacuum*, are more influenced by Imagination than by Reason" (p. 115); and "The fiction of a material finite Universe, moving forward in an infinite empty Space, cannot be admitted. ... These are Imaginations of Philosophers who have incomplete Notions. ..." (P. 181) "Methinks I see the revival of the *odd* Imaginations of Dr. Henry More (otherwise a learned and well-meaning Man), and of some others ..." (p. 205).

Meanwhile, to Clarke, Leibniz' account of divine cognition is "a mere fiction of the Schoolmen, without any proof" (p. 325) and his "pre-established harmony" a mere "Word or Term of Art," which explains nothing (p. 143).

Leibniz' arguments are grounded in certain principles, chiefly the *principle of sufficient reason*, the *principle of plenitude*, and the *principle of pre-established harmony*. The last of these, as we have seen, is invoked to solve the problem of epistemology, although its relevance is not limited to that problem. The second principle, particularly familiar to students of the *great chain of being* and Professor Lovejoy's account of it, is in part derived from the first principle of sufficient reason. This, then, is the most fundamental of Leibniz' principles, and the source of the most primary conflict with Clarke and Newton. In his second paper, Leibniz expounds the principle as the proper basis for demonstrating not only the Being and attributes of God, but also the dynamic principles of the natural world (pp. 21ff). He accordingly invokes it in his discussions of space and time; if space is something in itself, then the placing of bodies in space would be arbitrary, and against the principle of sufficient reason, that is, there would be no reason for their having been placed in one part of space rather than another. And so too with time; if time itself is distinct from *things* in time, no reason can be given for creation at a particular time, and not, say, a year earlier (pp. 59–61). Similarly, his argument against the existence of atoms and the homogeneity of matter is based upon the principle – choice must be founded on reason; if there were individuals indiscernible from each other, there could be no rational ground for choice in relation to them (p. 93). And again, "there is no *possible* Reason that can limit the quantity of Matter"; therefore there is no limitation, no *vacuum* (p. 103). There are reasons to limit the duration of matter, hence the universe is not eternal and created from eternity; but since there are no reasons to limit its extension, there must be a plenum (p. 231).

Against this doctrine, which is the extreme Rationalist one, in which the divine reason takes priority over the divine will, Clarke asserts a moderate *voluntarism*. He constantly asserts the free choice of God; God's will is a sufficient reason in matters indifferent – even if space were relative, as Leibniz maintains, the order of the particles in space is still a matter finally of choice (pp. 39, 72). For Leibniz, that choice must be a rational one, the choice of a "best possible"; for Clarke, to suggest that God had to choose between a best possible and a second best, with the choice inevitable, is to limit his freedom (p. 63). It will be obvious that Newton and Leibniz are here involved in the long and bitter discussion, bitter because theology and ethics are as much involved as psychology, over freedom of the will. Leibniz' distinction (in the correspondence with Arnauld, especially May 1686) between "intrinsic" and "necessary" acts, between the ability *not* to do something and the certainty that one *will* do it, is rather like Milton's distinction between foreknowledge and foreordination. Leibniz makes his position most clear, perhaps, in his modification of Lorenzo Valla's dialogue *Of Free-will* at the end of the *Théodicée*. But to the Voluntarist tradition, free-will tends to mean will arbitrarily exercised, determined neither by physical mechanism nor by rational motives. To the Rationalist, freedom lies in rational choice; arbitrary choice is random, or chance. The positions of the two schools, in their extreme forms, give exactly opposite definitions of freedom. A similar confusion surrounds the terms fate, chance, determinism. One remembers Newton's observation that God, if he had so willed, could have constructed a universe with quite different mathematical laws. It would still have been a mathematically rational universe. The crux of the debate seems to be in Leibniz' conception of the exclusive nature of rational choice; for him there is always a single best possible choice, and no such thing as a choice in matters indifferent. There are no matters indifferent. The principle of sufficient reason carries with it as a corollary the *principle of the identity of indiscernibles.* "Choice must be founded on Reason"; there is no such thing as two individuals (or two situations) indiscernible from each other, and hence offering indifferent choice (p. 93). Leibniz subordinates will very thoroughly to reason: "a Will without Reason, would be the *Chance* of the *Epicureans*" (p. 103). God acts "in the most *regular* and *perfect* Manner"; "it cannot be *regular,* without being *reasonable* ..." (pp. 69, 271). This is, of course, why Leibniz rejects so vigorously Newton's view that the universe is not a perfect self-regulating machine. But for Newton and Clarke, it is Leibniz' doctrine which comes closest to the Epicurean: "The notion of the World's being a great *Machine,* going on *without the Interposition of God,* as a Clock continues to go without the Assistance of a Clockmaker, is the Notion of *Materialism* and *Fate,* and tends, (under pretence of making God a *Supra-Mundane Intelligence,*) to exclude *Providence* and *God's Government* in reality out of the world" (p. 15).

At this point in the controversy, we have clearly come to a very fundamental theological conflict, which we can illuminate by turning back to the 1713 *Principia.* One of the most important, oft-quoted, and least-analysed passages in the General Scholium which Newton added to that edition is the one in which he sets forth his views on the nature of God and of his relation to the created world. As recent study has shown, it is one of the most deliberate, and long-thought-out statements Newton ever made. I offer no apology for quoting it in full:

This Being rules all things, not as soul of the world, but as Lord of all. And on account of his dominion he is wont to be called Lord God Pantokrator. For *god* is a relative word and refers to servants: and *deity* is the dominion of God, not over his own body, but over servants. The *Supreme God* is a Being eternal, infinite, absolutely perfect; but a Being however perfect without dominion is not the *Lord God.* For we say *my God, your God,* the *God of Israel,* but we do not say *my Eternal, your Eternal,* the *Eternal of Israel*; we do not say *my Infinite, your Infinite,* the *Infinite of Israel*; we do not say *my Perfect, your Perfect,* the *Perfect of Israel.* These titles have no relation to servants. The word *God* usually signifies *Lord,* but every lord is not God. It is the dominion of a spiritual Being which constitutes a *God,* a true dominion the true God, a supreme the supreme, an imaginary an imaginary God. And from his true dominion it follows that the true God is living, intelligent, and powerful; from his other perfections that he is supreme, or most perfect. He is *eternal* and *infinite, omnipotent* and *omniscient,* that is, he endures from eternity to eternity, and is present from infinity to infinity; he rules all things and knows all things which are done or can be known. He is not eternity or infinity but eternal and infinite; he is not duration or space, but endures and is present. He endures always, and is present everywhere, and by existing always and everywhere constitutes duration and space, eternity and infinity. Since every particle of space is *always*, and every single indivisible moment of duration *everywhere*, certainly the Maker and Lord of all things will not be *never*, *nowhere*. He is omnipresent not only *virtually*, but also *substantially*: for virtue cannot subsist without substance. In him all things are contained and moved, but without mutual effect. God is not acted upon by the motions of bodies: bodies feel no resistance from the omnipresence of God. It is admitted beyond doubt that the Supreme God exists necessarily, and by the same necessity he exists *always* and *everywhere*. Whence also he is all similar, all eye, all ear, all brain, all arm, all power of perceiving, of understanding, and of acting: but in a manner not in the least human, in a manner not in the least corporeal, in a manner absolutely unknown to us. As a blind man has no idea of colours, so we have no idea of the ways in which the most wise God perceives and understands all things. He is absolutely void of all body and bodily figure, and can therefore not be seen, nor heard, nor touched, nor ought he to be worshipped under the image or likeness of any sort of corporeal thing. We have ideas of his attributes, but we in no way know what is the substance of any kind of thing. We see only the figures and colours of bodies, hear only the sounds, touch only the external surfaces, smell only the odours, taste the savours: the inward substances we do not know by any sense or by any reflection; much less have we any idea of the substance of God. We know him only by his properties and attributes, and by his most wise and best contrivances of things, and final causes; we venerate and worship him because of his dominion. For a God without dominion, providence, and final causes, is nothing other than Fate and Nature. And thus much concerning God, to discourse of whom, especially from the appearances of things, belongs to experimental philosophy.

(Hic omnia regit non ut Anima mundi, sed ut universorum Dominus; et propter dominium suum Dominus Deus παντοκρατωρ dici solet. Nam *Deus* est vox relativa et ad servos refertur: et *Deitas* est dominatio Dei non in corpus proprium, sed in servos. *Deus summus* est Ens aeternum, infinitum, absolute perfectum; sed Ens utcunque perfectum sine dominio, non est *Dominus Deus*. Dicimus enim *Deus meus, Deus vester, Deus Israelis*; sed non dicimus *Aeternus meus, Aeternus vester, Aeternus Israelis*; non dicimus *Infinitus meus, Infinitus vester, Infinitus Israelis*; non dicimus *Perfectus meus, Perfectus vester, Perfectus Israelis*. Hae appellationes relationem non habent ad servos. Vox *Deus* passim significat *Dominum*; sed omnis Dominus non est Deus. Dominatio Entis spiritualis *Deum* constituit, vera verum, summa summum, ficta fictum. Et ex dominatione vera sequitur, Deum verum esse vivum, intelligentem et potentem; ex reliquis perfectionibus summum esse vel summe perfectum. *Aeternus* est et *Infinitus, Omnipotens* et *Omnisciens*, id est, durat ab aeterno in aeternum et adest ab infinito in infinitum; omnia regit et omnia cognoscit quae fiunt aut Sciri possunt. Non est aeternitas vel infinitas, sed aeternus et infinitus; non est duratio vel spatium, sed durat et adest. Durat semper et adest ubique, et existendo semper et ubique durationem et spatium, aeternitatem et infinitatem constituit. Cum unaquaeque spatii particula sit *semper*, et unum-

quodque durationis indivisibile momentum *ubique*; certe rerum omnium Fabri-
cator ac Dominus non erit *nunquam nusquam*. Omni praesens est non per *virtutem*
solam, sed etiam per *substantiam*: nam virtus sine substantia subsistere non potest.
In ipso continentur et moventur universa, sed absque mutua *passione*. Deus nihil
patitur ex corporum motibus: illa nullam sentiunt resistentium ex omnipraesentia
Dei. Deum summum necessario existere in confesso est: Et eadem necessitate
semper est et *ubique*. Unde etiam totus est sui similis, totus oculus, totus auris,
totus cerebrum, totus brachium, totus vis sentiendi, intelligendi et agendi; sed
more minime humano, more minimo corporeo, more nobis prorsus incognito. Ut
caecus ideam non habet colorum, sic nos ideam non habemus modorum quibus
Deus sapientissimus sentit et intelligit omnia. Corpore omni et figura corporea
prorsus destituitur, ideoque videri non potest, nec audiri, nec tangi, nec sub specie
rei alicujus corporei coli debet. Ideas habemus attributorum ejus, sed quid sit rei
alicujus Substantia minime cognoscimus. Videmus tantum corporum figuras et
colores, audimus tantum sonos, tangimus tantum superficies externas, olfacimus
odores solos, et gustamus sapores; Intimas substantias nullo sensu, nulla actione
reflexa cognoscimus; et multo minus ideam habemus substantiae Dei. Hunc
cognoscimus solummodo per proprietates suas et attributa, et per sapientissimas
et optimas rerum structuras, et causas finales; veneramur autem et colimus ob
dominium. Deus enim sine dominio, providentia, et causis finalibus, nihil aliud
est quam Fatum et Natura. Et haec de Deo; de quo utique ex Phaenomenis dis-
serere, ad *Philosophiam Experimentalem* pertinet.)[10]

This passage on the nature of God is of the highest interest and importance,
since when Newton commits himself to theological definition, he writes with
the utmost deliberation. What strikes the reader of the passage is the elaboration of the definition of *Deus*. A modern reader might wonder why Newton
so emphatically singles out this activity of dominion as essential to the
definition. Not every ruler is a god, but a god must be a ruler – it is as a
spiritual Being *who rules* that we acknowledge God. His other attributes – and
they form a familiar list: he is living, intelligent, powerful, in perfect degree;
that is, eternal, infinite, omnipotent, omniscient – these "follow" from his
true dominion. Since Descartes defines God as the absolutely perfect Being,
Newton's definition can be taken as directed against the Cartesian, but there
seems more in it than this. Some further light might be cast on Newton's
intention here by bringing in for comparison one of the most popular of

10 *Principia* (1713), pp. 482–83. Cf. John Maxwell's *A Discourse concerning God* (1715),
   pp. 2, 4, 93: "My Proposition is, that God is not rightly defined, a Being absolutely
   Perfect but that he is more rightly defined, a Spiritual Being endued with Absolute
   Dominion." "A Perfect Being, without Dominion, would be only an object of contem-
   plation and admiration, not of worship. ..." "Defining God, A Being absolutely
   Perfect, does in consequences promote Atheism, as we may perceive by the Writings of
   Des Cartes. ..."

eighteenth-century traditions, that of the great chain of Being. This concept is most familiar to modern readers in Leibniz' *Théodicée* (1710), but English readers of Newton's time would be equally likely to know the version presented in Archbishop King's *De Origine Mali* (1702). As the titles of both King's and Leibniz' works indicate, the great chain of Being is a systematic attempt to explain the origin of evil, the imperfection of the created world, and to vindicate the justice of its divine creator. Where orthodox Christian theologians offer a theological explanation through the doctrine of the *fall of man*, as in Milton's "justification" of God's ways, the philosophers of the great chain offer a philosophical explanation through a doctrine of ontological necessity. Their argument starts from the nature of Being. Perfect Being must be totally unlimited and independent, not contingent for its existence on any other Being; it must be uncreated therefore, eternal and infinite. There can clearly be only one such Being, and all other beings must be contingent on this one. Among the attributes of the perfect Being a fundamental one is "goodness" or "bounty," the will to impart Being by creative act. The fulfilment of this will involves the creation of the maximum amount of Being. This is to be secured, not by multiplication of individuals possessing one limited degree of Being, but by creation of every possible degree of Being, from the barest kind of existence through a full range to the highest possible short of the infinitely perfect. All Being, all degrees of Being, are accepted as good – as better than non-Being. The system of creation, which of course includes a hierarchy of angelic natures superior to man, then man himself, then the whole of animal, vegetable, and mineral nature, down to the lowest form of unorganized matter, exhibits the greatest variety of possible, or, as Leibniz would say, of "compossible" modes of Being. The limitations in the scheme are those of ontological necessity – given the nature of Being, the scheme could not have been otherwise. This is why this world, with all its imperfections, is in the often misunderstood phrase "the best of possible worlds."Evil is explained as necessary deficiency of Being, as limitation.

There are very important differences between this system of thought and that expressed in Newton's passage. In the first place, God is defined in the great chain in terms primarily of ontological perfection; his other attributes follow from this. Next, the emphasis on ontological necessity in the created universe has at least in some degree the effect of reducing emphasis on divine providence, at least on what is termed "particular Providence," and on the beneficent rule of God over his individual creatures. And the generalized vastness of the concept, in which the degrees of Being represented by species are important, but not individual members of a species (who are in a sense merely temporary representatives of a permanent rank of Being or link in the chain), tends to shift attention away from the sense of man's individual relation to God. It is this relation, of God to man and of man to God, that Newton seems anxious to assert – of God as a ruler and man as servant. He is asserting eternal providence, and with it this personal relation – "we say, my God ..., but we do not say my Eternal ... my Perfect." If we make the obvious comparison between the scholium passage and Newton's earlier statements in the 1706 *Opticks*, we recognize that this is a new emphasis. In the *Opticks*, he seems concerned solely with the relation of God to the physical universe, as creator of it, and source of its motions and forces. The analogies he uses, of the sensorium, and of moving bodies by an act of will, suggest the relation of soul and material body in man. Although there is every reason to believe that Newton's views had undergone no change, it is nevertheless true that the *Opticks* passages could be interpreted as presenting the doctrine of God as *anima mundi*. In the Scholium, Newton specifically and emphatically rejects this doctrine. God governs all things, *not* as the soul of the world; his dominion is *not* over his own body, but over his servants. Newton thus in effect abandons his previous analogies, not, I think, with any change of doctrine, but with a recognition that analogies can be misleading. When he had said, in the *Opticks*, that God could move all the bodies in the world much more easily than man could, by his will, move an arm, the ordinary reader might readily (and understandably) be tempted to think an analogy was being offered as to the nature of the two processes. Consequently, Newton now emphasizes the incorporeality of God. He is *all* eye, *all* ear, *all* brain, *all* arm, *all* power to perceive, to understand, and to act – these functions are not, in short, performed, as in man, by organs. Divine perception, intelligence, will, action, are all immediate, single, and whole, not mediate and performed by parts. God performs his functions "in a manner not at all human, in a manner not at all corporeal, in a manner utterly unknown to us." Newton no longer speaks of a divine sensorium. In fact he redefines the relation of God and infinite space. He still rejects the doctrine of the "Nullibists," that the concept of location is inapplicable to God; the doctrine of omnipresence is to be taken literally – God is everywhere. Nor is he present in a special sense, as power without substance – he is present as infinite spiritual substance. By his infinite presence he constitutes space. Infinite space thus becomes the locus of the infinite spirit. In similar fashion, the eternity of God constitutes duration. One of Newton's arguments is particularly ingenious. By bringing in the temporal dimension of a particle of space, and the spatial dimension of a moment of time, each of which is for him infinite, he urges by implication the impossibility of parts having a kind of infinity which is denied to God.

When he turns finally to the extent of our knowledge of the divine substance, Newton drops back to the Lockean argument on the general unknowability of substance. As in Locke, the unknowability is combined with a certainty of its existence. "Virtue cannot subsist without substance." Since the divine substance is not corporeal, it cannot be perceived by the senses; the divine attributes are revealed by his works, his "most wise and excellent contrivances of things," and by his providence, seen as final causes. In this discussion of substance, one rather curious passage occurs. An allusion to the familiar text of Acts xvii, 27, 28, supports the familar doctrine that in God "are all things contained and moved," followed however by the apparently contradictory assertion, "yet neither affects the other." The affirmation that God is not affected by his creatures, that he is in no sense passive, the receiver of action, but is pure action, is common enough. But at first sight Newton seems to be saying that God does not act upon matter. Since we know that he often asserts the contrary, this is not likely to be his meaning here. When he particularizes, saying that bodies find no resistance from the omnipresence of God, we recognize that what he is really denying is the sort of mutual actions bodies have on each other – God does not act upon material bodies as a material substance would act, since he is not a material substance. (The modern reader, with his knowledge of Newton's unpublished papers, is likely to be surprised at this passage, as at so many others, where Newton, in spite of very long and careful thought on the matter, produces a statement expressed in curiously loose terms.)

The over-all effect of the General Scholium on the eighteenth-century reader, as a statement of Newton's religious opinions, would be on the whole that it was more clearly orthodox than the sensorium passages of the *Opticks*. It affirmed the immateriality of God decisively and repeatedly, his unity and indivisibility, his personal concern and providence. It called him God, and not merely "a living, intelligent, and powerful Being," and it offered a less dubious account of the nature of space. To the rigorously orthodox, of course, it would be apparent that it was limited in its orthodoxy to the range of natural theology; it made no allusion to the Trinity or to Christ, or to such central Christian doctrines as that of the Fall. There was nothing in it, in short, as a defence against a charge of Arianism or Deism.

The emphasis on God's providence, on God as *pantokrator*, which we have noted in the General Scholium, appears again in Clarke's replies as evidence of the conflict between the Newtonian doctrine and that of the great chain of Being: "God ... not only composes or puts Things together, but is himself the Author and continual Preserver of their *Original Forces* or *moving Powers*: 'tis ... the true *Glory* of his Workmanship, that *nothing* is done without his *continual Government* and *Inspection*" (p. 15). But this does not mean, Clarke further argues, that God's original scheme was less than perfect: "The *Wisdom of God* consists, in framing *Originally* the *perfect* and *complete Idea* of a Work, which began and continues, according to that Original perfect Idea, by the *Continual Uninterrupted Exercise* of his *Power and Government*. The Word *Correction*, or *Amendment*, is to be understood, not with regard to *God*, but to *Us* only. ... With regard to God, the present *Frame*, and the consequent *Disorder*, and the following *Renovation*, are *all* equally parts of the Design. ..." (P. 45)

It is clear that Leibniz and Clarke (and Newton) differ again in their conceptions of the perfection of the universe. In one sense, of course, the great-chain doctrine could be considered as a demonstration of the necessity of imperfection; the best of possible worlds contains the greatest possible number of degrees of imperfect Being; its perfection lies, paradoxically, in containing the most compossible kinds of imperfection. But in the controversy with Clarke, Leibniz does not call on this concept. He emphasizes rather the Cartesian concept of the physical universe as a perfect piece of mechanism, complete and self-regulating. It would seem, on the face of it, that he and Clarke might on this point have exchanged roles, with Clarke appealing to the ontological principles of the great chain to argue the necessary imperfection of a material mechanism, unless regulated by a higher degree of Being. But in fact Clarke has put forward a conception of perfection different both from the Cartesian and from the great-chain conceptions, and the disagreement between the disputants is at this point very significant. Leibniz conceives of a static "perfection," the establishment at a single moment by a single divine fiat of a finished, self-regulating mechanism. Clarke and Newton, with their emphasis on God's active rule, conceive of a dynamic scheme, constantly being realized through time. If Clarke had pursued his train of thought further on the subject of "correction or amendment," he would have come to the conclusion that the whole notion we form of correction and amendment arises from our trying to treat the system of the World as a static and fixed system; the terms suggest, as does Leibniz' analogy, the limited completeness of a watch mechanism. What Clarke partly enunciates in this passage is a view of the cosmos, not as a simple fixed mechanical structure, but as a process, developing, under God's providence, through time in accordance with the divine *Idea*. For Leibniz, as for the other great-chain philosophers, a "rational" universe is one totally, permanently explicable as a complete and completed structure.

The situation is somewhat the same in regard to the view of divine providence. If each disputant were pressed, each surely would have to express a measure of agreement. For Clarke and Newton, undoubtedly, the created universe is ultimately and completely a manifestation of total providence. The planets pursue their orbits, and the sparrow falls, in conformity with the foreknowledge and will of God. In this comprehensive view, Clarke and Newton might be considered at one with Leibniz. Clarke comes closest, perhaps, to recognizing this in his assertion that what seem to us aberrations in the celestial system which must be corrected by what seem special divine interventions, special acts of providence, are all foreseen parts of the divine plan. In short, ultimately the distinction between general providence and particular breaks down. The constant exercise of divine power in the universe cannot, for Clarke any more than for Leibniz, involve *ad hoc* emergency measures on God's part to correct oversight. When all providence is made uniformly general in this manner, the only difference between the two sides is in the conception of how providence operates. For Leibniz it operates through the pre-established harmony, for Clarke through a temporarily sustained activity of the divine power, exhibited partly as what we think of as ordinary causality.

But however true it may be that, in the last analysis, both sides agree about providence, it is obvious that during the controversy they are mainly at variance on the subject. For although Clarke, under pressure, virtually subsumes special or particular providence under the ordinary or general, his habit of mind is to think usually in the two separate categories. It is perhaps no exaggeration to say that although he accepts a total and comprehensive general providence, he thinks much more habitually in terms of the particular. Like Newton, he rejects the doctrine of the divine architect, whose function is completed with the building, in favour of the *pantokrator*, whose activity is permanently necessary. This is why, although he insists that God does not *exist* in time, he emphasizes his activity in time. And this is one reason why he rejects Leibniz' view of providence, which he sees simply as the pre-established harmony under another name.

This means, too, that Leibniz and Clarke differ in their concept of nature, and with it, of miracles. Leibniz thinks steadily in terms of a contrast between the natural and the supernatural: "natural" is that which can be explained by "the Nature of Bodies"; all else is supernatural, or miracle (p. 71). And the nature of bodies is totally mechanical; "whatever is performed in the Body of Man, and of every Animal, is no less Mechanical than what is performed in a Watch" (p. 269). Boyle is praised for having "made it his chief Business to inculcate, that every thing was done *mechanically* in natural Philosophy (p. 267). Nothing can be "natural," unless it can be explained by the Nature of Creatures" (p. 271).

Clarke rejects Leibniz' dichotomy and his definition of natural. "*Natural* and *supernatural* are nothing at all different in regard to God ..." (*ibid.*, p. 49). In other words, it is not a case of there being one set of events with which God does not concern himself or take an active part in, called "natural," and another set in which he does act, called "supernatural." He acts in all. The difference, then, between the natural and the miraculous does not lie in the non-exercise or exercise of God's power; it lies rather in the manner in which that power is exercised. "For a Body to move in a Circle round a Center *in Vacuo*, if it be *usual* ... 'tis *no Miracle*, whether it be effected immediately by *God himself*, or mediately by any *Created Power* ..." (p. 87). What makes an event natural is not the kind of cause operating, or the immediate source of the power employed, but whether it is a usual or regular event, whether, in theological terms, it is an example of God's ordinary or regular providence, or of his particular or special providence. If it is usual, it is not a miracle, however performed. When to this Leibniz offers the objection (p. 113) that in these terms monsters must be miracles, Clarke has no difficulty in pointing out (as he had similarly done in the matter of perception and presence) the fallacy in Leibniz' argument. Miracles, he says, are necessarily unusual, but not all unusual things are miracles; some are irregular and rare effects of *usual* causes (p. 149). Miracles, he implies, are rare effects of unusual causes. He will not, of course, equate *usual* with *mechanical*. In a passage reminiscent of Newton's letter to Bentley, Clarke uses attraction as an example, chosen because Leibniz has attacked it as a "miracle":

That *One Body* should *attract* another *without any* intermediate *Means*, is indeed not a *Miracle*, but a *Contradiction*: For 'tis supposing something to *act* where it *is not*. But the *Means* by which *Two Bodies* attract each other, may be *invisible* and *intangible*, and of a different nature from *mechanism*; and yet, acting regularly and constantly, may well be called *natural*. ... If the word, *natural Forces*, means ...

Mechanical, then all *Animals*, and even *Man*, are as *mere Machines* as a *Clock*. But if the word does not mean *mechanical Forces*, then *Gravitation* may be effected by *regular* and *natural* Powers, though they be *not Mechanical*. (P. 151)

And in his last reply to Leibniz, Clarke enumerates what appears to be a completely empirical view: "The terms *Nature*, and *Powers of Nature*, and *Course of Nature*, and the like, are nothing but *empty Words*; and signify merely, that a thing *usually* or *frequently* comes to pass" (p. 351). This definition might seem to place Clarke, in this particular matter, in agreement with Hume and T. H. Huxley. But it is by no means certain that Clarke is thinking in such exclusively empirical terms as those later writers. If one recalls the other comment of his already quoted, that "*Natural* and *Supernatural* are nothing at all different with regard to *God*," it seems much more likely that he is staying in his own tradition. For Hume and Huxley, Clarke's phrase "usually comes to pass" would have a purely empirical meaning – "is usually observed by us in sensation" – "nature" being the sum total of our regular and ordered sense experience. For Clarke, there is no doubt that nature includes more than sense experience; it obviously includes the "natural Powers," invisible and intangible, that he speaks of above. His assertion of the ultimate identity of natural and supernatural is significant. His position is, I would suggest, the same as that expressed by Bishop Butler (who belongs in the same tradition). In his *Analogy*, Butler writes:

The only distinct meaning of the word *natural* is *stated, fixed, settled.* ... And from hence it must follow that a person's notion of what is natural will be enlarged, in proportion to his greater knowledge of the works of God. Nor is there any absurdity in supposing, that there may be beings in the universe whose capacities, and knowledge, and views may be so *extensive* as that the whole Christian dispensation may to them appear *natural*, i.e. analogous or conformable to God's dealings with other parts of his creation; as natural as the visible course of things appears to us.[11]

Nature is, then, in this tradition ultimately the total rational order, evidenced for us in regularity and recurrence, and comprising not only the physical but also the spiritual. It might be asked then why Clarke calls *nature* and *natural* "empty Words." First, I would suggest, because of the ultimate invalidity of the distinction between natural and supernatural, and secondly because of the varied content of the terms according to the knowledge of the user. It is evident to him, for example, that Leibniz's "nature" will not include phenomena which are for Clarke and Newton scientifically

11 Joseph Butler, *Analogy of Religion, Natural and Revealed* (1736), pt. 1, ch. i.

and rationally demonstrated. Finally, Clarke is making the usual attack against the dogmatist. Leibniz' attempt to fix the term "nature," to define sharply what is natural and what is not, what sort of cause is a natural cause, imposes, in Clarke's view, *a priori* preconceptions on the interpretation of phenomena, nourishing a false science and a false philosophy. The separation of phenomena and of causes into natural and supernatural, the assumption that mechanical causation is readily intelligible, immechanical not, that there is no mystery or miracle in the action of matter upon matter – these are for Clarke empty assumptions standing in the way of a true understanding. "What greater difficulty is there," he asks, "in conceiving how an *immaterial Substance* should act upon Matter, than in conceiving how Matter acts upon Matter?" (P. 369) No mechanism can explain the adhesion of parts of a solid, or the reflection of rays of light without contact. "Is a manifest Quality to be called occult, because the immediate efficient cause of it (perhaps) is occult, or not yet discovered? ... The Phaenomenon itself, ... and the Laws, and Proportions, ... are now sufficiently known. ..." (P. 369) Like the Cartesians, with whom he has much in common, Leibniz finds in "mechanical" explanation and causation an ultimate quality which Newton and Clarke are sceptical of. They would like to find mechanical causes of phenomena but are less sanguine than Leibniz about understanding "the nature of bodies," "the nature with which things are endowed by God."[12] As far as Clarke is concerned, he has introduced no miracles, even in Leibniz' definition; he has not suggested that God is continuously "changing the laws of bodies," but merely how he is "preserving each substance in its course and in the laws established for it."[13]

It is only relatively occasionally that Leibniz moves the argument into the area of science, and when he does, Clarke has little difficulty. Leibniz does not seem to have grasped Newton's basic principle of *inertia*; he speaks only of gravitation. He offers, for example, a theory of gravity based upon a non-gravitating fluid:

Both Quicksilver and Water, are masses of heavy matter, full of Pores, through which there passes a great deal of Matter void of Heaviness; such as is probably that of the Rays of Light, and other insensible Fluids; and especially that which is it self the Cause of the gravity of gross Bodies, by receding from the Center towards which it drives those Bodies. For, it is a strange Imagination to make all Matter gravitate ...: Whereas the gravity of sensible Bodies towards the Center of the Earth, ought to be produced by the motion of some Fluid. (Pp. 187–89)

12 Leibniz, *The New System* (1696), Open Court ed., p. 123.
13 Leibniz, Letter to Arnauld, 14 July 1686. Open Court ed., p. 134.

He here shows no sign of understanding Newtonian gravitation, nor of having read those parts of the *Principia* dealing with motion in and through fluid media. Again, he argues that "it is not so much the quantity of Matter, as its difficulty of giving place," that makes resistance to a body in motion. A plenum of subtle matter offers less resistance than of heavy matter, and to illustrate this he gives the example of a boat moving through water and through floating logs (pp. 187–89). It must be remembered that he denies the homogeneity of matter, and the Newtonian atoms, but Clarke has to remind him that in Newtonian theory it is the *inertia*, not the *gravity* of matter, that makes motion in a plenum impossible (pp. 297–99). At another point, Leibniz becomes involved in a discussion of the motion of falling bodies and the preservation of motion, and so Clarke devotes a long footnote to a lesson in mechanics. Leibniz, it seems, ignores time in dealing with the force of a falling body, merely multiplying mass by distance, so that the force of a four-pound mass falling one yard equals that of a one-pound mass falling four yards (pp. 111, 253, 327–39). In all these scientific matters, of course, Clarke is a very able exponent of the Newtonian system, and would doubtless have been pleased to have more of the debate a confrontation between Cartesian and Newtonian physics, but science plays a relatively minor part in the controversy, since Leibniz keeps pressing on the metaphysical questions.

Clarke has the advantage of the last word, and takes the further advantage in the published text of adding twenty-five pages of appendix. Here he selects passages from Leibniz (from the *Acta Eruditorum* from 1694 to 1698, and from the *Théodicée* of 1710) in which he expresses views more in conformity with the Newtonian: "Though the Gravity or Elasticity may and ought to be explained mechanically by the Motion of Aether, yet the ultimate Cause of Motion in Matter, is a Force impressed at the Creation ..." (p. 377). And although at this time he is ascribing activity to matter ("this active Faculty I affirm to be in All Substance ... So that not even corporeal Substance, any more than Spiritual, ever ceases acting"), in 1698 he was talking much of natural inertia and the "Sluggishness of Matter" (*ibid.*). Clarke thus ends the volume with the implication that Leibniz, when not engaged in controversy, had at least moments of recognition of the truth of some elements of the Newtonian philosophy.

IV
Berkeley, Newton, and Space*

JOHN W. DAVIS

> It is usual with you to admonish me to look over a second time,
> to consult, examine, weigh the words of Sir Isaac. In answer to
> which I will venture to say that I have taken as much pains as (I
> sincerely believe) any man living to understand that great
> author, and to make sense of his principles. No industry, nor
> caution, nor attention, I assure you, have been wanting on my
> part. So that, if I do not understand him, it is not my fault but
> my misfortune. (Berkeley, *A Defence of Free-Thinking in
> Mathematics*)

I

Berkeley opens the account in *Principles*, sections 110–17 by mentioning
Newton with esteem: "The best grammar of the kind we are speaking of, will
be easily acknowledg'd to be a treatise of mechanics, demonstrated and
applied to Nature, by a philosopher of a neighbouring nation whom all the
world admire."[1] Personal polemics are reserved for "minute philosophers"
and mathematicians other than Newton. Since the *Principles* was written
in Ireland, it was quite in order for Berkeley to speak of Newton as a
"philosopher of a neighbouring nation." Because the work was published in
Dublin the likelihood of its having come to Newton's attention is somewhat
diminished.

* This paper has benefited from the careful criticisms of Professor F. E. L. Priestley
and my colleague Professor A. M. Schrecker.

1 George Berkeley, *The Works of George Berkeley*, ed. A. A. Luce and T. E. Jessop,
9 vols. (Edinburgh, 1948–57), II, 1st ed. variant, p. 89. All quotations from Berkeley's
Principles will be from the first edition. Quotations from the *Philosophical Commentaries* will be from Berkeley, *Philosophical Commentaries*, ed. A. A. Luce
(Edinburgh, 1944), referred to as *Commentaries*. Perhaps Berkeley's most characteristic remark about Newton is found in *Siris*, sec. 245 in *Works*, V, p. 117. "Sir Isaac
Newton, by his singular penetration, profound knowledge in geometry and mechan-
ics, and great exactness in experiments, hath cast a new light on natural science."
See also *Commentaries*, entry 372, p. 116; Berkeley's letter to Johnson of 24 March
1730 in *Works*, II, 292; and *A Defence of Free-thinking in Mathematics*, sec. 13, in
Works, IV, pp. 114–15.

But Berkeley, as was his custom, expresses reservations about the implications of key Newtonian doctrines:

I shall not take upon me to make remarks, on the performance of that extraordinary person: only some things he has advanced, so directly opposite to the doctrine we have hitherto laid down, that we shou'd be wanting, in the regard due to the authority of so great a man, did we not take some notice of them. In the entrance of which justly admired treatise, time, space and motion, are distinguished into *absolute* and *relative, true* and *apparent, mathematical* and *vulgar*: which distinction, as it is at large explained by the author, doth suppose those quantities to have an existence without the mind: and that they are ordinarily conceived with relation to sensible things, to which nevertheless in their own nature they bear no relation at all. (*Principles*, sec. 110, *Works*, II, 89–90)

Apart from Berkeley's criticism of Newtonian fluxions, his basic charge against Newton is the one levelled here: the Newtonian absolutes of space, time, and motion are quantities having an existence "without the mind" thus running counter to Berkeley's most characteristic doctrine that the *esse* of material objects is *percipi*. To be on the safe side, however, whenever one writes of Berkeley's "*esse* is *percipi*," that perception is the criterion of reality, the whole immaterialist doctrine should be remembered: "Existence is percipi or percipere (or velle i.e. agere)."[2] The relativization of space, time, and motion is implied by "*esse* is *percipi*".

In *Principles*, section 111, Berkeley's account of Newton's views is accurate, although in summary form. What Berkeley omits, as comparison with the Newtonian texts shows, is illustrative in character. Newton begins by defining, although not rigorously, his fundamental conceptions of space, place, and motion.[3] Berkeley says: "This celebrated author holds there is an *absolute space*, which, being unperceivable to sense, remains in it self similar and immoveable: and relative space to be the measure thereof, which being moveable, and defined by its situation in respect of sensible bodies, is vulgarly taken for immoveable space. ... Now because the parts of absolute space, do not fall under our senses, instead of them we are obliged to use their sensible measures."[4] The Newtonian definition of place, a consequence of

2 Berkeley, *Commentaries*, entries 429 and 429a, pp. 138–39. In this way both active mind and passive idea are stressed.
3 Newton also defined absolute and relative time, but since Berkeley refers his reader to his own account in *Principles*, secs. 97–98, it can be eliminated from this discussion.
4 Berkeley, *Principles*, sec. 111, p. 90. The English translation of Newton used will be Isaac Newton, *The Mathematical Principles of Natural Philosophy and His System of the World* [*Principia Mathematica*], Motte's trans. rev. and supplied with an historical and explanatory appendix by Florian Cajori (Berkeley, 1934), referred to as "Cajori."

the definition of space, follows immediately in both Newton's text and in section 111 of Berkeley's *Principles*. Berkeley writes: "*Place* he defines to be that part of space which is occupied by any body. And according as the space is absolute or relative, so also is the place."[5] Finally Berkeley summarizes the Newtonian doctrine of motion as follows: "*Absolute motion* is said to be the translation of a body from absolute place to absolute place, as relative motion is from one relative place to another."[6] After distinguishing absolute and relative time, space, place, and motion, Newton goes on to assert that absolute motion could be distinguished from relative motion by certain "properties, causes and effects."[7]

At the end of *Principles*, section 111, Berkeley skilfully summarizes these Newtonian contentions. They form the target of his criticism in sections 112 through 115. Berkeley's objections in these sections are dynamical in character; the theoretical difficulties and practical ambiguities which according to Newton require absolute space to be postulated do not convince Berkeley. "As the place," according to Berkeley, "happens to be variously defined, the motion which is related to it varies" (*Principles* 114, p. 91). A man may be at rest with respect to the sides of the ship but moving with respect to the land. Berkeley as a critic of the Newtonian philosophy of science is at his most astute here. As Berkeley sees, Newton is wrong in thinking absolute space is the only possible postulate; there is an alternative which Berkeley chooses. This is the conception of an inertial system with respect to which the Newtonian laws are valid. Up to a point the earth itself can be treated as such a system, as can certainly the system of the fixed stars. He writes:

In the common affairs of life, men never go beyond the earth to define the place of any body: and what is quiescent in respect of that, is accounted *absolutely* to be so. But philosophers who have a greater extent of thought, and juster notions of the system of things, discover even the earth it self to be moved. In order therefore to fix their notions, they seem to conceive the corporeal world as finite, and the utmost

5 Berkeley, *Principles*, sec. 111, in *Works* II, p. 90. The Newtonian text on place is to be found in *Principia*, Scholium to Definitium VIII, Book I. "Place is a part of space which a body takes up, and is according to the space, either absolute or relative" (Cajori, p. 6). Newton goes on to differentiate place as a part of space from either situation or the external surface of a body. This point is not brought out by Berkeley, nor is it a necessary part of his argument to do so.

6 Berkeley, *Principles*, sec. 111. Newton writes in the Scholium to Definitium VIII: "Absolute motion is the translation of a body from one absolute place into another; and relative motion, the translation from one relative place into another" (Cajori, p. 7).

7 In the same Scholium to Definition VIII (Cajori, p. 8) Newton distinguishes three properties, one cause and one effect, devoting a separate paragraph to each.

unmoved walls or shell thereof to be the place, whereby they estimate true motions. (*Ibid.*, pp. 91–92)

Furthermore, Newton in the *Principia* had used the rotating bucket experiment to illustrate that "the effects which distinguish absolute from relative motion are, the forces of receding from the axis of circular motion" (Scholium to Def. VIII, p. 10).

Berkeley's reply to Newton's experiment – or better, *Gedanken* experiment – was: "As to what is said of the centrifugal force, that it doth not at all belong to circular relative motion: I do not see how this follows from the experiment which is brought to prove it. See *Philosophiae Naturalis Principia Mathematica*, p. 9 in Schol. Def. VIII. For the water in the vessel, at that time wherein it is said to have the greatest relative circular motion, hath, I think, no motion at all."[8] For Berkeley all motion when defined operationally is relative: "so that to conceive motion, there must be at least conceived two bodies, whereof the distance or position in regard to each other is varied. Hence if there was one only body in being, it could not possibly be moved. This to me seems very evident, in that the idea I have of motion doth necessarily involve relation." (*Principles*, 112, p. 91) Berkeley's criteria of motion are such as to delight the eye, ear, and mind of an ordinary language philosopher. "For to denominate a body *moved*, it is requisite, first, that it change its distance or situation with regard to some other body. Secondly, that the force occasioning that change be impressed on it. If either of these be wanting, I do not think that agreeably to the sense of mankind, or the propriety of language, a body can be said to be in motion." (*Ibid.*, 112, p. 92) The very meaning of the term "motion" shows that motion is relative.

After pointing out Newton's dynamical difficulties and his own solution of them by the doctrine of the relativity of motion, Berkeley turns to criticism of the doctrine of absolute space. His argument here is that absolute space is

8 Berkeley, *Principles*, sec. 114, p. 92. It is usual to say that Berkeley's contention that all motion is relative anticipated Mach by a century and a half. For Berkeley as a precursor of Mach see G. J. Whitrow, "Berkeley's Critique of the Newtonian Analysis of Motion," *Hermathena*, LXXXII (1953), 90–112, esp. 190f.; Whitrow, "Berkeley's Philosophy of Motion," *British Journal for the Philosophy of Science*, IV (1953), 37–45 (a shorter version of the previous item); John Myhill, "Berkeley's *De Motu* – An Anticipation of Mach," in *George Berkeley*, ed. S. Pepper, K. Aschenbrenner, and B. Mates, University of California Publications in Philosophy, XXIX (1957), 141–57; and Karl R. Popper, "A Note on Berkeley as Precursor of Mach and Einstein," in *Conjectures and Refutations* (London, 1963), pp. 166–74. This view has recently been challenged. See W. A. Suchting, "Berkeley's Criticism of Newton on Space and Time," *Isis*, LVIII (1961), 186–97.

an abstract idea and abstract ideas are meaningless. Berkeley makes his move from dynamical considerations to epistemological considerations. He writes: "And perhaps, if we inquire narrowly into the matter, we shall find we cannot even frame an idea of *pure space*, exclusive of all body. This I must confess is above my capacity." (*Ibid.*, 116, p. 93) In this passage with its reference to "framing ideas," it is clear that Berkeley's epistemological objection to Newton's doctrine of absolute space is that we cannot imagine an idea of space "distinct from that which is perceived by sense, and related to bodies" (*ibid.*, 116, p. 93). This, of course, is his usual objection to abstract ideas; it is psychologically impossible to do what we are asked to do to form an abstract idea, in this case, think space apart from body. There are, of course, well-known difficulties in Berkeley's theory; at bottom his contention here depends upon the dubious thesis that thought is solely the manipulation of mental images.

We can turn next to the critical passage which so many commentators have cited as an inducement to Newton to publish his "General Scholium" in 1713. Berkeley writes:

But the chief advantage arising from it [Berkeley's relative view of space], is, that we are freed from that dangerous *dilemma*, to which several who have employed their thoughts on that subject, imagine themselves reduced, to wit, of thinking either that real space is God, or else that there is something beside God which is eternal, uncreated, infinite, indivisible, immutable etc. Both which may justly be thought pernicious and absurd notions. It is certain that not a few divines, as well as philosophers of great note have, from the difficulty they found in conceiving either limits or annihilation of space, concluded it must be *divine*. And some of late have set themselves particularly to shew, the incommunicable attributes of God agree to it. Which doctrine, how unworthy soever it may seem of the Divine Nature yet I must confess I do not see how we can get clear of it, so long as we adhere to the received opinions.[9]

Here Berkeley's fundamental concerns are reached, and they are theological and not dynamical. Although Berkeley mantained over a lifetime that the doctrine of absolute space had dangerous theological consequences, his prime account, the crux of his contention, is carried in the passage just quoted. The "dilemma" Berkeley finds is succinctly stated. On the one hand, if "real space is God," in other words if extension is treated as an attribute of God, God's immateriality is denied. The danger to a theistic Christian view of the world like Berkeley's is plain. On the traditional conception of

9 Berkeley, *Principles*, sec. 117, p. 94. He refers to this objection in *Commentaries*, entries 290, 298, 695, and 825; *Analyst*, Query xiv, *De Motu*, 56, *Siris*, 270, 271, 288. In other words, Berkeley condemned this doctrine from first to last.

God there are two main characteristics of God, immateriality and causality.[10] From God's immateriality flow his attributes of unity, simplicity, incomparability, and immutability. But to make God extended, to make him material and thus subject to generation and corruption, is to jeopardize just these attributes. On the other hand, to hold that there is "something beside God which is eternal, uncreated, infinite, indivisible, immutable etc." is to deny God's uniqueness; it creates an "anti-God." To say there is something co-equal with God is to deny God's infinite reality beyond the world of time and space; it is a denial of God's transcendence. Christian theism with its contention that God is both transcendent from the universe and also providentially immanent in the universe through his divine presence cannot countenance the divinization of space, however etherealized this space is conceived to be.[11]

II

In this section the question of Berkeley's sources in his criticism of Newtonian conceptions in 1710 is examined. First the question of Berkeley's Newton – what was available and what Berkeley used of the Newtonian corpus will be discussed. Secondly, it will be argued against some recent commentators that Joseph Raphson's *De Spatio Reali* (1702) does not by itself disclose the metaphysical background of Newtonianism to Berkeley, but that there were a variety of views from which Berkeley recoiled in forming a view of space which was directed primarily against the contention that extension is an attribute of God.

With regard to the problem of identifying Berkeley's Newton, opinions have differed on the relative importance of the *Principia* and the *Opticks*. Koyré, on the one hand, comments that "the 'Queries' to the *Opticks*, curiously enough seem to have been ignored by Berkeley."[12] Jessop, on the other hand, says that "Newton's writings in particular he had studied while he was an undergraduate, and there are indications that for a long time there-

10 Cf. Harry Austryn Wolfson, *The Philosophy of Spinoza* (New York, 1958), p. 301.
11 The preceding paragraph is a summary of the latent background of Berkeley's thought. As F. E. L. Priestley has reminded the author, however, Newton and Raphson do not accept the Cartesian identification of matter with extension; omnipresence to them proves the extension (infinite) of an immaterial substance (the divine spirit). But this in no way makes God material – unless in Cartesian fashion you make "extended" equal "material."
12 Alexandre Koyré, *From the Closed World to the Infinite Universe*, (New York, 1958), p. 207.

after the *Principia* probably, and the *Optics* almost certainly, were within the reach of his hand whenever he sat down to write on philosophy."[13]

Actually it would appear that the views of both Koyré and Jessop are inaccurate, and, since the question of Berkeley's Newton is of interest to this paper, the question can profitably be explored afresh.

Consider the Newtonian texts available to Berkeley in 1710. The *Principia* was first published in 1687. The work was re-edited by Cotes in a second edition of 1713 which contained for the first time the famous General Scholium, to be discussed later in this paper. In this scholium Newton presented his teleological argument for the existence of God and added the famous remark as it was going through the press "and thus much concerning God; to discourse of whom from the appearance of things, does certainly belong to Natural Philosophy" (*Principia*, p. 546). The definitive text of the *Principia* was established with the third edition of 1726, edited by Pemberton, the last edition to appear in Newton's lifetime.

The question of Newton's *Opticks* is more complicated. There were four English editions of the work appearing in 1704, 1717, 1721, and 1730 and a Latin edition translated by Samuel Clarke which appeared in 1706. There was also a second Latin edition of the *Opticks* in 1719. The first English edition (1704) has sixteen "Queries" attached, appearing on pp. 132–37. This was followed by the Latin edition of 1706 in which there were seven additional queries added at the end bringing the total number to twenty-three, occurring on pp. 293–348. In 1717 another edition of the *Opticks* was published referred to on its title page as the second edition. Actually this was the third edition. In this second English edition of 1717 eight new queries were intercalated between those of the first English edition and those of the Latin edition bringing the total and final number of queries to thirty-one. Furthermore, there were a variety of changes in the queries in the course of the several editions, some of them merely stylistic but others involving considerable substantial additions to or modifications of earlier views. It is not enough, therefore, to know that a particular passage is included in the edition of that date if its availability at a certain time is to be cited. All of which points out the need, long since recognized, of critical editions of at least the *Opticks* and the *Principia* to complement the magnificent collection of the letters at present being issued.

Queries XXVIII and XXXI are the interesting ones for our purposes, since

13 T. E. Jessop, "Berkeley and the Contemporary Physics," *Revue Internationale de Philosophie*, VII (1953), 90.

they contain Newton's contentions concerning the omnipresence of God. These passages were later to become a crux in the Leibniz-Clarke correspondence (1717) over space. The text of Query XXVIII was available to Berkeley in Clarke's Latin edition of the *Opticks* in 1706 and received only minor stylistic changes in later editions. In this query Newton, arguing against the Cartesian plenum, points out that those who invoke a vacuum and the gravity of atoms tacitly attribute the cause of gravity to something other than matter. Reflection upon the first cause of Nature, not itself mechanical, leads the mind to God. The query ends with the much disputed passage that space is the sensorium of God. Newton writes:

And these things being rightly dispatch'd, does it not appear from Phaenomena that there is a Being incorporeal, living, intelligent, omnipresent, who in infinite Space, as it were in his Sensory, sees the things themselves intimately, and thoroughly perceives them, and comprehends them wholly by their immediate presence to himself: Of which things the Images only carried through the Organs of Sense into our little Sensoriums, are there seen and beheld by that which in us perceives and thinks. And though every true Step made in this Philosophy brings us not immediately to the Knowledge of the first Cause, yet it brings us nearer to it, and on that account is to be highly valued.[14]

Another well-known passage asserting God's omnipresence is Query XXXI in which Newton speaks of God "Who being in all Places is more able by his Will to move the Bodies within his boundless uniform Sensorium, and thereby to form and reform the Parts of the Universe, than we are by our Wills to move the Parts of our own Bodies" (*Opticks*, p. 403). Berkeley thus had available in 1710 the first edition of the *Principia* (1687), without the General Scholium, and the queries to the *Opticks*, including the metaphysi-

14 Sir Isaac Newton, *Opticks*, Introduction by I. B. Cohen (New York, 1952), p. 370. This edition is based on the fourth edition of 1730. The quoted portion reproduces the Latin text (Query XX) of the edition of 1706. Newton probably identified space literally with the sensorium of God, despite the "as it were" of the above passage, and Clarke's contention that Newton only had a "similitude" in mind. The evidence for this interpretation is David Gregory's memorandum, dated 21 December 1705, written out shortly after he had visited Newton and Newton had described the additional queries added to the Latin edition of the *Opticks*. Gregory writes: "His doubt was whether he should put the last quaere thus. *What the space that is empty of body is filled with.* The plain truth is, that he believes God to be omnipresent in the literal sense; and that as we are sensible of objects when their images are brought home within the brain, so God must be sensible of every thing, being intimately present with every thing: for he supposes that as God is present in Space where there is no body, he is present in space where a body is also present." *David Gregory, Isaac Newton and Their Circle: Extracts from David Gregory's Memoranda, 1677–1708*, ed. W. G. Hiscock (Oxford, 1937), p. 29. The thesis presented in the foregoing is by now the classic interpretation. For a carefully argued challenge see F. E. L. Priestley's paper in this volume.

cally interesting ones now numbered XXVIII and XXXI.[15] What then of Newton did Berkeley read? The easy answer is everything, but this answer does
not hold. What Newtonian writings did Berkeley criticize, recoil from, and
which by way of criticism helped him form his own views? Consider first
the period through the publication of the *Principles* in 1710, the date with
which this paper is most concerned.

The *Philosophical Commentaries*, Berkeley's workshop, were begun in
June or July of 1707 and completed in August or September 1708.[16] Berkeley's references to and discussions of Newton in this work fall into five
categories. First of all, Berkeley comments on the Scholium to Definition
VIII in entries 30, 450–52, and 455–56 and in particular reminds himself in
entry 316 to discuss this scholium carefully – a task completed in the
Principles and repeated in the *De Motu*. Secondly, fluxions, as one would
expect, come up for discussion fairly frequently in the *Commentaries*, for
example in entry 333 where Newton's fluxions are declared needless. Thirdly,
Berkeley frequently attacks mathematicians, often unfairly, in the *Commentaries*, for instance in entries 368 and 370–76 in particular. Although
Newton is mentioned in connection with these attacks, he is spared with the
comment that "I see no wit in any of them but Newton, the rest are meer
triflers, meer Nihilarians" (*ibid.*, 372, p. 116). Fourthly, Berkeley launched
an attack against the Newtonian conception that gravity is proportional to
matter in entries 361 and 618, claiming that Newton's argument was circular,
a charge he made persistently.[17] Finally, consider references to the *Opticks* in
the *Commentaries*. They occur, as far as I can see, in connection with the

15 The unpublished material with which Berkeley conceivably might have been familiar is
Newton's correspondence with Bentley which took place between 1692 and 1693.
Newton's letters to Bentley, the Queries to the *Opticks*, and the General Scholium to
the second edition of the *Principia* are the most important documents available in
studying God and natural philosophy in Newton's thought. It has been suggested more
than once that the essentials of Newton's views in the letters to Bentley had been made
public by the use Bentley made of them in his lectures. Cf., e.g., Victor Monod, *Dieu
dans l'Univers* (Paris: Fischbacker), p. 158. I can find no evidence, however, that
Berkeley criticized Bentley, or knew his Newton by way of Bentley. The Newton-
Bentley correspondence, it would appear, can be eliminated safely as forming part of
Berkeley's Newton. It would, of course, be hard to believe that Berkeley had not read
Bentley.
16 For this dating see A. A. Luce, "Editor's Introduction" in Berkeley, *Philosophical
Commentaries*, pp. xxviii–xxxii.
17 Berkeley indirectly makes this point in *Principles*, sec. 103, and directly in the "Three
Dialogues," *Works*, II, 242 and 279–80. Berkeley's most complete discussion of gravity
did not come until *Siris*, secs. 231–54, a work unjustly neglected by almost all commentators on Berkeley except John Wild. Anyone interested in Berkeley's philosophy
of science must study the work with care.

composition of colours as in entries 502–5 and 562. There is no reference in the *Commentaries* to the metaphysical queries of the *Opticks*.

The *Essay Towards a New Theory of Vision* (1709), of course, draws on the *Opticks* for the study of light and colours and Berkeley experimented along Newtonian lines. But the metaphysical queries to the *Opticks* make no appearance. Finally, as we have already seen, Berkeley's Newton in the *Principles* is the Newton of the *Principia*, particularly the Newton of the Scholium to Definition VIII of Book I.

Next turn to the *De Motu* (1721) and the correspondence with Johnson of 1729 and 1730, works that along with the *Commentaries*, the *Principles*, and the *Siris*, contain Berkeley's philosophy of science. In the *De Motu* gravitation and force come under fire, and in *De Motu*, sections 52–65, the doctrine of absolute space and motion are criticized in substantially the same terms as in the *Principles*, 110–16. But no mention is made of the teachings of the *Opticks*. In his letter of 5 February 1730 Johnson gave Berkeley a specific chance to comment on the queries but Berkeley made no reply.[18]

When we reach the *Siris* of 1744, however, Berkeley's last great foray in the philosophy of science, there is no longer the comparative neglect of the *Opticks* and their metaphysical queries which we have thus far observed. Gravity as having another cause than matter is discussed in *Siris* 225, with explicit reference made to the "fits ... of easy transmission and reflection" of Query XXVIII. In *Siris*, 289, p. 134, space as God's sensorium is denied, although Newton is not quoted by name. In this passage the doctrine of absolute space is referred to as a "modern mistake," with the clear implication that it is not only Newton that Berkeley has in mind as he rejects the doctrine. In *Siris* 241 and 250, there is criticism of the Newtonian doctrine of forces and reference is made to Query XXXI of the *Opticks*. In addition to references to the queries more specific reference is made to the *Opticks* proper in the *Siris* than elsewhere, particularly to the Newtonian conception that light is a heterogeneous medium (*ibid.*, 148, 165, 238).

The summary of this rather tedious compendium is that, discussion of

---

18 Johnson, in describing his own adherence to Newton's views, wrote: "And in his *Opticks* calls space *as it were God's boundless sensorium*, nor can I think you have a different notion of these attributes from that great philosopher, tho' you may differ in ways of expressing or explaining yourselves" (Samuel Johnson in Berkeley, *Works*, II, 287). Johnson is usually called an astute critic of Berkeley and I suppose he was, but this passage is a parody. Berkeley's reply, however, was laconic. He once again referred to the fact that Newton drew a distinction between absolute and relative motion and space, and pointed out that he himself held a doctrine of relative space, ending with the comment "For my meaning I refer you to what I have published" (*ibid.*, p. 292).

fluxions excluded, Berkeley's Newton until the *Siris* (1744) is the Newton of the *Principia*, particularly the Scholium to Definition VIII of Book I, and the Newton whom entry 27 of the *Commentaries* criticized for holding that gravity is proportional to matter (cf. entry 361, p. 115). Newton's *Opticks* is a minor influence on Berkeley compared with the *Principia*. Jessop's contention that the *Opticks* is from the beginning of prime importance in Berkeley's writing on science is not borne out by the facts of the case. Nor is Koyré's comment accurate that Berkeley ignored the queries, if the *Siris* is taken into account. The conclusion that it was the *Principia* and not the *Opticks* which influenced Berkeley in his formative period is somewhat of an anomaly; as I. B. Cohen emphasized some years ago, the image of Newton in Britain as a theoretical scientist was based upon the *Opticks*, which was read, rather than on the *Principia*, which was only admired.[19]

Berkeley was always his own man, however, and more often than not seemed to be swimming against the major currents of thought in his own time. On the Continent those scientists best in a position to understand the *Principia*, men like Leibniz and Huygens, rejected its teachings mainly because of the doctrine of universal gravitation. It is a measure of Berkeley's greatness that not only did he read the *Principia* when most of his fellow countrymen lacked the ability, but that, Leibniz excepted, he subjected it to the most profound critique this great work on science has ever received.

I wish to turn next to consideration of an interesting but I think erroneous view advanced by Koyré that the metaphysical background of Newtonianism was disclosed to Berkeley by Joseph Raphson's *De Spatio Reali* (1702). Koyré writes: "It is certainly Raphson's interpretation, or it would be better to say, Raphson's disclosure of the metaphysical background of Newtonianism, that Bishop Berkeley had in mind, when in 1710, in his *Principles of Human Knowledge*, he not only made a vigorous attack upon its fundamental concepts, absolute space and absolute time, but also pointed out the great danger that they implied from the theological point of view."[20] If this view were correct, it would answer the question of why the criticisms of Newton by Leibniz and Berkeley were so long delayed. The *Principia* came out in 1687, and the critiques of Leibniz and Berkeley were not published until after the turn of the century, in Berkeley's case twenty-three years after the first edition of the *Principia*. Toulmin writes: "What was it then, that roused Berkeley and Leibniz to attack Newton? Not so much, it appears, the

19 I. B. Cohen, *Franklin and Newton* (Philadelphia, 1956), p. 124.
20 Koyré, *Closed World to Infinite Universe*, p. 221.

mathematical doctrines of the *Principia* as the theological doctrines which were subsequently read into it by Raphson and the like."[21]

The thesis that Berkeley's criticism of Newton's conceptions is at bottom theological and not dynamical is, I think, correct. But nevertheless the line taken by Koyré is misleading. I shall show that Raphson is only one among several sources for Berkeley's critique in 1710, and that indeed to view the attack in *Principles* 110–17 as directed solely at Newton's conceptions of absolute space, with or without the disclosure of the metaphysical background by Raphson, is to misread it.

First consider Raphson as a source of Berkeley's critique. There is no question that he was *one* influence on Berkeley; the frequency with which he is mentioned in contexts of discussion of absolute space shows this beyond question. At least once Berkeley refers to Raphson in terms which, if taken in isolation, suggest that Raphson's influence was critical in the formation of Berkeley's criticism. In Berkeley's letter to Johnson on 24 March 1730, he writes:

As to Space. I have no notion of any but that which is relative. I know some later philosophers have attributed extension to God, particularly mathematicians, one of whom, in a treatise, *De Spatio Reali*, pretends to find out fifteen of the incommunicable attributes of God in Space. But it seems to me that, they being all negative, he might as well have found them in Nothing; and it would have been as justly inferred from Space being impassive, increated, indivisible, etc. that it was Nothing as that it was God.[22]

But neither this passage, nor others in which Berkeley refers to Raphson, show that Raphson's influence provided Berkeley with a "disclosure of the metaphysical background of Newtonianism."

Consider first of all the dates. When Berkeley began the *Commentaries* in June or July of 1707 he was twenty-two years of age. It seems unlikely that even a Berkeley could have written on Newton prior to the turn of the century. He did not enter Trinity College, Dublin, until 1700, at fifteen years of age; when Berkeley published his *Principles* in 1710 he was only twenty-five. Berkeley's age can account for the timing of the publication of his attack on Newton at least as readily as his discovery of Raphson.

21 Stephen Toulmin, "Criticism in the History of Science: Newton on Absolute Space, Time, and Motion II," *Philosophical Review*, LXVIII (1959), 203.

22 Berkeley, *Philosophical Correspondence with Johnson* in *Works*, II, 292. Raphson is also mentioned in *Commentaries*, entries 298, 827 and in the essay *Of Infinities*, *Works*, IV, and probably is referred to in *Principles* 116 and 117. Joseph Raphson FRS published his *Universal Analysis of Equations* in 1697. He added an appendix to the work in 1702 entitled "De Spatio Reali seu Ente Infinito conamen Mathematico Metaphysicum."

There is evidence, however, that Raphson is less decisive in the formation of Berkeley's theological objections to Newton than Koyré's thesis would suggest. In *Principles*, 117, where Berkeley's attack on Newton comes to a focus, Berkeley refers to "several" writers who hold the doctrines condemned by Berkeley. In the next sentence he writes "not a few divines as well as philosophers of great note" hold the doctrines he is attacking. On the evidence of this passage the only person we can be reasonably sure is in Berkeley's mind is Newton, named uniquely in *Principles*, 110 and alluded to in *Principles*, 117. When we turn to the *Commentaries* (1708), entry 298, p. 97, it is Locke, More, Raphson, who "seem to make God extended." At 825 and 827 Hobbes, Locke, Spinoza, and once again Raphson are mentioned. Leroy has shown in a few beautifully constructed and succinct pages the views of space with which Berkeley was familiar and adds to the above-mentioned list Malebranche, John Norris, Arthur Collier, and John Toland. Leroy concludes:

Toutes ces conceptions de l'espace et de la matière, Berkeley les juge soit imprudentes et dangereuses, soit fausses et malignes. Il cherche donc à les saper à la base en montrant l'inanité de l'espace absolu. Il reprend à son compte la formule traduite d'Aristotle: la matière est un *nec quid nec quantum nec quale*, que les controversistes ont déjà utilisée à des fins adverses. Cette lutte de Berkeley contre les notions d'espace absolu et de matière au bénéfice de l'espace relatif et des corps sensibles se poursuit à travers tout l'œuvre de Berkeley, des *Commentaires philosophiques* à la *Siris*.[23]

Berkeley's critique of absolute space as theologically dangerous was not something brought up in the *Commentaries* and spelled out only in the *Principles* in the passage we have examined. His objection persisted over his whole lifetime, from the *Commentaries* to the *Siris*.[24] The correct answer to the question of the source of Berkeley's doctrine is not that he rejected absolute space after Raphson had disclosed the metaphysical background of Newtonianism, but that Berkeley found a variety of modern writers holding doctrines of absolute space or the sufficiency of matter independent of perception, all of which were in his mind as he wrote his critique in 1710. Newtonianism is thus only one important strand in Berkeley's attack in *Principles*, sections 110–17.

23 Andre-Louis Leroy, *George Berkeley* (Paris, 1959), p. 55. Curiously Leroy does not mention Spinoza, who was, I suspect, an important influence in the formation of Berkeley's view.
24 For example, *Commentaries*, entries 290, 298, 695, and 825; *Analyst*, Qu. 14; *De Motu*, sec. 56; and *Siris*, 270, 271, and 288.

III

The question posed in this final section of the paper is this: Did Berkeley influence Newton? It has been widely held that Berkeley's attack on Newton in the *Principles* in 1710 was a major influence – the other influence being Leibniz – inducing Newton to publish the famous General Scholium to the second edition of the *Principia* in 1713.[25] I wish to challenge the general opinion that Berkeley influenced Newton. My argument is a simple one in two stages. There is no evidence from the General Scholium itself, nor is there evidence connected with the publication of the second edition of the *Principia*, to link Berkeley to Newton's General Scholium. In the absence of such evidence, and without knowledge of third parties to whom Newton was referring, the case for Leibniz as the proximate cause inducing Newton to publish the Scholium has to be taken as sufficient.

There are three documents which enable us to assess Berkeley's possible role in inducing Newton to write the General Scholium of the second edition of the *Principia* in 1713: Cotes' letter to Newton of 18 March 1713; Cotes' Preface to the second edition of the *Principia*; and the scholium itself. First consider Cotes' letter to Newton. The critical passage is as follows:

25 Newton, *Principia*, editor's note, pp. 668–69. Cajori writes: "In the first edition of Newton's *Principia* no statement is made on the nature of God. Nevertheless, criticism was passed upon the *Principia*, on theological grounds, by two prominent thinkers, Bishop Berkeley, who in 1710 published his *Principles of Human Knowledge*, and Leibniz, who on 10 February 1711 wrote a letter to Hartsoeker, a Dutch physician at Düsseldorf, which was published on 5 May 1712 in the Memoirs of Literature, a weekly sold in London. ... And so, in 1713, twenty-six years after the first appearance of the *Principia*, Newton, then seventy-one years old, prepared the famous General Scholium printed at the end of the second edition of the *Principia*."

E. W. Strong, "Newton and God," *The Journal of the History of Ideas*, XIII (1952), 149 makes a more guarded statement. He writes: "The criticisms of Bishop Berkeley in *A Treatise Concerning the Principles of Human Knowledge*, published in 1710, may also have come to Newton's attention." Koyré (*Closed World to Infinite Universe*, p. 223) says: "Berkeley's attack, though it certainly did not affect Newton as strongly as was thought by some of his historians, seems nevertheless to have been the reason, or at least one of the reasons – the second being Leibniz's accusation of introducing, by way of his theory of universal gravitation, the use of a senseless occult quality into natural philosophy – that induced Newton to add to the second edition of his *Principia* the famous *General Scholium* which expresses so forcefully the religious conceptions that crown and support its empirico-mathematical construction and thus reveal the real meaning of his 'philosophical method.'" Max Jammer, *Concepts of Space* (New York, 1960), p. 111 writes: "Of greater relevance for our subject, however, is Berkeley's attack on Newton's theory of space, which Cotes had certainly in mind, although he did not mention Berkeley by name." R. H. Hurlbutt, *Hume, Newton, and the Design Argument* (Lincoln, Nebraska, 1965), p. 5, comments that Newton's "response" to the criticisms of Leibniz and Berkeley was to add the General Scholium. See p. 13 where this assertion is repeated.

I think it will be proper [to] add somethings by which your book may be cleared from some prejudices which have been industriously laid against it. As that it deserts Mechanical causes, is built upon Miracles and recurrs to Occult qualitys. That You may not think it unnecessary to answer such Objections You may be pleased to consult a Weekly Paper called *Memoires of Literature* and sold by Ann Baldwin in Warwick-Lane. In the 18th Number of ye second Volume of those papers which was published May 5th, 1712, you will find a very extraordinary letter of Mr. Leibnitz to Mr. Hartsoeker which will confirm what I have said. ... I do not propose to mention Mr. Leibnitz's name; 'twere better to neglect him, but the Objections I think may very well be answered and even retorted upon the maintainers of Vortices.[26]

The reference in this critical passage is specific, clear, and unequivocal. It is Leibniz, and except for the phrase "maintainers of vortices" in the last sentence of the quotation which refers to the Cartesians, only Leibniz who is referred to; there is no reference either direct or implied to Berkeley, and in no way can this passage be construed as referring to him. The "prejudices" which Cotes says have been laid against the first edition of the *Principia* are Leibniz' charges which over and over from 1690 he had laid against Newton: gravity is an occult quality, and universal attraction is a miracle. In Edleston's edition of the correspondence concerning the second edition of the *Principia*, there is no mention of Berkeley.[27]

The next text to be considered is Cotes' Preface to the second edition of the *Principia* (Cajori, p. xx–xxiii).[28] The document, although of great historical importance, can be dealt with very briefly here. Three subjects are discussed in turn. The Preface opens with a defence by Cotes of Newton's experimental "method of philsophy" (*ibid.*, p. xx). Secondly, an examination of Leibniz' objections is undertaken beginning with a remark about those who "mutter something about occult qualities" (p. xxvi).[29] Finally, Cotes' Preface con-

---

26 Quoted in J. Edlestone (ed.), *Correspondence of Sir Isaac Newton and Professor Cotes* (London, 1850), pp. 153–54. In his Preface to Newton, *Opticks*, 1952, p. liii, I. B. Cohen notes that "In the second edition of the *Memoirs of Literature*, 'revised and corrected', Leibniz's letter appeared in vol. 4 (London, R. Knaplock, 1722), Art. LXXXV, p. 425ff."

27 Nor is Berkeley mentioned in this connection by Newton's biographers. Berkeley is mentioned by Brewster only in connection with Berkeley's subtitle for the *Analyst*, viz. "A Discourse addressed to an Infidel Mathematician." See Sir David Brewster, *Memoirs of the Life, Writings, and Discoveries of Sir Isaac Newton* (New York, 1965), II, 164. Louis Trenchard More, *Isaac Newton, A Biography* (New York, 1962), pp. 322–23, discusses Berkeley's empiricism as a criticism of Newton, but does not suggest any influence or direct contact of Berkeley with Newton.

28 Newton wrote a very short Preface to the second edition containing nothing germane for our purposes.

29 Presumably the slur that caused Leibniz to write on 9 April 1716 that Cotes' Preface was "pleine d'aigreur."

tains an examination of the Cartesian system of vortices, which Cotes, of course, finds good reason to reject. No direct reference is made to Berkeley, and there is no passage in it, so far as I can see, which can even remotely be construed as having reference to Berkeley.

Consider finally the General Scholium (Cajori, pp. 543–47) itself, which, compared with Cotes' Preface, is a serene document.[30] The first two paragraphs discuss critically the vortex theory of Descartes which according to Newton is "pressed with many difficulties" (p. 543) and contains nothing which could be said even remotely to refer to Berkeley. In the third paragraph Newton denies that "mere mechanical causes" (p. 544) could give rise to the regular movements of the heavenly bodies. "This most beautiful system of the sun, planets, and comets could only proceed from the counsel and dominion of an intelligent and purposeful Being" (p. 544). In other words, the paragraph is a statement of Newton's teleological proof for the existence of God. Paragraph four discusses God's nature. Although recognizing that God has other attributes than space, Newton contends that God "constitutes duration and space" (p. 545). In discussing God's omnipresence Newton insists that God is always (*semper*) and everywhere (*ubique*) not only in action but in substance. Whether Newton's divinization of space was learned from Henry More, as commentators generally contend, is a subject that requires further study. But whatever Newton's source, it is not a critique of Berkeley. In the penultimate paragraph Newton turns to the vexed question of the cause of gravity, and pronounces his famous "Hypotheses non fingo." The scholium ends by alluding to a "certain most subtle spirit which pervades and lies hid in all gross bodies" (p. 547), a possible explanation of how gravity might work. Berkeley does not figure in the General Scholium in any way, shape, or manner.

Let us consider the evidence against Berkeley's possible influence on Newton. There is no reference to Berkeley in any of the correspondence between Newton, Cotes, and Bentley over the publication of the second edition of the *Principia*. The General Scholium does not suggest such an influence. Berkeley did not go to London until 1713. In 1710 he was a relatively unknown Irishman of twenty-five whose *Principles*, published in Dublin, had largely been ignored. It is true that when he came to London early in 1713 to publish the *Three Dialogues* he got a good reception from the London wits, but this was too late to have influenced Newton's General Scholium.

---

30 There are six changes in the General Scholium in the third edition of 1726. These are listed by Cajori on pp. 669–70. They do not affect the summary as presented here.

Newton had long held the views he expressed in the Scholium, but in general had tried unsuccessfully to keep his natural religion, his revealed religion, and his science apart. In the absence of textual evidence to the contrary, it is an entirely unsupported conjecture to suppose that Berkeley influenced Newton in the General Scholium or anywhere else.

With Leibniz, however, the case is very different. In 1712 Leibniz was sixty-six years of age, a friend of royalty, and had already been involved with Newton in the ugly controversy over the priority of the calculus. This controversy which began in 1699 had in 1708 boiled up again with the publication by Keill of a paper in the *Philosophical Transactions* making a flat claim for Newton's priority. It was known that Leibniz had the support of the Continental men of science. It is not surprising that Cotes, and the ever suspicious Newton, who by 1708 had a cold and implacable hatred of Leibniz, were disturbed by Leibniz' charge that gravity was a senseless occult quality, that is incapable of being known in experience. The reply to the charge that gravity is an occult quality occurs in the General Scholium (Cajori, p. 547) in which Newton admits that he has not in the *Principia* assigned gravity a cause and ends with the comment "And to us it is enough that gravity does really exist, and acts according to the laws which we have explained, and abundantly serves to account for all the motions of the celestial bodies and of our sea" (*ibid.*, p. 545). Cotes also replies vigorously to Leibniz' charge in the Preface to the second edition.

In sum, there is ample evidence that Leibniz' charges induced Newton to write the General Scholium and no evidence that the young and unknown Berkeley had anything to do with it. (This is not, of course, to say that the scholium contains nothing but a reply to Leibniz.) Berkeley was one of Newton's most profound critics, but Newton never knew it.

V

Gravity and Intelligibility: Newton to Kant

GERD BUCHDAHL

I

One of the problems created by Newton's dynamics was that of the intelligibility of gravitational attraction; and it is this which I want to make the central topic of this paper. I want to show how the resulting perplexities led, particularly in the Kantian reaction to Newton's work, to a more articulated methodological structure of scientific hypotheses. The story of Newton's complex views on gravitation has been told in recent years with increasing finesse, so there is no need to tell it again in detail.[1] I shall select for attention only some of the logical aspects of the situation, enough to enable us to grasp the precise nature of subsequent attempts to grapple with Newton's methodology. The complexity and shifts in Newton's attitude are partly due to philosophical difficulties internal to his theory, partly to his reaction to attacks by others on the conception of gravity, attacks which reinforced Newton's own misgivings. To start, let us distinguish between the law and the concept of gravitation, or force of gravitational attraction; a related concept being Newton's "centripetal force" (cf. Definitions v–viii; *Principia*, pp. 2–4).[2] Now Newton's view concerning the inductive status of the law of

1 See, among many, the writings of A. Koyré and I. B. Cohen.
2 The following are works frequently cited throughout this paper: Immanuel Kant *Critique of Pure Reason*, trans. by Norman Kemp Smith (London, 1953); abbreviated to *Critique*.
——— *Kant's Logic*, in *Kant's Introduction to Logic*, translated by T. K. Abbot (New York, 1963); abbreviated to *Logic*.
——— *Metaphysische Anfangsgründe der Naturwissenschaft* (*Metaphysical Foundations of Natural Science*), in *Kants gesammelte Schriften* (Preussische Akademie der Wissenschaften, Berlin, 1900–42), iv, 465ff; abbreviated to *Foundations*.
——— *Prolegomena to any Future Metaphysics*, trans. by P. G. Lucas (Manchester, 1953); abbreviated to *Prolegomena*.
Alexandre Koyré *Newtonian Studies* (London, 1965); abbreviated to *Studies*.
G. W. F. von Leibniz *New Essays Concerning Human Understanding*, trans. by A. G. Langley (La Salle, 1949); abbreviated to *New Essays*.
Sir Isaac Newton *Opticks* (New York, 1952).
——— *Mathematical Principles*, trans. by A. Motte, rev. by Florian Cajori (Berkeley, 1960); cited as *Principia*.

gravitation is well known. That law, like the laws of motion, is "inferred from the phenomena and afterwards rendered general by induction" (*Principia*, p. 547; at *Opticks*, p. 401 it is "derived from the phenomena"). This apparent paradox has worried later logicians. If the law of gravitation is an explanatory hypothesis or principle, in what sense can it be said to be derived from the phenomena? To appreciate Newton's view, and to understand both his own position as well as that of later writers, concerning the relation between the law and the concept of gravity, we must be clear on the formal development of the law within the body of the *Principia*. To facilitate the discussion, I will limit it to a consideration of a component of the inverse-square law, the law of centripetal force, since this incorporates most of the formal aspects of Newton's treatment that I want to emphasize.

To start with, let us note that in the *Principia* this law is proved as a "theorem." It is displayed as a deductive consequence, utilizing the "axioms" (or "laws of motion") as well as certain propositions of Euclid's *Elements*.[3] In colloquial language, this theorem says that if a body moves round a stationary point in such a way that radii drawn between the body and the point sweep out areas proportional to the times, then the body "is urged by a centripetal force directed to that point" (*Principia*, p. 42). To get from the kinematical antecedent to the dynamical consequent, the proof, apart from geometry, employs the first law of motion, according to which since the body is not moving in a straight line, it must be subject to "the action of some force that impels it" (*ibid.*). It also uses the second law, from which it follows that the acceleration of the body takes place in the direction of the straight line in which the force is impressed (*Principia*, p. 13).[4]

So far we have been dealing with the supposition of an idealized material particle, moving in a curved path round a point. In Book III, for example Proposition II, this is applied to astronomical reality, here the planets. The proposition states that the forces by which the planets are "drawn off from rectilinear motion, and retained in their proper orbits, tend to the sun" (*Principia*, p. 406). This is proved by using the theorem concerning central forces, together with what Newton labels "Phenomenon V," according to which the areas which the planets "describe by radii drawn to the sun are proportional to the times of description" (*Principia*, p. 405), that is Kepler's-

---

—— *Newton's Philosophy of Nature* ed. by H. S. Thayer (New York, 1953); abbreviated to *Nature*.

3 Book I, sec. II, Prop. II, Th. II; cf. *Principia*, p. 42.

4 Note also that prior to this theorem, Newton has proved the converse, i.e. given "an immovable centre of force," the areal velocity is constant (*Principia*, p. 40).

second law of planetary motion. A similar logical account holds also for the complete law of gravitation, for which, among other things, Newton in addition invokes the results of certain experiments with vibrating pendula.

It only remains to mention that, apart from the "phenomenon" of gravity being denoted by a universal law, the explicit "universality" of the law and property of gravity is "inferred" by Newton in accordance with his third so-called Rule of Philosophizing, prefixed to the astronomical part of the *Principia* (p. 398), according to which we are authorized to extend gravity from earth and moon to all regions of space, and thus "universally [to] allow that all bodies whatsoever are endowed with a principle of mutual gravitation," as Newton explicitly states in the *Principia* at p. 399 (cf. p. 413).

This brief résumé of the structure of Newton's argument will perhaps help to explain the sense in which Newton holds the universal law of gravitation to be derivable "from the phenomena." It was an argument supposed to entitle Newton to reject the charge that the law was an "hypothesis," if by hypothesis we here mean (as Newton does) the making of certain uncorroborated explanatory assumptions; for instance, concerning the motions of unobservable particles, purportedly explaining certain inductive generalizations, as instanced in the present case by mutual attraction. It was this part of the argument, with its imposing deductive façade, that led Newton's contemporaries and followers (friend and foe alike) to regard the inverse-square law as an inductive statement with a probability approximating to truth, and not as a mere hypothesis; and it yields one of Newtons' grounds for asserting, as he does in the *Principia* (p. 547), that "gravity does really exist."

But it might be said that there is nevertheless an hypothesis smuggled into the argument, which is that the "force" mentioned in the first law of motion, which implies, according to Newton's argument, that a force is responsible for the curvilinear motion of the planets, is to be *identified* with an actual physical attractive force, acting between planet and central body. Now although Newton's language undoubtedly suggests such an interpretation, he did not explicitly invoke it. As we shall see presently, it is his view (rightly or wrongly) that the presentation of the *Principia* is neutral as to the question whether there *is* a physical property corresponding to the concept of attractive force, or whether the centripetal motion is due to extraneous circumstances, not involving "attraction."

This brings us to the second aspect of gravitation, the concept itself. For trouble only arose when it was asked: what is it that is actually asserted by the law of gravitation? And when the question of the nature of the centripetal force involved in Newton's argument came to be faced; when it was realized that the concept of gravitational force was not clear.[5] And it was only over this question that people parted company. To see this, let us look once more at our Theorem II, where Newton says that the area-law implies a centripetal force by which the revolving body "is urged" towards the centre. At this point, two different questions often come to be confused. The first is this: *how* is the moving body "urged" towards the centre? This implied a request to spell out a *modus operandi*, a detailed description, for instance, of the way in which some medium or other might be understood to act on the revolving body. The request for this information was due to two considerations; first that Newton's demonstration involved no reference to an intervening medium; secondly that it was assumed that the presence of such a medium was a *sine quâ non* of a satisfactory "explanation."

Behind this there lies, as I said, a second and more general question: what in (or about) the central body is it that *causes* the revolving body to be "turned aside" from its straight path? (A question which was particularly pertinent for those who assumed that Newton himself – contrary to historical fact – was not invoking such a medium.) And associated with this was a further question: how can this force be made manifest, since it looks as though Newton had merely "assumed its existence"?[6]

I think it is important to distinguish all these questions, for only in this way can we appreciate the immensely complex set of considerations which were mixed up in the disputations that resulted; considerations which involved preferred explanation-patterns (preferred "paradigms", such as "action by impulse") on the one hand; and on the other, questions concerning the logical status of "force," with which (for good measure) came to be entangled the problems surrounding the concept of causation.

5 A paradoxical situation: avowed belief in the *truth* of the law, coupled with a worry about what its constituent *concepts* may mean!

6 As already noted, Newton frequently denies that he makes any physical assumptions. The logic of the situation is however confused because on other occasions Newton claims that he does not so much assume the existence of gravity as he asserts it as an established inductive truth (cf. *Principia*, p. 547). But what he has then in mind is the corresponding *law* of gravitation; any assumptions would, as just noted, concern only the physical interpretation of this law.

But it was perhaps also a peculiar request to demand that gravitational force be made "manifest," for such a request treats "forces" as though they had the logical status of substantival entities, e.g. "particles." A similar confusion will emerge presently when we come to discuss the "causal" aspect of gravity.

II

We need not spend too much time on Newton's answers to these various different questions since they are fairly well known. Moreover, his answers are often, confusedly, replies to all these questions at once. Thus, he usually assumes that there is no difficulty in speaking of the accelerated motion of a revolving body as being "caused." He then thinks of a force as something *producing* a change; witness the language of the definitions, for example, IV (*Principia*, p. 2). On the other hand, as explicitly mentioned in Definition VIII, he pleads agnosticism with respect to the "seat" of this cause, for example, whether or not (as seemingly implied in our centripetal force example) it does really lie in the "central body" (*Principia*, pp. 5–6). Indeed he goes here even further, moving in the direction of a formalist position with the famous proviso, that in the *Principia* he means

only to give a mathematical notion of those forces, without considering their physical causes and seats; [and that quite generally, he is] considering those forces not physically, but mathematically; [that he does not want to] define the kind, or the manner of any action, the causes or the physical reasons of these forces; [does not want to attribute] in a true and physical sense [forces] to certain centres (which are only mathematical points); when at any time ... [he happens] to speak of centres as attracting, or as endued with attractive power (*Principia*, pp. 5–6).[7]

This long proviso is complex and needs unravelling. Its minimum contention is that Newton in this part of the *Principia* is not concerned with the *modus operandi* of any medium. Secondly, and more strongly, it leaves unsettled the question as to what physical medium, or what physical property in general, corresponds to the centripetal force, the force which is "directed towards the centre." But thirdly, and still more strongly, he does not want here to treat of gravitational force as a *physical* property at all, wishing to "consider" it only "mathematically." Now this last restriction can hardly mean that Newton wants us to take the logical status of his force to be that

7 This agnosticism explains the liberality with which Newton employs locutions which suggest "transeunt activity" on the part of centripetal force. At *Principia*, p. 406, the planets are "drawn off from rectilinear motion" by this force; at p. 56, centripetal force "tends towards the focus" of an ellipse; at p. 40, it is the geometrical "radii" that are "drawn to an immovable centre of force" (inviting an unconscious pun); according to p. 42, a revolving body "is urged by a centripetal force directed to" the centre. Most clearly the effect of Newton's agnosticism on this variety of characterizations of force as a possible physical action appears at p. 2, where centripetal force is defined as "that by which bodies are *drawn or impelled, or any way tend towards* a point as to a centre."
 Note also that the expression "gravitational force" is not synonymous with "attractive." But as we shall see the "action" language retains its unconscious hold.

of a "number"; after all, we are dealing with a physical situation; a force is "an action exerted on a body" (Def. IV). So Newton must mean *either*, that when speaking of this centripetal force he is solely concerned with the numerical (quantitative) expression of the measure of *physical* force; *or*, that he is concerned only with the spatio-temporal measures of the *deviations of bodies* from straight lines, that is, with the *kinematical effects* of this force.

The last-named alternative, attractive though it sounds, is not really an adequate account of Newton's actual procedure. Consider the account previously given of Theorem II, the law of areas. This is couched in a language, according to which the deviation from the straight line is *caused by something*, whose magnitude is measured by the magnitude of the deviation; a reference both to the causal, that is, physical, as well as the mathematical aspects of the situation. Newton need not specify, of course, in what way the central and revolving bodies are, if at all, causally concerned in the total situation; nor does he need to introduce any third element, for instance, a medium such as is represented by the ether. He may in fact just want to say, as in Mach's later formulation, that the existence of the two masses is *determinative* of certain accelerations in the revolving bodies; "determination" being the most neutral locution possible for a causal state of affairs, and compatible with a post-Newtonian theory which includes considerations of variations in the metric of "space" in the neighbourhood of "matter"; compatible even with an abandonment of any straightforward notion of "cause."

And it is perhaps true to say that here lies one of the cruxes of Newton's difficulties. While his formalist disclaimers at the end of Definition VIII seem almost to go to the ends of disavowing any intention of introducing a causal account at all, the implications of the language of the first law, as well as of Definition IV, clearly implied *some* causal account or other, and thus an ontological commitment in the direction of a *physical* account. It is then easy to understand why some of Newton's opponents should have charged him with framing hypotheses, a ceremonial locution by which these critics really meant, *either* that they had noticed that he had after all been operating with a causal account, particularly if they chanced themselves to be possessed of metaphysical worries concerning the very concept of causation itself, and were thus confusedly making a metaphysical point through the language of a physical or methodological complaint; *or*, alternatively, that they meant to censure Newton's supposed identification of that cause, as for instance, in the form of a physical, attracting link; a cause which in the language-use of Leibniz and Berkeley was deemed to be thoroughly "occult."

To this I shall return presently. For the moment I note that Newton's agnosticism with respect to any "interpretation" of the term "force," although seemingly offering his readers a thoroughly *formal* account, was made plausible (at least partly) by this concealed causal element in the situation, a non-specified reference to its physical aspects, which enabled Newton both to say that he was not concerned with the physical (but only "mathematical") nature of force, and yet prevent the theory from being pure mathematics. It was this combination of formalism with an unspecified physics that gave him sufficient freedom to claim that – given his presentation of the law as an inductive inference – the law of gravitation was an inductive *truth* concerning a physical state of affairs. Indeed, with this account, we can understand more clearly why Newton should have affirmed so emphatically that – as we have already noted him saying – "gravity does really exist." For when in his agnostic mood, this affirmation is for him reducible simply to the inductive inference (in the way explained) of a "general law of nature," a "principle of motion" (*Opticks*, p. 401) – though with the concealed physicalist interpretation just noted!

The term "principle" itself admirably symbolizes the logical ambiguity of the situation. For it enabled Newton to speak of gravity not only as "existing," but as "an active principle" (*ibid.*). Now when challenged on this, he was quick to defend himself against the tempting conclusion that such a "principle" must be an "occult quality,"[8] by remarking that this "quality" (*sc.* law) of gravity is perfectly "manifest"; adding that only the "cause" of this quality "is occult" (*ibid.*).[9] He thereby concealed from himself the existence of a "causal" element in the law itself. Newton's critics sometimes share this confusion. One is then never clear whether their complaints are about gravity as a *primary*, putatively "manifest" cause, or about the secondary cause (i.e. explanation) of that "cause." This is once again the

8 Similarly, he denies that though "universal", gravity is an "essential property" of matter; again a move to rebut ontological interpretations (cf. *Nature*, p. 53). Sometimes, this is supported by a Lockean phenomenalism, according to which we know nothing about the essential properties of matter, and have to do only with its phenomenal qualities, not the substances or real things that lie behind the qualities (cf. *Principia*, p. 546). At p. 400, however, Newton denies to gravity the status of being an "essential" property on the grounds that, unlike *inertia*, it is not "immutable," but "is diminished" as we "recede from the earth."

In another, rather ceremonial, move, "occult qualities" are occasionally rejected because they are "supposed to result from the specific forms of things" (*Opticks*, p. 401), a point which does perhaps no more than cash in on the prevailing anti-Aristotelianism of the time.

9 For the reference to the "hypotheses" concerning "the cause of this power" of gravity, see *Principia*, p. 546.

confusion between the logical status of gravity itself, as a "primary" cause, and the *modus operandi*, if any, of a "secondary" explanatory mechanism for gravity.

III

At this point, it will be useful to introduce a finer structure of methodological components, defining criteria for the choice of hypotheses (in the neutral, or logicians', and not of course Newton's special, sense of that term); a structure which itself comes to be developed only in the course of the present historical debate. I will distinguish between, (a) the "comprehensibility" of an hypothesis or hypothetical concept, a notion which itself eventually we shall find to split up into (i) its "possibility" and (ii) its "intelligibility"; (b) the "probative strength"; and finally, (c) the "reasonableness," or "rationality" of an hypothesis.[10] Thus in the context of our present problem, we find that all of Newton's critics agree with him about the probative, that is, for them, inductive, strength of the law of gravity; they only question the other pair of aspects, and indeed frequently at first confuse them (as does Newton himself).

Let us first note an historical fact. Newton was at one with some of his bitterest critics (such as Huygens and Leibniz; though they were not always aware of this) that to regard gravity (in the sense of an attracting agency) as an uncaused cause was unintelligible. Thus in the famous letter to Bentley he states that the assumption of gravity as "innate", that is, the assumption of one inanimate "body acting on another at a distance through a *vacuum*, without the mediation of something else ... is to me so great an absurdity that I believe no man who has in philosophical matters a competent faculty of thinking can ever fall into it" (*Nature*, p. 54). There are two components in this complaint: first, gravity as a primary cause is absurd; second, the absurdity is removed if we can "explain" it – that is, explain the manifest accelerations in accordance with law through the action of a medium. In

10 As will be seen later, "rationality" as here used, is an oblique reference both to the incorporation of an hypothesis in a larger theoretical framework ("consilience of inductions"), as well as to certain "regulative" ingredients which determine its preferment. "Comprehensibility" for the time being will have a neutral and rather vague sense, involving, and being at first almost equivalent to the equally vague notions of "conceivability" and "intelligibility." (Since a considerable part of this paper deals with Kant, I also add that "intelligible" is here never used in the technical sense implied by the Leibnizian or Kantian contrast between "intelligible" and "phenomenal.") It is part of the object of this essay to trace the growing articulation of this concept, especially through the work of Kant.

my terminology, Newton holds that gravity can be made "intelligible" or "comprehensible" only by making it "rational," or "consilient." The two are absorbed into each other.[11] Leibniz sometimes shared this conflation. Thus he asserts in his *New Essays* (p. 61) that matter cannot "naturally possess ... attraction because it is impossible *to conceive* how this takes place, *i.e. to explain it* mechanically" (my italics). Again "conceivability" and "explanation" are treated synonymously.

Was there then any excuse (historically speaking) for the strictures of Newton's critics? I believe there was. By constantly seeking escape from the problem of intelligibility by postulating a secondary explanation in terms of impulse action, Newton did not seem to face the issue of intelligibility of gravity as such, that is, of the causal implications of his language, as already hinted before. He sought, as we have seen, to avoid this issue, by attempting to "explain away" gravity through reference to the action of other physical agents; and further by arguing that, since it is an inductive inference, the *law* of gravitation may be employed for the explanatory purposes of the *Principia*, even though no successful *secondary* explanation had been given; for good measure insisting that he is only concerned with the formal expression of the law.

But here lay just one of the chief difficulties. The *Principia* was rightly regarded as giving a *primary explanation* of kinematical phenomena. And Newton unconsciously interprets this so himself, by speaking of "gravity" as a "manifest property," as an "active principle" that "really exists." With this terminology he does admit to a feeling that a purely formal approach (such as gravitation would be in its pure mathematical interpretation) can hardly be said to give an "explanation."

Now this was perhaps a confusion – philosophers are still arguing about the question of the explanatory power of purely formal laws.[12] But in any

11 And we know from both his unpublished and published writings (e.g. the Queries to his *Opticks*) how Newton struggled all his life without avail to construct a theory of the secondary causation of gravity. Huygens and Leibniz both made similar attempts. For this, see for instance *Studies*, p. 115, ch. III, Appendix A.

12 Compare the aftermath of the Campbellian schema of theory-construction in science. It might of course be said that though Newton's "interpretation" was physicalist, this need have no ontological implications, since we can always understand the "interpretation" to have the logical force a "model" for the force-term. Of course, much depends here on the meaning of model. But if the point of the argument is that the introduction of a model helps us to bypass the ontological question of the "reality of force," it can hardly be said to do so, since if model is here used – as it must be – in its normal sense, it must be as something which is believed to have (to a greater or less degree) a *resemblance* to a possible physical state of affairs.

case, we have seen that Newton himself unawares slips the existence of some causal element into his conception of the law of gravitation. (Remember: he has only desisted from *specifying* this cause in detail!) It was easy for his critics to construe this on lines which implied that an additional quasi-material detail has been postulated. Holding that no genuine explanation is forthcoming until causality (or lawlikeness) has been "materialized," they construed Newton's admissions as the postulation of a cause (as gravity here seems to be); only of course in order immediately to charge him with intro-ducing a cause which they regarded as "occult."[13]

Newton found himself thus in a cleft stick. He either admitted that ulti-mately there was no such thing as gravity, and then there was no explanation. Or he allowed that there was such a "quality," and then it would be objected that the latter was occult. And his puritanism, expressed as not "wishing to specify" anything about "the nature of gravity" made matters only worse.

Newton's critics should then not be dismissed too easily. If the law of gravitation was given a genuinely physical import, then the question of the physical nature of the gravitational effect could easily be raised. And if one omitted from view the hypothesis of a physical medium, then however much one admitted the probative (inductive) establishment of the law, one could still demand that the process involved be made comprehensible – at least as long as one was not prepared to accept the effect as an ultimate and opaque fact. And this was not possible as long as the physical implications of the view of gravity as a quality were still competing with alternative physical theories; or if these seemed less and less tenable, with alternative conceptual schemes. In the appropriately conceived historical situation we have thus an interplay, not to say warring conflict, between our various criteria, a fact which gives the present case-study some general interest.

IV

So far, we have limited ourselves to those parts of our story where intelligi-bility shades into what I have termed, 'rationality," that is making gravitation

---

13 This is precisely how Berkeley interprets the situation in his *Principles*. See George Berkeley, *A Treatise Concerning the Principles of Human Knowledge* (New York, 1957) secs. 103–4. His proposal, especially in *De Motu*, is that we should give up the claim that Newton's theory "explains" anything, and instead regard the law of gravity, and especially the corresponding concept, as no more than "a mere mathematical hypo-thesis"; i.e. to substitute formal "derivation" for "explanation." See his *De Motu* in *Berkeley's Philosophical Writings*, ed., D. M. Armstrong (New York, 1965), secs. 6, 17, 28, 37.

consilient with impulse mechanism. I have suggested that frequently the issue was faced only in these terms. But the question might naturally be asked, as indeed it was: why must a mechanical explanation be given at all; why not accept gravity as a basic quality? And it is well known that some of Newton's own immediate scientific pupils, for example, Cotes, were much tempted to embrace such a solution.

Here, however, appeared again the old stumbling-block which had after all been the original motive for the supposed need for explanation: it was that gravity, regarded as "action at a distance," seemed unintelligible, impossible to conceive, indeed self-contradictory, as hinted in Newton's letter to Bentley.[14] However, as time goes on, and Newtonianism gains in prestige, the temptation to meet the charge of unintelligibility via explanation tends to seem less and less attractive, though the charge itself is not abandoned. For this had to await the reconstruction of the concept without recourse to "explanation"; an approach of which Kant's method (to be discussed presently) is a supreme example. But this took time; and we must study the more immediate attempts that were made to escape from the difficulty.

Before turning to this, we must however briefly consider an objection that may perhaps be raised. For one might question this whole problem of the unintelligibility, not to mention contradictoriness, of gravitation on several quite general grounds. To start with, one might insist that it was absurd to hold that action without contact is a self-contradictory concept, objecting to this either on the ground that what is clearly observed to be the case can hardly be self-contradictory, or on the ground that the concepts of matter and of action do not logically clash with the concept of "not being in physical contact." More seriously, one might demand that an explication of the notion (or of the various notions) of unintelligibility here involved be given before proceeding any further.

Now it seems to me that recent discussions have shown that notions like

14 Impossibility in the sense of self-contradictoriness of the conception was averred by Locke as well as by Clarke, both holding that for one body to act on another "without intermediate means" (Clarke), or "where it is not" (Locke) was either "a contradiction" (Clarke) or "impossible to conceive" (Locke). Clarke inferred from this that one *does* necessarily require a medium, though for him one that was "invisible and intangible." Locke's conclusion, on the other hand, was quite different, making – as we shall see presently – a virtue out of the supposed deficiency. For Clarke's view see *The Leibniz-Clarke Correspondence*, ed., H. G. Alexander (New York, 1956), Clarke's fourth reply, sec. 45. Locke's comments may be found in *An Essay Concerning Human Understanding*, 1st to 3rd eds. (London, 1790–95) Book II, ch. VIII, sec. 2.

self-contradictoriness, or the closely related one of analyticity, are even now not yet clear-cut; and the same goes for our understanding of what it is for anything to be "conceivable," or again, intuitable. Certainly, therefore, while it would be rewarding and important to subject these concepts to a general critique, yet since the present essay is predominantly organized in an historical mode, it has seemed preferable to let the senses of these controversial concepts emerge gradually through the study of the ways in which they occur in the discussions of the period under review. Such a study does, not very surprisingly, show graphically that the concepts in question were not clear. And the thrusts and counter-thrusts which we here meet are therefore simply part of a method of reaching a greater degree of clarity on the general question.

Certainly we meet with a whole spectrum of cases, from one extreme of straight logical impossibility, via Hume's approach which proceeds from his contention that *actio in distans* is contrary to one of his criteria for causal action, spatial contiguity, via a supposed lack of "familiarity," and "inability to frame a picture," via the supposed clash with predominant physical theories or conceptual schemes, all the way to the other extreme of straight muddleheadedness or even prejudice.

This general comment involves also the answer to the more specific objection that has been mentioned. One should not argue that Clarke was simply wrong in insisting that action at a distance constitutes a contradiction, until we are clearer on the place such notions as "contradiction," "intuition," "conception," played during this period and in such contexts. Above all, we cannot urge against such a view the observation that action at a distance is an "established fact" – in the first place, because most of the writers in the period under consideration are aware of this fact, and in the second, because the relation between established fact and intelligibility is precisely what here (if not later) is still in question.

In this way we shall find that Clarke posits logical impossibility, and Locke some rather different form of inconceivability. By the time we come to Kant, although the objection of *logical* impossibility is now rejected as absurd (*Foundations*, pp. 513–14), the *real* possibility of "a force of action without any contact" is still questioned (cf. *Critique*, p. 613). An analysis of this contention, and Kant's attempt to substitute an interpretation of *actio in distans* that will satisfy the criterion of real possibility, must itself be regarded as one of many attempts to articulate the notions of intelligibility and possibility.

Let us then proceed by noting that, initially at any rate, we meet with two possible moves to avoid the need for explanation of gravity, despite its supposed unintelligibility, moves which still proceed without much awareness that it is the concept of comprehensibility itself that is here really in question. The first move was to let the "inconceivability" of attraction stand as an opaque fact. To this answer (which was that given, among others, by Locke) I shall turn in a moment. The second move was to take Newton's agnosticism seriously, and to designate attraction as reducible simply to the combined action of several *laws*; that is, briefly, that in the neighbourhood of a massive central body other bodies just moved in the way described by Newton's laws (formulated above, pp. 75–6).

Both views formed the chief butt of attack from the side of Leibniz. To the second in particular he objects that non-linear motion, in the absence of externally interfering impulse-action, is not "natural" (*New Essays*, p. 61); that we cannot "account for it from the nature of the object" (*Studies*, p. 141); and that it is therefore not "distinctly conceivable" (*New Essays*, p. 61).[15] To leave gravitation standing as something unintelligible, as though due to "a simple primitive quality, or by a law of God, who produces that effect without using any intelligible means, [makes this] an unreasonable occult quality ... (*Studies*, p. 141).

The reference to God brings us to the first of the counter-moves against the request for the necessity of explanation, in the sense of making the concept of gravity intelligible: let gravity stand as an opaque, unintelligible quality. This was Locke's view; but the end to which it is used by him is most interesting. Locke, as much as anyone at that time, usually assumes – he is not always consistent – that intelligible causal physical action must involve spatio-temporal contiguity, subsequently one of Hume's criteria for causality. Also, Locke is equally certain that "free" non-linear motion cannot be "made conceivable by the ... essence of matter in general" (*ibid.*, p. 155). At the same time, however, he contends that the unintelligibility of gravitational action is no argument against the phenomenon as such.

The basic source of this new response springs from the fact that Locke is a convinced "Newtonian," in the sense that by now the emphasis is all on the

15 This is not the place to go into the sources of Leibniz's views on "natural motion," connecting as they do with his whole conception of substance and force, not to mention the principle of continuity. But when everything is said and done, it does seem that Leibniz's position involved a certain amount of mere prejudice, owing to the inconsistency of this philosophical interpretation of Newton's intentions with his own system.

inductive truth of the law of gravitation, and its wonderful power to system-
atize the phenomena of dynamics[16] – a consideration strong enough to convince him that the unintelligibility of gravitation is no argument against its
employment in "natural philosophy." In his reply to Stillingfleet, he thus
writes: "I have been convinced by the judicious Mr. Newton's incomparable
book ... that the gravitation of matter towards matter in ways *inconceivable*
to me is not only a demonstration that God ... can put into bodies powers and
modes of acting beyond what can be derived from our idea of body or explained by what we know of matter: but it is furthermore an incontestable
instance that he really does so" (*Studies*, p. 155; my italics).

But there was more to it than this, for actually the kind of unintelligibility
which concerns us here is for Locke an important tool for distinguishing the
province of empirical science from that *scientia* whose aim (mostly futile, in
Locke's eyes) had been to produce knowledge in the older, Aristotelian,
sense. Lacking any "insight," we are reduced to study the phenomena – by
which Locke of course does not just mean simple observations, but rather
those inductive generalizations that may be suitably systematized as in the
example of the *Principia*.[17] So, to admit unintelligibility is at the same time to
claim inductive prestige for Newton's conceptions; and *per contra*, Newton's
successes guarantee that we need not be afraid of unintelligibility. (Modern
parallels will not be lost on the reader.) From being a deficiency, unintelligibility becomes a merit, a veritable criterion of factual, contingent scientific
statements, as I shall show presently.

Now Locke usually phrases all this by saying that the power of matter
to attract (though not, as our passage shows, conceivable as an essential
property) is the result of God's action; a theological way of saying that
gravity is a basic opaque matter of physical fact. And this was, of course,
just the position which Leibniz was still fighting, referring to Locke's
assumption pejoratively as a "perpetual miracle."[18] We must, and we have
the right to deny, he argues against Locke, "what is absolutely neither
intelligible nor explicable" (*New Essays*, p. 6).[19]

Actually Locke's position is more radical than has so far been noted, since

16 Cf. Locke's characterization of the logic of the *Principia*, "Mr. Newton['s] ... never
   enough to be admired book," in his *An Essay Concerning Human Understanding*, ed.
   J. W. Yolton. Everyman ed. (London, 1961), II, Book IV, ch. VII, sec. 11.
17 See Locke, *Essay*, Book IV, ch. VII, sec. 11.
18 See *The Leibniz-Clarke Correspondence*, fifth reply to Clarke, sec. 122; cf. *New
   Essays*, p. 55; *Studies*, p. 144.
19 Note that *here* the two methodological components of intelligibility and rationality
   are *distinguished*.

in the passages just referred to, the *un*intelligibility of action at a distance is still being contrasted with the intelligibility of action by contact, for instance, during collision. Elsewhere in the *Essay*, however, he goes further. Thus at ii. 21. 4, communication of motion by impulse itself is declared to be too "obscure" to yield a clear idea of "power." In another place he adds that this phenomenon is so hard to comprehend that it is "inconceivable," even though, he adds, the fact of the matter is of course observed "by daily experience" (ii. 23. 28). More radically at iv. 3. 29, the "original rules and communication of motion" are declared to be unintelligible; and he adds that since "we can discover no natural connection with any ideas we have, we cannot but ascribe them to the arbitrary will and good pleasure of the wise Architect."[20]

Now it is important to realize that the contrast to which Locke is here alluding by way of an eccentric locution is that of Hume's later distinction between "relations of ideas" and "statements of matter of fact"; and the true significance of Locke's "lack of intelligibility" will then be appreciated. His is simply a confused way of defining empirical "unmediated" contingency.[21]

Still, Locke's manner of opting for contingency, by exalting unintelligibility, was eccentric. Therefore, as soon as this notion of empirical contingency had come to harden, as for instance through the criticism of Hume (who used quite a different set of logical tools to define it), the old problems of intelligibility might be expected to raise their heads again. Surprising perhaps to some, though easy to understand if one follows the logical sequence of these events, this turns up in some of the very writings of Hume himself.

To start with, let us note once more that spatio-temporal contiguity is for Hume one of the criteria for causality. Secondly, I mark that Hume is opposed also to empty space, for certain epistemological reasons that need not concern us here. With these preliminaries in mind, let us turn to his argument, to be found in the *Enquiries*.[22] Malebranche and his followers had held that there

20 Communication of motion is one of the concepts that Kant will later seek to reconstruct in *Foundations* (pt. 3), in order to prove it to be comprehensible, in the sense of "really possible."

21 Naturally, Leibniz, whose picture of contingency was so very different, could have no sympathy with such a doctrine. Continuity, as a heuristic or "architectonic" principle, was for him an analogical mirror, at the physical level, of the "rational" connection between all things (via "sufficient reason") at the metaphysical level and could permit no such approach.

22 See David Hume, *Enquiries Concerning the Human Understanding and Concerning the Principles of Morals*, ed. L. A. Selby-Bigge, 2nd ed. (Oxford, 1902), pp. 72–73, and 73n.

is no causal activity in the world, and hence that causal efficacy must be located in God. Now in part they had sought support for this conclusion from the semi-empirical argument that gravity is plainly not a candidate for causation, since, being action at a distance, it is incomprehensible, and hence no more than an opaque concatenation of events.

This argument Hume now counters, first by way of his general doctrine that in the sense required there is no causal necessity anywhere, since causal arguments involve only matters of fact. But what is of greater interest to us in the present context is that he supports his basic point by the additional contention that it is quite impermissible to seek support from Newton's authority, since the latter, Hume insists, has himself opted for contiguity, via his "hypothesis" of an ether (Hume obviously here being on the side of Newton).

Now knowing (as I have pointed out) that Hume is as such in favour of physical – though not of course metaphysical – contiguity, the whole argument evidently amounts to saying that the question of causal necessity (or the lack of it) must be clearly distinguished from that of the intelligibility or otherwise of the Newtonian concept of gravitation – not to mention its inductive strength, in respect of which the fact of attraction reduces for Hume quite simply to the truth of the corresponding law. Unlike Locke, Hume refuses to employ the apparent "logical" gap in gravitation as a support for his general thesis of metaphysical atomism, thereby incidentally clarifying considerably the philosophical status of the latter as an attempt to explicate empirical contingency. Moreover, the logical fact of contingency (as exemplified in the inductively established law of gravitation) being quite neutral to the question of the intelligibility of the concept of gravitational action, that problem is once again wide open.

V

However, with the increasing realization that mechanical explanations were not going to be successful in making gravitation "reasonable" or "consilient," and the growing paradigmatic entrenchment of the concept itself, the interest in the question of its "possibility" or "intelligibility" temporarily begins to wane; all the more so, since the fluidity of these notions themselves made it more and more difficult to grasp their logical import.

Here, it was Kant who (long before Mach) revived the old interest in the subject, not only by raising the question of the possibility of gravitational attraction afresh, but by supplying a richer logical framework in which to articulate the various methodological notions involved, such as possibility, rationality, probability.[23] Unlike Mach, however, and despite the dust raised concerning the need for subjecting gravitation to a critique, Kant will in the end be found to underwrite the Newtonian theory, this being simply an extension of his general approach which always sets itself to explore the conditions of the possibility of what (on other grounds) he accepts as the cultural, here scientific, heritage of his time.[24]

Naturally, this subject is too vast to treat adequately within the limited confines of the present essay.[25] But the preceding account will perhaps have prepared the way for us to grasp the general trend of Kant's distinction between "intelligibility," "possibility," and "inductive probability," especially as it affects our problem.[26]

To start, since inductive probability is a function of empirical evidence, viewed of course not as crude generalization, but in the manner of Newton's development presented at the start of this paper, we must expect any *a priori* aspects of dynamics to belong only to the "possibility" component.[27] And this we find in fact to be the case. Contrary to what is implied by the majority of commentators, Kant (here at one with both the scientists as well as with his own philosophical predecessors and contemporaries) regards the law of gravitation as altogether empirical. This he states explicitly (*Foundations*, p. 534), emphasizing that we are not entitled "through *a priori* conjectures to hazard a law of attractive ... force, [but that] universal attraction (as a cause

23 Thus, the possibility of an hypothesis, as distinct from its probability (which in certain circumstances may "be raised to an analogue of certainty" [*Logic*, p. 75]), is singled out for attention at *Logic*, pp. 75–76. At greater length, the contrast between the possibility of the hypothesis of a universal force of attraction and its inductive truth (as an "inference from the data of experience") is noted explicitly at *Foundations*, pp. 533–34 (see also *Critique*, p. 613). To this I shall return.
    The delineation of a satisfactory concept of "real" (as contrasted with "logical") possibility was of course one of the chief objects of Kant's whole philosophical career, both pre-critical and critical.
24 Which is not to say that the critical notions thus developed – as here in Kant's "dynamics" – were not to be vital *elements of change* in the subsequent history of science.
25 As regards the general architectonic of Kant's system, I shall also avail myself of certain results that I have argued elsewhere. See for instance my paper "The Relation between 'Understanding' and 'Reason' in the Architectonic of Kant's Philosophy," *Proceedings of the Aristotelian Society*, New Series, LXVII (1967) 209–26.
26 The major part of Kant's discussion will be found in pt. ii of *Foundations*.
27 That this is an *a priori* matter becomes clear from Kant's saying that "in every hypothesis there must be something apodictically certain." And the main element of this apodictic certainty, apart from the logical validity of the deduction of the consequences from the hypothesis, and its self-sufficiency to account for the former, is "the possibility of the supposition itself" (*Logic*, 76).

of gravity), together with its law, must be inferred from the data of experience" (cf. *ibid.*, pp. 517–18) – words which almost reproduce those of Newton. Kant, likewise, follows Newton's reduction of "attraction" to its "law": "to attract each other without contact, means, to approach each other according to an invariable law" (*ibid.*, p. 514).

Not only does Kant thus treat the law of gravitation as an inductive truth, he also (like Locke) regards gravitation as a basic property. But unlike Locke he does raise the questions of intelligibility and possibility in a far more positive way – partly because, like Hume, he has an entirely different approach to empirical contingency; though his is not of course Hume's approach. Above all, Kant echoes the realization, clear to most people by the time of his writing, that the attempt to "explain" attraction by impulse, through the use of intervening media, must be regarded as hopeless, and indeed circular. It must therefore be basic and irreducible (see *ibid.*, p. 514).

In an ironical passage he rejects the habit of explaining away attraction by reference to the escape of framing hypotheses (*Hypothesenspiel*), left open by Newton's puritanical abstemiousness as expressed through his "purely mathematical" approach (*ibid.*). No wonder, Kant says, that Newton himself declined to frame hypotheses in the *Principia*, this being a "mathematical" treatise, whereas the question of attraction is "either a physical, or a metaphysical one" (*Foundations*, p. 515) – a clear allusion to the "hypotheses non fingo" passage in the General Scholium (*Principia*, p. 547). It was, Kant goes on to say, merely the fact that Newton's contemporaries, and perhaps he himself, were (wrongly) scandalized by the assumption of attraction as something basic that caused Newton to be "at variance with himself" (*Foundations*, p. 515).[28]

The intelligibility or possibility of the concept of gravitational attraction can thus not be certified by mechanical explanation; the question is an entirely different one. But, as noted, Kant does think that the concept requires certification, though whether this will result in actually establishing its "possibility" remains to be seen. What *is* important is that the question of any *a priori* foundation in respect of gravitation is now seen to have to do entirely with non-probative considerations belonging to the fields of possibility, intelligibility, and rationality.

And here it is interesting to find that not only does Kant entertain the

---

28 Kant notes that as late as the second edition of the *Opticks*, Newton still expressed dissatisfaction at not having discovered the "cause of gravity," refusing to "take gravity for an essential property" (*Foundations*, p. 515).

question of possibility; he also has a novel way of distinguishing this from the question of rationality, a notion for which, having excluded the aspect of consilience or secondary explanation of attraction, he supplies an altogether fresh context as well. This is done by emphasizing the *methodological function* of the concept of gravitational force at the level of what is called "reason in its hypothetical [also "regulative", "theoretical"] employment" (cf. *Critique*, pp. 535, 546). When viewed in this light, the force of gravity plays the role of a theoretical construct which functions as a vehicle for the systematization of the phenomena of dynamics so to speak from above. Regulative notions such as "manifoldness," "affinity," "unity" all point to and are concretely expressed "by [the idea of] one and the same moving force" (*ibid.*, p. 545). Without such constructs, according to Kant, there would be no science, no "order of nature." They have a "creative" function with respect to nature, viewed as a system of laws. Moreover, since it is ourselves who inject system into nature, we can be certain of always meeting it again in our research into nature (see *ibid.*, p. 564). We thus get a more complex and sophisticated account of the component of "rationality" of hypotheses, defined in terms of the function of Kantian "reason."

Let us note here in passing that this is *one* of the several senses in which Kant's apparent talk about the *a priori* nature of gravitation in paragraph 38 of the *Prolegomena* must be understood. He writes, in apparent contradiction to what he said in the *Metaphysical Foundations*: "No other law of attraction than that of the inverse square of the distances can be thought out as suitable for a cosmic system. Here then is nature resting on laws which the understanding knows *a priori*, and in fact primarily in virtue of universal principles of the determination of space." (*Prolegomena*, p. 83)

Now although he here does not explicitly remind us of his so different-sounding declarations concerning the law's inductive basis which makes it a statement of contingent fact, we clearly must take these remarks as referring to "rationality," "intelligibility," and "possibility." The aspect of rationality is affirmed when Kant says that the systematic and explanatory power of the concept of gravity in physical astronomy is so extensive that it is difficult to believe that an alternative law could be "thought out as suitable" (*schicklich erdacht*). This certainly does not mean that an alternative is *logically inconceivable* – a view that would obviously clash with the contingent status of the law.[29]

What confuses the issue is that in the same paragraph Kant seems to link

29 English translations are here particularly misleading. Lucas translates *schicklich*

the inverse-square form of our law with the *geometrical* relation that obtains between the area of a spherical surface and its radius. But again on inspection this turns out to have nothing to do with either probability, nor even possibility or rationality, but rather with a more technical sense of intelligibility. For once again there can be no question of Kant's wanting to say that this property of space can *settle* the fate of an inductive conclusion, such as instanced by our law. The real intention is made clear only in the *Metaphysical Foundations* (p. 524) where Kant puts forward the geometrical analogue of the properties of the sphere as something which we may "perhaps *a priori* conceive [*denken*] ... without contradiction," but which is only a "possible construction" (p. 518). This phrase must be carefully distinguished from Kant's notion of "construction" *simpliciter*, which, as we shall see presently, determines the "real possibility" of a concept.[30] But since gravity is only a "[logically] possible construction," we must beware, Kant goes on, of arguing from this to the "actuality" of a force of attraction, let alone to its "law" (cf. *ibid.*, pp. 524–25).[31] In other words, "possible construction" presents a methodological feature to which we would refer nowadays as the provision of a mathematical analogy; it is thus precisely something which we should suggest as increasing the plausibility or intelligibility of a conception.[32]

There remains however the important task of articulating the old quest for (what Kant, echoing Newton, had alluded to as) a "physical or metaphysical" account of the concept of gravity; to see how far we can establish its "possibility"; or if not that (as it will turn out in the case of Kant), how far

erdacht as "conceived as suitable"; Carus puts "imagined as fit" (Open Court ed. [1902], p. 83). Cassell's German dictionary gives the following uses for *erdenken*: think out, devise, invent, excogitate, conceive, imagine. "To think out" gives probably the closest rendering of what Kant intended.

30 For such "possible constructions," see *Foundations*, pp. 518–21. Evidently, it would be easy for the careless reader to confuse "possible construction" with "construction as possibility"!

31 We shall subsequently see that an additional reason for the illegitimacy of this inference is that in the end Kant is not capable of establishing the "real possibility" of forces either.

32 What makes the text of the *Prolegomena* so confusing here is that both "possible construction" and "regulative conception" are meant to supply the reader with analogies through which Kant seeks to explain his *a priori* view of geometry. Space, regarded as a form of intuition, he argues, is so altogether "indeterminate" that it cannot yield axioms. For this we require that the understanding should inject its own principles, since only what is thus injected can be recognized as determining space *a priori*—an argument which seeks to explicate a possible sense of an *a priori* synthetic body of geometry, supposing Kant's belief that there is such a science be granted (see *Prolegomena*, pp. 82–4). There is thus a relative discrepancy between the main argument and the analogies used; and the complexity of the geometrical argument only increases our confusion concerning the true status of the analogies themselves.

its place in the whole scheme of dynamics can be made comprehensible. In Kant's architectonic this task is accomplished at the level of the understanding and its schematized categories, applied to the empirical concept of matter; all of which results in a "metaphysical" exposition, in the sense of a "metaphysics of nature" (*Foundations*, p. 470).[33]

The old quest for "comprehensibility" is now interpreted as follows. We must explicate the concept of matter (its essential properties) in such a way that its attractive (and repulsive) properties are seen to "belong" to it more intimately and "essentially" than had been the case in the traditional conceptions (e.g. of the "corpuscularians").

Since it is possible to sketch here only one or two facets of Kant's ideas concerning these "metaphysical foundations" of dynamics, let us approach this matter by reverting for a moment to Kant's requirement that apart from the "probability" of an hypothesis, we always must first establish, and that with "apodictic certainty," its "possibility."[34] Take for instance the old Newtonian conception of "a force of attraction without any contact," and, in the case of two or more bodies, the associated concept of mutual dynamic interaction. Granted that these are not "borrowed directly from experience," says Kant, then, before we can frame any hypotheses which involve any such concepts, we must first establish their possibility *a priori*. And as he contends in the *Critique*, this can only be done if – as purportedly shown for the case of interaction in the Third Analogy – the concept is "understood" as a presupposition of possible experience in general; in the present case, of our perception of bodies in space (*Critique*, p. 214).

It is otherwise with the concept of "attraction without contact." According to the section on "hypothesis" of the *Critique*, we are not "entitled to invent [*erdenken*] such new primary forces," in our attempt to formulate explanatory hypotheses (*ibid.*, p. 613). Or rather – though this is not men-

---

33 It is metaphysical because it involves (putatively) reference only to *a priori* principles, i.e. those principles which in the analysis of the transcendental deduction are presuppositions of "experience in general." It follows that the synthetic *a priori* status of this "metaphyics" is not of the "dogmatic" but of the "critical" kind (and hence, according to Kant, permissible). It should be understood, however, that the propositions which thus result (e.g. concerning universal attraction and repulsion, inertia, impact) are not presuppositions of "experience in general," but at best only of the lawlike principles of Newtonian physics which hold *at* the level of fully fashioned experience. They are, in this guise, not conditions of experience in general, though they may in turn presuppose the latter, and its general principles – but, so to speak, at one remove.

34 Cf. above, n. 23 and n. 27. Note that the old Rationalist ideal of certainty and necessity is here re-located at a new level, moved from physics to the "metaphysics" of science.

tioned here and only emerges when we turn to the *Metaphysical Foundations* – we must first establish an interpretation of *actio in distans* which shows the latter to be an essential part of any "possible construction" of the concept of matter, proceeding under the guidance of the categories (see *Foundations*, pp. 524–25).

Kant thus does clearly not abandon *actio in distans* as such; and he certainly rejects as groundless and due to a misunderstanding the Locke-Clarke objection that matter cannot act where it is not. As he sees it, action at a distance is otiose only if it is construed under the model of material indivisible atoms, separated from one another by empty space, yet subject to attracting forces, apparently added arbitrarily and altogether "externally" (*ibid.*, p. 525). For the trouble with such an atomistic scheme is that it involves the positing of self-contained parcels of "solid" matter,[35] residing in a type of space the status of which furthermore is precisely what Kant's "critical" philosophy of space denies. It follows that under the traditional scheme these "solid" particles are endowed with the ability to attract and repel one another purely for the sake of physical theorizing.

Against this Kant advances his own doctrine. Its basic position is that forces must not be regarded as a "foreign element," logically superadded to matter; instead they must "belong to matter" and be regarded as essential for its possibility as such. [36] In this scheme matter becomes simply a "primitive term," defined implicitly by certain functions listed under the guidance of the major categories; for example, as the movable in space (quantity); as that which "fills space" (quality), has "moving force" (relation), and so on. It is the seat (picture it as a geometrical point) of these functions, that is, of forces acting in accordance with various laws of dynamics. It lies at the logical intersection of these laws. (It follows that all matter is continuous, is infinitely divisible, and fills all of space, though to varying degrees of intensity.)

To all this we must add, as just noted, the Kantian concept of space. According to the *Foundations* (pp. 503–8), the proof of the infinite divisibility of matter requires (as do of course many other Kantian arguments stated in the *Critique*) that the latter be regarded as mere appearance, with space a form of intuition of that appearance, instead of being a "property of things in themselves." It follows further that force (as a criterion or

35 Whose "solidity" is not made "intelligible" either; cf. *Foundations*, pp. 497–98.
36 *Ibid.*, p. 525. Actually, only repulsive force is a basic "criterion" of matter; but attraction is "proved" by Kant to be entailed by the former; and both are said to be "required for the possibility of matter" (*ibid.*, pp. 509–10).

"proprium" of matter) "requires space," which thus itself becomes a "presupposition of matter"; space "contains the conditions of the laws of propagation of force" (*ibid.*, p. 534). Space, matter, force, thus become *complementary terms*, each logically incomplete without the others.[37]

"So we may endow matter with a force of attraction," writes Kant, "in so far as it occupies surrounding space in which attraction occurs" (*Foundations*, p. 535). And in this sense, there may be interaction between attracting bodies "at a distance," even without contact (*ibid.*, p. 512); except that we should remember, as Kant remarks, that what is called action by contact, for instance, in cases of collision, can be explicated itself only by first invoking repulsive forces, and the attractive forces associated therewith. It is these and not "contact," that are basic in this phenomenon. In other words attraction (as well as repulsion) logically "precede the possibility of physical contact," as its condition, for without them there would be no parcels of matter in contact (see *ibid.*, p. 516). Similarly, the question of "empty space" completely loses its former importance. This is now a relative matter, Kant points out; we speak of empty space where repulsive forces are minimal (see *ibid.*, pp. 534–35).[38]

There is thus no need (according to Kant) to introduce hypothetical explanations of gravitational action; the latter is a basic property of matter in space, which possesses "dynamical" potentialities in so far as it "fills

37 More precisely, as the argument of the Third Analogy shows, the space "in which" material substances coexist, or more properly, our perception of such substances co-existing in extended space (regarded as "formal intuition," as distinct from "form of intuition") *presupposes* the concept of dynamic interaction. This aspect of space is thus dependent on, being complementarily associated with, the concept of dynamic interaction, though only in a transcendental manner. Earlier, in *Thoughts on the True Estimate of Living Forces* (see Immanuel Kant, *Gedanken von der wahren Schätzung der lebendigen Kräfte, Gesammelte Schriften*, I, parag. 9), the forces presupposed as a condition of this space had been *physical* in nature, whereas in *Inaugural Dissertation* (see Kant: *Selected Pre-Critical Writings*, trans. G. B. Kerford and D. E. Walford [Manchester, 1968], parags. 17, 22) they were "grounded" in something "metaphysical," in the old-fashioned sense of a "necessary" and "extramundane being." Here also it is these forces which are presupposed in order first to give us "space," defined as the "relation of all substances" (parag. 16). In the "critical" doctrine, space is divided into "form of" and "formal intuition" (see *Critique*, p. 170a); and it is the latter that is treated on the lines of the *Estimate* and the *Dissertation*, except that what is "presupposed" is a *transcendental* concept of force; whereas "form of intuition" covers that aspect of space which is given as the *locus* for all "appearances" as such.

38 It is not possible within the confines of this paper to provide a complete account of Kant's theory of matter, and the use he makes of the category of "quality," and its corresponding principle of the "anticipations of perception." Still less is it possible to criticize here the probably unworkable doctrine of attractive and repulsive forces as such. Besides, it is the intentions that interest us at present.

space" at all (*ibid.*, p. 534) – no doubt a comforting conclusion for a philosophy that wishes to reconstruct the foundations of Newtonian mechanics.
On the other hand, it is true to say that Kant himself saw his position through
progressivist spectacles. The "advantage of such a methodological metaphysics," he writes, whose "negative" aim is to constrain the "equally metaphysical" claims of the mechanistic-mathematico-atomistic scheme, is "to
enlarge the field of action for the scientist" (*ibid.*, p. 524).[39] Besides, this en-
largement, by adding philosophical respectability to the scientist's conception of force, had the accidental result of heightening considerably the importance of that concept during the nineteenth century.

VI

Unfortunately, Kant did not quite make good his avowed original hope,
completely "to construct the concept of matter," which for him means "to
exhibit it as possible in intuition"; and hence possible *simpliciter* (*ibid.*, pp.
524–25). His failure is largely due to the fact that forces, as "intensive"
entities with an ineluctably *a posteriori* content, can neither be "anticipated
a priori," nor "constructed." At most, this can be managed only for the
spatio-temporal characteristics of matter, for example, velocity, acceleration.[40] But forces cannot as such be made intelligible – their possibility cannot be "conceived" (*einsehen*) (*ibid.*, p. 524). Especially is this true of the
fundamental forces of attraction and repulsion; not only can they (like all
forces) not be constructed; they are also incomprehensible in a second sense,
our special sense of "irrationality," which is that of their not being "derivable" from any other forces, especially those of impact (*ibid.*, pp. 513–15).[41]

39 It should be noted that Kant is not opposed to the atomistic scheme on any grounds
  connected with the *unobservability* of atoms. He opposes hypotheses concerning
  "unobservables" only, where the concepts concerned are not in agreement with the
  demonstration of their "possibility."
40 Again, we cannot here give an adequate account of the Kantian concept of "construction." An example may serve: the construction of the concept of the composition of
  velocities (see *Foundations*, pp. 486–94). Suppose a body to be subject to two velocities,
  equal in magnitude but opposite in direction. According to Kant, the "thought" by
  which we try "to represent two such motions in one and the same space in the same
  point" is "impossible" (*ibid.*, p. 491). To "construct" such a possibility involves
  "subjectivizing" space, as a transcendental entity, and splitting it up into two spaces,
  one "empirical and relative," the other (though only as an "idea of reason") absolute.
  Composition of velocities is thus shown to be "possible" by shunting it into the transcendental structure of space and time. And only as such, does matter (in its spatio-
  temporal aspects) become possible.
41 It is true that concepts like cause (of which force is the aspect in physics), and dynami-

They, together with the estimation of their quantitative values, can only be "derived from experience" (*Foundations*, p. 487; cf. *Critique*, p. 230).

Accordingly, it is impermissible to give an "*a priori* explanation of the particular, let alone specific determination and diversity of the properties of matter" (*Foundations*, p. 524) – something belonging only to the inductive enquiry. Nor does the freedom with which we frame ("logically conceive," *denken* [*ibid.*, p. 524]) those "possible constructions" of quantitative relations under the guidance of mathematical analogies (the significance of which for the notion of "intelligibility" we have noted previously), entitle us to assume that we are dealing with anything of *real* possibility, allowing us to speak, even hypothetically, of the possibility of "actual" forces; the reason being that "we have no insight into the possibility of fundamental forces" (*ibid.*, p. 524).

From all this it becomes clear that although Kant made the question of possibility quite distinct from that of an inductive foundation, in the end he did not manage to offer the kind of rationale for the concept of attractive force that approaches his ideal of cognitive grasp. If nevertheless he makes force an essential component of the conception of matter as such, this must (ironically) be dictated by the nature of the ruling dynamic theory, his method thus displaying an unconscious borrowing from the inductive, or hypothetico-deductive procedure of the empiricist scientist.

However, if Kant did not admit defeat, this was because basic forces, even though they might not be capable of "construction,"[42] had in his scheme nevertheless been shown to be intimate requirements of the concept of matter. For this reason he writes that in *this* sense at least they "make possible the *general* concept of matter" (*ibid.*, p. 524), even though it is not possible to "construct this concept [in detail and thus] represent it as possible

cal interaction, function in the first *Critique* as transcendental categorial concepts. But they do this only by yielding "analogies of experience"; and they are not employed "constitutively" with respect to intuition, i.e. for purposes of "construction," but only "regulatively," in order "to bring the *existence* of appearances under rules *a priori*" (*Critique*, p. 210). On the other hand, to tell us what actually happens – as the discussion of the Second Analogy notes – we require knowledge of "actual forces, which can only be given empirically ... or what amounts to the same thing, of certain actual successive appearances, as motions, which indicate such forces" (*ibid.*, p. 230).

42 As implied in our account of "construction" on p. 97, n. 40, this comes down ultimately to elucidate velocity and acceleration in a way as to function like vectorial quantities. But if this is what makes them constructible, i.e. "possible," it is puzzling that Kant did not take the step of applying precisely the same mode of procedure to "forces," now recognized as "vector" quantities. A similar comment would also apply to the third part of *Foundations* where Kant seeks to "make comprehensible" the concept of "transmission of motion" in collision phenomena.

in intuition" (*ibid.*, p. 525). The "dynamical viewpoint" can at most thus bring us to the threshold of construction (see *ibid.*, p. 534).

Similarly with repulsion. If I explain the impenetrability of matter on the older traditional lines of Locke and Lambert, by reference to the concept of "solidity," Kant complains, this is not only to add a "foreign" term, but does no more than supply us with an analytic proposition, "according to the principle of contradiction" (*ibid.*, p. 498).[43] Only when we "conjoin with the concept of matter" that of repulsive force, do we come to "*understand*" that there is something contradictory about one body being in the same space as another simultaneously (*ibid.*). Here again this is described as yielding *at least* "a *datum for* the construction of the concept of matter" (*ibid.*) – even though force itself is not capable of construction.

The fineness of all these distinctions shows that Kant is here hard-pressed to maintain a semblance of consistency. Altogether, his position amounts perhaps to no more than making the notion of force basic, in the belief that it will thus lead naturally to the method of construction and with that to the applicability of mathematics to nature (as actually asserted at *ibid.*, p. 534); spatio-temporal construction being the mediating link between the realms of concept and of empirical objects.

Kant has thus channelled the old Lockean complaint concerning incomprehensibility into a different direction, replacing it by "unconstructability" (which registers a bare echo of the older qualms) and at the same time recognizing that there is nothing logically otiose about saying that bodies simply attract each other in space, just as they repel each other during impact.[44] In general, what has been done is to show that the concept of attraction (like that of collision) is acceptable at least to the extent of showing that it can serve as an integral part of the "general concept of matter," a concept so envisaged as not involving properties like solidity (repulsion) and attraction as "foreign ingredients," but as criteria which it possesses *ab initio*.[45]

Force and space thus yield a possible scheme, as primary conditions for

43 Cf. his famous saying: "The law of contradiction does not repel any material body" (*ibid.*).
44 It is not possible within the confines of this paper to discuss Kant's account of the Newtonian laws of motion, and in particular, that of "action and reaction." But the major principles of approach resemble those presented here in the context of Kant's "dynamics."
45 Kant speaks of this characteristic of the concept of attraction as "making the general concept of matter possible" (*Foundations*, p. 524), but since he also says that this concept cannot be "constructed" (*ibid.*, p. 525), this clearly leads to a less powerful sense of "possibility"; a distinction which he never acknowledged explicitly.

building up the general concept of matter. Moreover, since the concepts which guide the whole enquiry are the categories, this (in Kant's eyes) no doubt lends further respectability to the enterprise. Nor would I want this remark to be construed in any particularly pejorative sense, since I believe that it was not Kant's view that the logical force of the transcendental deduction literally overflows into the metaphysical foundations of science.[46] The realm of scientific experience, in respect of the basic Newtonian laws, is half-way between that of individual experience (whose possibility *in general* alone the categories guarantee) and that of a full-fledged science, whose theories comprise the systematic manifold of *empirical laws*. The categories "support" the *basic* framework of that science only indirectly; though more directly than they support the complex system of particular empirical laws. What is common to both cases is that the categories are employed without reference to *particular a posteriori* data; in the transcendental context they apply to the content of experience in general; in the case of the "metaphysics" of science, they apply to the "empirical concept of matter" (*Foundations*, p. 470).

Unkindly, we might summarize that the notion of "construction" and the various moves connected therewith boil down to exhibiting Newtonian happenings as taking place in Kant's type of space. This is supposed to make the "metaphysics of nature" respectable, especially when the metaphysics is apparently sustained by the Kantian architectonic of the understanding and of reason. But what are thus made respectable, are always just those facts of science already known or better, those facts and concepts to which Kant wants to accord a privileged status. But perhaps that is after all the gist of the transcendental method. Besides, in the enterprise, the facts and concepts selected, and made respectable, come to exert a stronger historical influence, by appearing as competing *physical* conceptual frameworks (such as the "dynamical" vs. the "mechanistic" approach). If the underwriting of contemporary science was a gesture of conservatism, the articulation of the "foundations" was pregnant with new ideas. It yielded a more complex methodological structure for an interpretation of particular scientific systems and, in Kant's case at least, thereby linked these to the more general problems of his philosophical edifice. A greater degree of self-consciousness concerning the nature of the questions and perplexities of the earlier philosophers and scientists was the result; witness the novel articulation of comprehensibility, and its explicit distinction from the inductive basis of science.

One might ask whether or not it is the legitimate business of a philosopher

46　This should be read in conjunction with what was said above, p. 94, n. 33.

to interpret scientific discoveries so as to make them conform to his general philosophical position; or whether he should always be ready to modify his position, though at the risk of inconsistencies with his own previous philosophical writings.

The answer is that somehow Kant represents both sides of this process. His interpretation of action at a distance was meant to integrate this concept within the general framework of critical philosophy. Yet, on the other hand, he was willing to surrender something, too. The Preface to the *Metaphysical Foundations* had said that there was only "as much science as there is in it of applied mathematics," that is as can be constructed (*Foundations*, p. 470). But forces, and hence matter, cannot be constructed. Despite this, the doctrine of forces was made by Kant an integral element of dynamics. He could of course have concluded that Newtonian dynamics needed rewriting – to eliminate the concept of force as a basic entity, in the fashion of Hertz. (Besides, after all, as subsequent history has shown, the last word had not been said on action at a distance.) Alternatively, he could have admitted to a blemish in his basic philosophical assumptions. He does neither, but instead uses the vastness of his system to underwrite the Newtonian scheme, though with its basic concepts interpreted in a novel fashion. If this is in part something of a shadow-play, it is not a total loss. For not only is there much greater methodological articulation; the enriched background also provides a point of departure for future generations (particularly for those with "anti-atomistic" preconceptions), by broadening the perspective of "force."

In sum then, any theoretical concept (of which gravity is a prominent example) maintains itself against a number of pressures, however well probatively entrenched it may be. The request for comprehensibility is an expression of demands that the concept be integrated within the broader background of ruling conceptual schemes, and of a more general philosophy.

His own philosophical system offered Kant a way of articulating this notion of comprehensibility. The general idea behind such an attempt may be right, and the attempt indeed perhaps inescapable. On the other hand, Kant's procedure is essentially a conservative one of adapting a given and fairly narrow scientific conception without taking into account the broader developments of science taking place even in his time. Thus, the impression is conveyed that the general philosophy provides a *backing* for the theoretical concept, when in fact such a backing is not really forthcoming. Not only is there a "looseness of fit" between Kant's general transcendental procedure and the specific formulations of Newtonian science; even Kant's special demonstrations adopt as their basis the ruling scientific doctrine as it stands.

One might say, adapting one of Whitehead's tags about simplicity, that one should welcome attempts to integrate concepts within the widest possible conceptual field, while at the same time distrusting them.

VI

Thomas Reid and the Newtonian Turn of British Methodological Thought

L. L. LAUDAN

Introduction

In the famous passage in the preface to his *Treatise*, Hume expressed the fervent hope that he could do for moral philosophy what Newton had done for natural philosophy.[1] In eighteenth-century ethics, literature, political theory, theology, and of course, natural science, similar sentiments were expressed openly and frequently.[2] Newton's *Principia* seemed to have established, almost overnight, new standards for rigour of thought, clarity of intuition, economy of expression and, *above all*, the certainty of its conclusions. At long last, natural philosophy, which had hitherto been open to such controversy and speculation, was established on an unshakable foundation. It was tempting to believe that conjecture had given way to fact and that an infallible system, based on rigorous inductions from experimental evidence, had finally been found.[3] Outside of the natural sciences, where Newton's

1 David Hume, *A Treatise of Human Nature*, ed. L. A. Selby-Bigge (Oxford, 1896), p. xx. Newton himself had suggested that his new methods might well have bearing on moral philosophy: "And if natural philosophy in all its parts, by pursuing this Method shall at length be perfected, the Bounds of Moral Philosophy will be also enlarged." See Sir Isaac Newton, *Opticks* (New York, 1952), Query xxxi. Taking up this theme, Pope insisted that we should "Account for Moral, as for nat'ral things." See Alexander Pope, *An Essay on Man* (London, 1786), Epistle iv.
2 In each of these domains, and others as well, one can point to several figures who wanted to "Newtonize" their subject in various ways. The most overt of these are the attempts to model works of politics or theology strictly along the deductive lines of the *Principia*. For example, George Cheyne in pt. 2 of his *Philosophical Principles of Religion: Natural and Revealed* (London, 1715), constructs an elaborate theological system beginning with definitions and axioms and then proceeding to a series of theorems, lemmas, and corollaries deduced from the axioms.
3 Even a brief sampling of eighteenth-century texts illustrates how enthusiastically physicists adopted Newton's call for a non-conjectural science. Thus, Oliver Goldsmith described how science had progressed from being an "hypothetical system" to an "authentic experimental system" (*A Survey of Experimental Philosophy* [London, 1776], p. 4). W. 'sGravesande, an eminent Dutch Newtonian, observed that, thanks to Sir Isaac, "all hypotheses are to be rejected" in natural philosophy (*Mathematical Elements of Physics, Proved by Experiments* [London, 1720], i, 5). 'sGravesande went

real achievements were obscured by what scientific non-initiates took them to be, the enthusiasm for Newton reached an even higher pitch. Newton's great contribution, it was said, was not so much his cosmological synthesis *per se*, but rather the formulation of a new conception of science and its methods. Newton was seen as the harbinger of an inductive, experimental learning which proceeded by a gradual ascent from the particulars of observation to general laws which were true and virtually incorrigible. What Bacon had prophesied in the way of an inductive interpretation of nature, Newton had brought to fruition.

Not surprisingly, therefore, many of Newton's casual remarks on scientific method, especially the famous "Hypotheses non fingo," were taken up as slogans and catch-phrases for intellectual reformers in almost every branch of human thought, especially in Britain. The eighteenth century has often been called the Age of Newton, and rightly so; but it was Newtonian, not so much in its physics or its metaphysics, as in its conception of the aims and methods of science. Putting it another way, it was Newton's inductivism and experimentalism – in short, his peculiar kind of empiricism – rather than his optics or his mechanics that motivated the leaders (and the charlatans) of eighteenth-century English intellectual history.

There is, of course, nothing particularly new or original about the brief account I have just given; to the contrary, it represents the view of most his-

on to insist that "He only, who in physics reasons from phenomena, rejecting all feigned hypotheses, and pursues this method to the best of his power, endeavors to follow the steps of Sir Isaac Newton, and very justly declares that he is a Newtonian philosopher ..." (*ibid.*, p. xi). Henry Pemberton, in his *View of Sir Isaac Newton's Philosophy* (London, 1728), contrasts the unreliable hypothetical method which "makes a hasty transition from our first and slight observations on things to general axioms" with the Newtonian and Baconian method of cautious ascent (p. 5). Writing about the same time, 1731, the Dutch physicist Musschenbroek asserted that as a result of Newton's work, "all hypotheses are banned from physics" (cited in Rosenberger's *Geschichte der Physik* [Braunschweig, 1887], III, 3). Earlier still, one of Newton's first followers, George Cheyne, asserted that "... imaginary or *Hypothetical* Causes, have no place in true Philosophy" (above, n. 2, pt. 1, p. 45).

Perhaps the most explicit claim as to the infallibility of Newton's physics was Emerson's observation that "It has been ignorantly objected by some that the Newtonian philosophy, like all others before it, will grow old and out of date, and be succeeded by some new system ... But this objection is falsely made. For never a philosopher before Newton ever took the method that he did. For whilst their systems are nothing but hypotheses, conceits, fictions, conjectures, and romances, invented at pleasure and without any foundation in the nature of things. [*sic*] He, on the contrary ... admits nothing but what he gains from experiments and accurate observations ... It is therefore a mere joke to talk of a new philosophy ... Newtonian philosophy may indeed be improved and further advanced; but it can never be overthrown; notwithstanding the efforts of all the Bernoulli's, the Leibnitz's ..." (*Principles of Mechanics* [London, 1773], n.p.).

torians of ideas who have studied the period. But there is a curious flaw in this oft repeated account of the development of British thought in the Enlightenment; namely, where do the professional philosophers come into the picture and how was the "Newtonian message" (which, as we have seen, was primarily a methodological and epistemological one) received among British philosophers? Although histories of philosophy often bracket Newton with the classical British empiricists, Locke, Berkeley, and Hume, such a conjunction is more misleading than illuminating, at least so far as the history of the philosophy of science is concerned. Indeed, those three empiricists are surprisingly un-Newtonian when it comes to questions of scientific method. Locke, for instance, died before most of Newton's pronunciamentos on methodology were published, so we look in vain for signs of Newtonian influence there.[4] Berkeley, on the other hand, though undoubtedly aware of Newton's inductive empiricism, developed a theory of scientific method and concept formation which is almost as alien to Newton's views as any could be.[5] Indeed, Berkeley's *De Motu* can be read as a poorly disguised critique of Newtonian empiricism and inductivism. The situation is not vastly different with Hume, who seems to have taken little or no cognizance of Newton's numerous methodological *obiter dicta*. In fact, when Hume did come to grips with methodological issues (e.g. induction or causality), his conclusions were diametrically opposed to the then usual interpretation of Newton's doctrines. Of course I do not mean to suggest that Newton's physics, his theory of space and time, or his theology were without influence on Locke, Berkeley, and Hume; on the contrary, his work was profoundly important on each of these scores. But, and this is the anomaly, on the crucial questions of scientific method and the philosophy of science – the very areas where Newton ventured most openly and frequently into the philosophers' domain – there seems to be very little evidence indeed that the early British empiricists were either very impressed by, or paid much heed to, Newton's much publicized views.

4 Many historians of philosophy have overlooked the fact that the major sources of Newton's methodological views were not available when Locke's *Inquiry* was written. This has led to two serious errors: (1) the suggestion that Locke, as a presumed Newtonian, was a vehement opponent of hypotheses in science, and (2) the claim that Locke's general theory of method, including his supposed aversion to hypotheses, was derived from Newton. For a discussion of these questions, see my "The Nature and Sources of Locke's Views on Hypotheses," *Journal of the History of Ideas*, xxvii (1967), 211–23.

5 Cf. K. Popper's "A Note on Berkeley as a Precursor of Mach," *British Journal for the Philosophy of Science*, iv (1953), 26–36, and G. J. Whitrow's "Berkeley's Philosophy of Motion," *ibid.*, 37ff.

Within the next century, however, circumstances had changed considerably. English philosophical works of the early and middle nineteenth century are teeming with references to Newton's philosophy of science, to his *Regulae Philosophandi*, to the "General Scholium" to the *Principia*, and to Queries XXVIII and XXXI of the *Opticks* (where Newton discusses scientific method). Indeed, almost all of the major figures of nineteenth-century English philosophy, logic, and philosophy of science (e.g., Brown, Herschel, Whewell, Mill, Hamilton, DeMorgan, Jevons, and even Bradley) devote a great deal of time and space to a discussion of Newton's methodological ideas. More important, their philosophical doctrines show signs of having come to grips, at a fundamental level, with the epistemological implications of both Newtonian physics and Newtonian philosophy of science.

How is the historian to explain this profound transformation? When, and by whom, was Newton introduced into the mainstream of British philosophical thought on epistemology and the philosophy of science? What happened within British empiricism that caused it to take Newton the methodologist as seriously as it had previously taken Newton the scientist? I submit that a partial and tentative answer to all these questions will come from a close analysis of the methodological writings of Thomas Reid (1710–96), leader of the Scottish school of common-sense philosophy. Indeed, most of the available evidence seems to indicate that Reid was the first major British philosopher to take Newton's opinions on induction, causality, and hypotheses seriously.

Of all the British philosophers of the eighteenth century, Reid was ideally suited to serve as Newton's spokesman. Trained in the natural sciences, Reid lectured at Aberdeen and Glasgow in physics and mathematics as well as philosophy in the narrower sense. His first publication was a defence of Newtonian mechanics in the *Philosophical Transactions*.[6] A close friend of the Newtonians, James Stewart and David Gregory, and the nephew of James Gregory, he was a devout partisan of Newtonian physics and gave lectures on the *Principia* for some twelve years. (It is significant that the first section of Reid's surviving lecture notes on natural philosophy – written by one of his students – was devoted to Newton's *Regulae Philosophandi*; maxims which, as we shall see, were later to play so important a role in Reid's philosophical works.) Reid, in short, was a well-read, capable physicist who knew Newton's work first-hand and could see that there was more in it of

6 For a discussion of, and excerpts from, Reid's paper in the *Phil. Trans.*, see my "Postmortem on the *Vis Viva* Controversy," *Isis*, LIX (1968), 131–43.

methodological interest than the popularized works of Newtoniana could begin to suggest.[7] But if Newton was Reid's scientific inspiration, it was Hume who seems to have stirred his first serious philosophical interests.[8] Reid evidently read the *Treatise* and the *Enquiry* avidly for he wrote to Hume in 1763: "I shall always avow myself your disciple in metaphysics. I have learned more from your writings in this kind, than from all others put together."[9]

However, his self-avowed debt to Hume was a curious one; for almost all of Reid's philosophical works are concerned with showing that the Humean scepticism with regard to the senses and the predilections of common sense as well as Hume's critique of the sciences are without foundation. Reid believed that the Humean account of knowledge, causality, and induction was so far-fetched as to constitute a *reductio ad absurdum* of the basic premises of classical empiricism. He felt it was necessary to start again at the foundations in order to give an account of knowledge and the means of obtaining it which distinguished various degrees of certainty and reliability in our knowledge. As Reid interpreted Hume, empiricism was no longer able to distinguish between the merits of, say, the astrologers and the classical mechanicians and therefore was no longer appealing as a philosophy of science.[10] While granting Hume's point that no empirical knowledge was infallible, he maintained that there were degrees of fallibility and he insisted that an epistemology and philosophy of science should offer guide-lines for deciding between reliable and unreliable propositions or systems. In constructing such an epistemology, Reid drew extensively on the insights which he had gleaned from his lengthy familiarity with the writings of Newton. It is

7 Few intellectuals, besides trained physicists, could read the *Principia*, or even the *Opticks*, without great difficulty. As a result popularized works were much in vogue, such as Voltaire's *Elements of Newton's Philosophy*, Pemberton's *View of Sir Isaac Newton's Philosophy* (London, 1728), and Maclaurin's *Account of Sir Isaac Newton's Philosophical Discoveries* (London, 1750). Although these books all praised Newtonian science for the certainty of its conclusions and the experimental bias of its founder, none of them did justice to Newton's theory of scientific method. For a discussion of some of these works, see I. B. Cohen's *Franklin and Newton* (Philadelphia, 1956).

8 In this as in other respects, the intellectual careers of Reid and Kant are much alike.

9 Reid to Hume, 18 March 1763, *Works of Thomas Reid, D.D.*, ed. Hamilton, 6th ed. (Edinburgh, 1863), I, 91. Hereafter all page references will be to the *Works* unless indicated otherwise.

10 This reading of Hume as a total sceptic, unable to distinguish sound from unsound judgment, is not as far-fetched as it might seem. After all, it was Hume who wrote "The intense view of these manifold contradictions and imperfections in human reason, has so wrought upon me, and heated my brain, that I am ready to reject all belief and reasoning, and can look upon no opinion even as more probable or likely than another."

important that we point out, however, that Reid had more than one reason for taking Newton seriously; for he saw his own work as an attempt to create a scientific mental philosophy, that is, psychology.[11] He continually preached that the mental sciences (viz., psychology and epistemology) were so backward precisely because no one had tried to construct them according to the canons of scientific evidence and proof. What finer aim could one have, he reasoned, than to seek to structure the philosophy of mind along scientific lines, and this, of course, meant trying to shape the mental sciences so as to conform to Newton's methodological insights.

The Polemic Against Hypotheses. One of the foundation stones of Reid's philosophical system, and the basic point he adopted from Newton, was his suspicion of, if not overt contempt for, any theories, hypotheses, or conjectures which are not *induced* from experiments and observations. He maintained that a patient and methodical induction coupled with a scrupulous repudiation of all things hypothetical was the panacea for most of the ills besetting philosophy and science. Thus, in his *Essay on the Intellectual Powers of Man,* he writes:

[Scientific] discoveries have always been made by patient observation, by accurate experiments, or by conclusions drawn by strict reasoning from observations and experiments, and such discoveries have always tended to refute, but not to confirm, the theories and hypotheses which ingenious men have invented.

As this is a fact confirmed by the history of philosophy in all past ages, it ought to have taught man, long ago, to treat with contempt *hypotheses in every branch of philosophy, and to despair of ever advancing real knowledge in that way.*[12]

Elsewhere, he notes that "philosophy has been, in all ages, adulterated by hypotheses; that is, by systems built partly on facts, and much upon conjecture" (*Intellectual Powers*, p. 249). Reid was particularly antagonistic to hypotheses when discussing his programme for transforming the philosophy of mind into a science. "Let us," he insists, "lay down this as a fundamental principle in our inquiries into the structure of the mind and its operations – that no regard is due to the conjectures or hypotheses of philosophers, however ancient, however generally received" (*Intellectual Powers*, p. 236).

Reid has several objections to the hypothetical method, some logical, others historical or psychological:

11　"... if ever our philosophy concerning the human mind is carried so far as to deserve the name of science, which ought never to be despaired of, it must be by observing facts, reducing them to general rules, and drawing just conclusions from them," *An Inquiry into the Human Mind* (1765), abbreviated to *Human Mind*, in *Works* I, 122.

12　*Essays on the Intellectual Powers of Man* (1785), hereafter abbreviated *Intellectual Powers*, in *Works*, I, 235.

(1) *As a matter of historical fact, hypotheses and conjectures have not been very productive, and have tended to mislead rather than enlighten us.* Despite Reid's familiarity with the history of science (he would probably have said because of it), he maintained that there was not a single law or discovery which was made by conjecturing about nature. He argued that if even *one* "useful discovery" could be credited to the hypothetical method then "Lord Bacon and Sir Isaac Newton have done great disservice to philosophy by what they have said against hypotheses. But, if no such instance can be produced, we must conclude, with those great men, that every system which pretends to account for the phaenomena of Nature by hypotheses or conjecture, is spurious and illegitimate, and serves only to flatter the pride of man with a vain conceit of knowledge which he has not attained" (*Intellectual Powers*, p. 250).

(2) *The adoption of an hypothesis prejudices the impartiality of the scientist.* In so far as a conjecture or hypothesis is a creation of our own minds, we tend to take a vested interest in it and are less eager to test it severely.[13] Reid argues that science floundered so long in the Middle Ages precisely because the Galenic hypotheses in medicine, the Ptolemaic hypotheses in astronomy, and the Aristotelian hypotheses in physics dissuaded the Schoolmen from making the sorts of experiments which eventually led to the downfall of these systems.

Moreover, once we discover an hypothesis that is appealing on *a priori* grounds, we are prone to decide the truth or falsity of empirical propositions by their accord with that hypothesis rather than by testing our hypothesis against empirical statements whose truth has been determined independently.[14] Almost a century earlier, Newton himself had been forced to develop an argument very like Reid's in his early optical controversy with Hooke, Huygens, and Pardies.[15] Reid points out that preconceived hypotheses even

13 "When a man has, with labour and ingenuity, wrought up an hypothesis into a system, he contracts a fondness for it, which is apt to warp the best judgment" (*Intellectual Powers*, p. 250). "When a man has laid out all his ingenuity in fabricating a system, he views it with the eye of a parent; he strains phenomena to make them tally with it, and makes it look like the work of nature" (*Intellectual Powers*, p. 472).

14 "These facts are phenomena of ... nature, from which we may justly argue against any hypothesis, however generally received. But to argue from a hypothesis against facts, is contrary to the rules of true philosophy." (*Human Mind*, p. 132.)

15 Newton wrote to Oldenburg: "For the best and safest method of philosophizing seems to be, first diligently to investigate the properties of things and establish them by experiment, and then seek hypotheses to explain them. *For hypotheses ought to be fitted merely to explain the properties of things and not attempt to determine them ...*" (Turnbull, ed., *Correspondence of Isaac Newton* [Cambridge, 1959], I, 99, my italics). See also Newton's fourth *regula philosophandi*.

tend to influence the way in which we interpet observations: "A false system once fixed in the mind, becomes, as it were, the medium through which we see objects: they receive a tincture from it, and appear of another colour than when seen by a pure light" (*Intellectual Powers*, p. 474).

(3) *The hypothetical method presupposes a greater simplicity in nature than we find there.* In any given domain of science or philosophy, there are certain obvious phenomena which require explanation. If we indulge in hypotheses, and if we are sufficiently ingenious, we can always find several different hypotheses which will "save" or explain those phenomena. The most common way of choosing between such explanatory hypotheses is to select the simplest of the set. But, and here Reid uses the historical argument again, the development of the sciences shows conclusively that those hypotheses that seem the simplest are generally quite wide of the mark. Nature, in his view, is highly complex and "correct" theories like Newton's only seem simple in retrospect because they are sufficiently complex to match nature's intricacy. He particularly objects to the tendency of many philosophers to give *a priori* preference to a system just because its structure is simple or its principles few.[16] Even Newton comes in for criticism here since he was, on Reid's view, sometimes "misled by analogy and the love of simplicity" (*Human Mind*, p. 207; cf. *Intellectual Powers*, p. 471).

(4) *The use of hypotheses assumes that man's reason is capable of understanding the works of God.* In Reid's view, nature is complex because it is the handiwork of a Being whose wisdom and ingenuity are infinitely greater than man's. If we were presented with a machine or other contrivance (say a clock) made by another human being, then it would not be unreasonable, prior to our empirical inspection of its clockwork, to conjecture about its internal arrangement. Because its maker is no more ingenious than we are, we might have a reasonable chance of guessing the correct arrangement. But,

The works of men and the works of God are not of the same order. The force of genius may enable a man perfectly to comprehend the former, and see them to the

16 Thus, he writes: "Men are often led into error *by the love of simplicity which disposes us to reduce things to few principles, and to conceive a greater simplicity in nature than there really is.* ... We may learn something of the way in which nature operates from fact and observation; but if we conclude that it operates in such a manner, only because to our understanding that appears to be the best and simplest manner, we shall always go wrong." (*Intellectual Powers*, pp. 470–71.) Cf. ch. VII of *Human Mind* (p. 206) where Reid similarly notes that: "There is a disposition in human nature to reduce things to as few principles as possible." Cf. this sentiment with Bacon's remark that "the human understanding is of its own nature prone to suppose the existence of more order and regularity than it finds" (*Novum Organum*, Book I, Aphorism xlv).

bottom. What is contrived and executed by one man may be perfectly understood by another man. ...

But the works of nature are contrived and executed by a wisdom and power infinitely superior to that of man; and when men attempt, by the force of genius, to discover the causes of the phaenomena of Nature, they have only the chance of going wrong more ingeniously. Their conjectures may appear very probable to beings no wiser than themselves; but they have no chance to hit the truth.[17]

(5) *Hypotheses can never be proved by "reductio" methods.* Although proponents of the hypothetical method were aware of the fallacy of affirming the consequent, and conceded that hypotheses could not be proved directly by comparing their predictions with observation, many of them maintained that an hypothesis could be proven indirectly by a series of crucial experiments.[18] It was then said that there could be no other explanation besides the hypothesis that survived the crucial experiments. Newton was probably the first to point out the fallacy in this reasoning,[19] by showing the unlikelihood of being able to enumerate all the possible hypotheses, and Reid follows him in dismissing the notion that hypotheses can be proved in this way: "This, indeed, is the common refuge of all hypotheses, that we know no other way in which the phaenomena may be produced, and therefore, they must be produced in this way" (*Intellectual Powers*, p. 250).

(6) *The use of hypotheses usually violates Newton's first "Regula Philosophandi."* Newton's first rule – that no more causes are to be admitted than those which are both true and sufficient to explain the appearances – was often used by Reid, but rarely so effectively as in his critique of the hypotheticalists.[20] The first rule, he argued, requires not only that hypotheses be

---

17 *Intellectual Powers*, p. 472. Earlier, he had written in a similar vein: "Now, though we may, in many cases, form very probable conjectures concerning the works of men, every conjecture we can form with regard to the works of God has as little probability as the conjectures of a child with regard to the works of a man" (*ibid.*, p. 235). "Men," he writes, "only begin to have a true taste in philosophy when they have learned to hold hypotheses in just contempt; and to consider them as the reveries of speculative men, which will never have any similitude to the works of God" (*ibid.*, p. 309).
18 Reid's opponent, David Hartley, had been one of the more important exponents of *reductio* techniques, as well as a vigorous advocate of the hypothetico-deductive method. Cf. especially Hartley's *Observations on Man* (London, 1749), I, ch. I, Prop. V.
19 Newton wrote: "I cannot think it effectual for determining the truth to examine the several ways by which the phenomena may be explained, unless there can be a perfect enumeration of all those ways" (Turnbull, above, n. 15, I, 209).
20 Of all Newton's four *regulae*, it was the first that Reid regarded most highly. It is, he argues, "a golden rule; it is the true and proper test by which what is sound and solid in philosophy may be distinguished from what is hollow and vain" (*Intellectual Powers*, p. 236). In the light of Reid's opposition to the principle of simplicity, it may seem curious that he could speak so glowingly of the first *regula* since that rule seems to

adequate to explain all the appearances, but also that the mechanisms and entities postulated in those hypotheses be true, and not merely fictions of the human imagination. Reid asserts, with some justice, that the "votaries of hypotheses" were generally satisfied if their hypotheses saved the appearances and that they were not concerned to know whether their hypothetical entities and mechanisms corresponded to physical reality. In an important letter to Lord Kames, Reid elaborates on this point and on the meaning of that cryptic Newtonian phrase "true cause":

All investigation of what we call the causes of natural phenomena may be reduced to this syllogism – If such a cause exists, it will produce such a phenomenon; but that cause does exist: Therefore, &c. The first proposition is merely hypothetical. And a man in his closet, without consulting nature, may make a thousand such propositions, and connect them into a system; but this is only a system of hypotheses, conjectures, or theories; and there cannot be one conclusion drawn from it, until he consults nature, and discovers whether the causes he has conjectured do really exist.[21]

Five years later, and indicating still more clearly his debt to the first rule, Reid wrote:

When men pretend to account for any of the operations of nature, the causes assigned by them ought, as Sir Isaac Newton has taught us, to have two conditions, otherwise they are good for nothing. *First*, they ought to be true, to have a real existence, and not to be barely conjectured to exist, without proof. *Secondly*, they ought to be sufficient to produce the effect.[22]

There are, I think, two important points involved in Reid's argument concerning the *regula prima*:

(*a*) He is suggesting, in the first place, that a scientific law must deal only with observable or (at least) instrumentally detectable entities and properties. This insistence on observable causes seems to follow from Reid's claim that the scientist must consult nature in order to discover "whether the causes he has conjectured do really exist." If the general form of a law is "If A, then B," Reid's claim amounts to the assertion that the states of affairs

presuppose the simplicity of nature. On the other hand, as I point out later, Reid has a rather novel interpretation of the meaning of the first rule.

21 Reid to Kames, 16 December 1780, *Works*, I, 57.
22 *Intellectual Powers*, p. 261. In the same work, he observes that Newton "laid it down as a rule of philosophizing, that no causes of natural things ought to be assigned but such as can be proved to have a real existence. He saw that ... the true method of philosophizing is this: From real facts, ascertained by observation and experiment, to collect by just induction the laws of Nature, and to apply the laws so discovered, to account for the phenomena of Nature." (*Ibid.*, pp. 271–72.)

described by both A and B must be capable of being observed in any particular case where we hope to use the law for explanation. If A (the cause) is unobservable in principle, then it cannot possibly qualify as a *vera causa*. (Of course, to be a *vera causa* it must be true as well as observable.) This is tantamount to the demand that every explanation must contain what we should now call descriptive statements of initial conditions. Unless we know the initial conditions (which, for Reid, are generally the causes of the event to be explained), then it is impossible to give an explanation. Scientific laws or hypotheses alone are, as he puts it, "merely hypothetical." Until we know that the causes and effects which those laws correlate are present in any particular process under examination, then those laws are void of any explanatory content. From a modern point of view, this insistence on having initial conditions which instantiate the antecedent of the law seems so obvious as to be an almost trivial description of the logic of explanation. However, Reid seems to have been the first philosopher of science to make the point explicitly, and it certainly deserved making in the context of eighteenth-century science. The hypotheticalists would often offer an "explanation" of an observable event by formulating causal hypotheses which asserted that events of the kind in question resulted from the behaviour of forces or agents or micro-particles whose existence was, in principle, not directly confirmable. (Consider, for instance, the claim that the transmission of images from the eye to the brain was caused by the non-detectable vibrations in an immaterial, imperceptible fluid in the optic nerve.) On Reid's view, until it becomes possible to test directly for the presence of this fluid, it cannot figure as a cause in any authentic scientific explanation. Reid's insistence that *verae causae* are observable antecedent events is closely connected with his view, which we shall discuss below, that all proper scientific causes are capable of being discovered by inductive inference. Since simple inductive generalization of correlations between observable events cannot produce any (non-logical) predicates referring to unobservable entities, it was natural for him to insist that the only legitimate causes we can invoke are observable ones.

(*b*) A related argument concerns the common hypotheticalist stratagem for the confirmation of unobservable entities. Basically, this consisted in propounding an hypothesis of the form "If A, then B," where A was a statement describing an imperceptible property or condition and B was a statement of observation. If B was found to be true, it was assumed that A was true as well and that the existence of the hypothetical entities to which it referred was established or at least made likely by the success of the conditional statement in accounting for the outcome of experimental tests.[23] Reid plausibly argues that such a procedure only establishes the *possibility* of the hypothetical entities (i.e., their compatibility with observation) and does not establish their actual existence. He goes on to insist that there are no grounds whatever for deducing the existence of such entities from their consistency with the date of observation:

Supposing it [viz., a certain hypothesis] to be true, it affirms only what may be. We are, indeed, in most cases very imperfect judges of what may be. But this we know, that were we ever so certain that a thing may be, this is no reason for believing that it really is. A *may-be* is a mere hypothesis, which may furnish matter for investigation, but is not entitled to the least degree of belief. The transition from what may be to what really is, is familiar and easy to those who have a predilection for a [*sic*] hypothesis. ...[24]

(7) *The hypothetical method substitutes premature theoretical ingenuity for painstaking experimental rigour*. As a general rule, inductivists have been suspicious of the sharp mind and the quick wit of genius. They have sought to reduce scientific discovery to a mechanical process, where differences of intelligence have little or no role to play and where, to use Bacon's phrase, "all wits and understandings [are] nearly on a level."[25] Bacon, Hooke, Newton, Herschel, and Mill – the classic English inductivists – all shared the belief that a "logic of discovery" should establish rules for discovering scientific laws and theories and that these rules should be so nearly mechani-

23 Reid's perennial adversary, David Hartley, had used an argument very like this to establish the existence of the aether. "Let us suppose," he wrote, "the existence of the aether, with these its properties, to be destitute of all direct evidence, still if it [viz., the aether] serves to account for a great variety of phaenomena, it will have an indirect evidence in its favour by this means" (*Observations on Man* [London, 1749], I, 15). Perhaps the most specious argument of this kind was Bryan Robinson's defence of the aether: "This *Aether* being a very general material Cause, without any Objection appearing against it from the Phaenomena, no Doubt can be made of its Existence: For by how much the more general any Cause is, by so much the stronger is the Reason for allowing its Existence. The *Aether* is a much more general Cause than our Air: And on that Account, the Evidence from the Phaenomena, is much stronger in Favour of the Existence of the *Aether*, than it is in Favour of the Existence of the Air." (*A Dissertation on the Aether of Sir Isaac Newton* [London, 1747], preface, n.p.)
24 *Intellectual Powers*, p. 397. Years earlier, he had written to Kames: "A cause that is conjectured ought to be such that, if it really does exist, it will produce the effect. ... Supposing it to have this quality, the question remains – Whether does it exist or not? ... If there be no evidence for it, even though there be none against it, it is a conjecture only, and ought have no admittance into chaste natural philosophy." (16 December 1780, *Works*, I, 57.)
25 Francis Bacon, *Works*, ed. Ellis & Speeding (London, 1858), IV, 63.

cal and foolproof that there would be little need for a facile mind or a fertile imagination.[26] Reid unreservedly sides with this point of view. "The experience of all ages," he maintains, "shows how prone ingenious men have been to invent hypotheses to explain the phaenomena of nature; how fond, by a kind of anticipation, to discover her secrets. ... Instead of a slow and gradual ascent ... by a just and copious induction, they would shorten the work, and by a flight of genius, get to the top at once."[27] Genius and the creative intellect have only a very circumscribed role to play in science, properly inderstood: "[Genius] may combine, but it must not fabricate. It may collect evidence, but it must not supply the want of it by conjecture. It may display its powers by putting Nature to the test in well-contrived experiments, but it must add nothing to her answers." (*Intellectual Powers*, p. 472)

One of the severe limitations to the hypothetical method is that it relies too heavily on the ingenuity of the theoretician to second-guess nature, to anticipate the outcome of unperformed experiments. Given Reid's opinions on the complexity of nature and the limitations of man's genius compared with God's, it is clear why he held no hope that genius unaided by extensive experimentation could advance very far. So adamant was Reid on this point, that he even chided Newton for his occasional lapses into the language of hypothesis. After pointing out several errors in the hypothesis in the fifteenth query to the *Opticks* (regarding the transmission of images from the eye to the brain), Reid concludes that even "if we trust to the conjectures of men of the greatest genius in the operations of nature, we have only the chance of going wrong in an ingenious manner."[28]

Feeble as an instrument of discovery, and therefore impotent as a probe

---

26 George Turnbull, Reid's teacher, particularly stressed the mechanical character of scientific discovery: "And by the discoveries made in natural philosophy, we know, that no sooner are facts collected, and laid together in proper order than the true theory of the phenomenon in question presents itself" (*Principles of Moral Philosophy*, [London, 1740], p. 59).

27 *Intellectual Powers*, p. 472. Earlier he put the point even more candidly: "The world has been so long befooled by hypotheses in all parts of philosophy, that it is of the utmost consequence to every man who would make any progress in real knowledge, to treat them with just contempt, as the reveries of vain and fanciful men, whose pride makes them conceive themselves able to unfold the mysteries of nature by the force of their genius" (*ibid.*, p. 236).

28 *Human Mind*, p. 181. Reid's contemporary, Jean D'Alembert, was similarly sceptical about finding truth by the hit-or-miss method of conjectures and refutations: "It may be safely affirmed that a mere theoretician (*un physicien de cabinet*) who, by means of reasonings and calculations, should attempt to divine the phenomena of nature and who should afterwards compare his anticipations with facts would be astonished to find how wide of the truth almost all of them had been" (*Melanges de Littérature, d'Histoire, et de Philosophie* [Amsterdam, 1767], v, 6).

for truth, the hypothetico-deductive method emerges from Reid's attack with very little to recommend it.

It was not only hypotheses that Reid found objectionable; theories, too, were anathema to him. Indeed, he tended to conflate the terms theory, hypothesis, and conjecture and to attack them indiscriminately.[29] He leaves us in no doubt that it was from Newton that he inherited his aversion to all things hypothetical: "I have, ever since I was acquainted with Bacon and Newton, thought that this doctrine [i.e. never to trust to hypotheses and conjectures] is the very key to natural philosophy, and the touchstone by which everything that is legitimate and solid in that science, is to be distinguished from what is spurious and hollow. ..."[30] Elsewhere, he speaks of the example "the great Newton" set in the *Opticks*, an example which "always ought to be but rarely hath been followed" (*Human Mind*, p. 180), whereby he distinguishes his speculations (which he put "modestly" in the queries) from his indubitable conclusions.[31] It was, Reid tells us, precisely because Newton took such care to distinguish his hypotheses from his inductively established theories that he "considered it as a reproach when his system was called his hypothesis; and says, with disdain of such imputation, *Hypotheses non fingo.*" (*Intellectual Powers*, p. 250)

Like Newton, Reid maintained that there was an important difference in kind between the laws and properties discovered by induction and the hypotheses and theories devised to explain those laws and properties. Moreover, the same kind of vacillation that scholars have detected in Newton's writings[32] between an explicit denunciation of all hypotheses and a grudging admission of the possible utility of some hypotheses is echoed by a similar sort of ambiguity in Reid's position. At one moment, he tells us that hypo-

29 Thus, he writes: "Conjectures in physical patters have commonly got the name of *hypotheses*, or *theories*" (*Intellectual Powers*, p. 235). Sir William Hamilton in his *Lectures on Metaphysics* took Reid to task for confusing theories and hypotheses; see especially *ibid.*, p. 120.
30 Reid to Kames, 17 December 1780, *Works*, I, 56.
31 He makes a similar point when he notes approvingly that: "Sir Isaac Newton, in all his philosphical writings, took great care to distinguish his doctrines, which he pretended to prove by just induction, from his conjectures, which were to stand or fall according as future experiments and observations should establish or refute them" (*Intellectual Powers*, p. 249). In his own work, Reid follows Newton's example, separating "facts" about the human mind from conjectures. He has, for instance, a separate chapter in the *Inquiry* called "Some Queries Concerning Visible Figure Answered," and a chapter in his *Intellectual Powers* on an "Hypothesis concerning the Nerves and Brain." One of Reid's main criticisms of David Hartley's psychological writings was that they mingled hypotheses with facts.
32 For a discussion of this point, see I. B. Cohen's *Franklin and Newton* (Philadelphia, 1956) as well as his more recent publications.

theses should be "treated with contempt," that they are "apocryphal and of no authority" and that they "cannot produce knowledge"; but when pressed on this point he concedes that "conjecturing may be a useful step even in natural philosophy"[33] and that hypotheses "may lead to productive experiments."[34] Nonetheless, the thrust of almost all Reid's arguments is towards discrediting those philosophers (e.g., David Hartley) and scientists (e.g., the Cartesians) who did use hypotheses, however sparingly.

Fundamentally, what seems to have disturbed Reid more than anything else about the hypothetical method was the subtle way in which, so far as he was concerned, it distorted and perverted the true aims of science. For Reid, the chief goal was the discovery of how nature operated and a faithful description of those operations. But once the natural philosopher was allowed to indulge his fancy with hypotheses, such hypothesizing became the chief aim, to which all else was subordinate. The situation had become so bad that Reid was forced to observe that "... the invention of a [sic] hypothesis, founded on some slight probabilities, which accounts for many appearances of nature, has been considered as the highest attainment of a philosopher."[35] Reid, of course, was not alone in interpreting Newton's "Hypotheses non fingo" literally and in applying it even more broadly than Newton had done. It was a characteristic of the time to lampoon hypotheses and their proponents and to treat them as anachronistic legacies from the pre-Newtonian era. As Benjamin Martin noted shortly after the appearance of Reid's *Human Mind*: "The Philosophers of the present Age hold [hypotheses] in vile Esteem, and will hardly admit the Name in their Writings; they think that which depends upon bare Hypothesis and Conjecture, unworthy the name of Philosophy; and therefore have framed new and more effectual Methods for philosophical Enquiries."[36] Reid was, however, the only one of his philosophical colleagues to take a great deal more from Newton's methodology than his anti-hypotheticalism.

33 Reid to Kames, 16 December 1780, p. 56.
34 *Ibid*. Elsewhere he makes a similar point: "Let hypotheses be put to any of these uses as far as they can serve. Let them suggest experiments or direct our inquiries; but let just induction alone govern our belief." (*Intellectual Powers*, p. 251)
35 *Intellectual Powers*, p. 235. More than a century earlier, Newton had deplored the preoccupation with hypotheses and phenomena – saving among his scientific colleagues. He observed that finding a general hypothesis accounting for all the appearances had become "the philosophers' universall topick" (Turnbull, above, n. 15, I, 96–97; cf. I. B. Cohen, ed., *Isaac Newton's Letters and Papers on Natural Philosophy* [Cambridge, 1958], p. 179).
36 B. Martin, *Philosophical Grammar*, 7th ed. (London, 1769), p. 19. Martin was rather more sympathetic to hypotheses than most of his British contemporaries.

In a very real sense, Reid's conception of an "hypothesis" and his rather shabby treatment of the hypothetico-deductive method are logical extensions of the trend which was started by Newton and which reached its culmination in the work of Comte and Mill. By gradual stages, the meaning of the term hypothesis was eroded and altered, much to the confusion of subsequent methodological inquiry. In the early seventeenth century, hypothesis had signified any general proposition which was assumed, but not known, to be true. It was used especially to refer to the unproven postulates, axioms, or first principles of any science, and this meaning of the term had been common since Aristotle and Euclid. Even Newton used "hypothesis" in this sense in the first edition of the *Principia* (1687) and it carried no particularly pejorative connotations there.[37] But the signification of the term was gradually transformed in Newton's later writings. In a constant battle with the Cartesians, Newton would often find his opponents offering theories or conjectures which were patently false when tested empirically. Thus, six of Descartes' seven laws of motion were obviously incompatible with the most elementary impact experiments. Similarly, Descartes' vortex hypothesis was demonstrably false, even if its refutation was rather more elaborate than in the case of the laws of motion. Undeterred by such anomalies, many Cartesians continued to hold to Descartes' laws of motion and vortex theory, defending them in terms of their *a priori* cogency. Understandably, Newton had no patience with such an approach and he tried to discredit it with methodological arguments. The "a priorists," he insisted, were using hypotheses; so the natural way to eliminate their non-empirical techniques was to insist, as he finally did, that "hypotheses have no place in experimental philosophy."[38] Unfortunately, Newton's blanket denunciation of hypotheses not only discredited the "a priorists," it also left no place for an *empirical* hypothetico-deductive method, which insisted on the experimental testing of all conjectures. What tended to happen, therefore, was that the older meaning of hypothesis (as an axiom or postulate) came to be confounded with the notion of an unempirical or untestable proposition. Where before the two had been clearly distinguished, they were now indiscriminately confused and the legitimate arguments against *a priori* and un-

---

37 For a discussion of the evolution of the meaning of "hypothesis" in Newton's work, see Cohen's *Franklin and Newton*.

38 Newton, *Principia*, General Scholium. Compare this with Reid's remark that "hypotheses ought to have no place in the philosophy of nature" (*Essays on the Active Powers of the Human Mind* [*EAPHM*], 1788, *Works*, II, 526). It is significant that whereas Newton's disclaimer of hypothesis was confined to "experimental philosophy," Reid broadens it to apply to all of the philosophy of nature.

testable hypotheses were mistakenly used against all hypotheses whatever.[39] By Reid's time, as we have seen, the hypothetical method was in such ill repute that Reid, although perfectly able to distinguish the two senses of hypothesis, considered them equally objectionable and demanded that both were to be avoided scrupulously.[40] Indeed, so vague had the term hypothesis become that Reid could include "theory" in its connotation and could claim that Newton's arguments against hypotheses were equally arguments against theories!

In assessing the propriety, let alone the validity, of Reid's attack on hypotheses, one must take certain mitigating circumstances into account. Reid was concerned, above all else, with founding a science of mind or pneumatology, as he called it. He took methodological questions so seriously because he felt it was necessary to see that the new science had adequate criteria for explanation and sound guide-lines for investigation. Comparing the fledgling mental science with natural science, one thing was evidently clear to him: although hypotheses in physics could easily be detected and exposed if they were false, hypotheses dealing with mental phenomena were not so easily disposed of. To take an elementary example, if one adopts the conjecture that the mind at birth is a *tabula rasa* there is no clear-cut way of confirming or refuting such an hypothesis. Reid, sensitive to the extent to which hypotheses about mental events were insulated from observable phenomena, took the extreme course of insisting that hypotheses must be consistently rejected.

One must remember, too, that Reid could well afford to be so cavalier about hypotheses and so indiscriminate in his deprecation of them. Reid, after all, thought he had a method which dispensed with hypotheses once and for all – the method of induction.

Induction and the Uniformity of Nature. Before we examine the origins and structure of Reid's views on induction, a word should be said about "Newtonian" and "Baconian" induction; otherwise, it will be difficult to decide whether Reid's theory of induction derives from one or the other. At the outset, it must be noted that Reid writes as if the Baconian and Newtonian

---

39 Reid's contemporary, James Gregory, perceived that the then predominant disdain for hypotheses was due to such terminological ambiguities as I have described briefly above. "The prejudice against hypotheses which many people entertain is founded on the equivocal signification of a word. It [viz. hypothesis] is commonly confounded with theory. ..." (Quoted by Dugald Stewart in his *Works* [London, 1854], II, 300)

40 It would scarcely be an exaggeration to say that a great deal of the history of eighteenth-century methodological thought could be gleaned from carefully attending to the changing nuances in the meaning of this crucial term.

theories of induction amount to the same thing and he is continually paying lip-service to both. Generally, he maintains that Bacon developed the theory of induction and that Newton subsequently applied it in a brilliant fashion to astronomy and optics.[41] Newton, moreover, simplified and codified the principles of Baconian induction in his *Regulae Philosophandi*. This might lead one to believe that Reid was a Baconian essentially and only incidentally a Newtonian methodologist. But to take such a view would be a serious mistake. Baconian induction was concerned with the discovery of *forms* by a study and classification of *simple natures*.[42] Bacon's method was essentially the Aristotelian one of definition by genus-species relationships. It was not so much a method of determining laws as it was a technique for generating definitions. However, with Newton, as with Reid, induction is conceived in an entirely different mode. In their work, there is no analogue for Bacon's forms or simple natures; nor is their induction foolproof as Bacon's was. Moreover, the method of elimination, which was such an integral part of Bacon's scheme, is repudiated by both Newton and Reid.[43] Accordingly, all the evidence I can find points to this conclusion: that Reid was only vaguely familiar with the details of Bacon's *Novum Organum* and that he assumed, as was common to that time, that Newton (whose work he did know well) got his ideas on induction from Bacon and that Newton's writings on method were enlargements on, but perfectly compatible with, Bacon's views.[44]

Basically, Reid's inductive method had three components: (1) observation of facts and experimentation; (2) "reduction" of these facts to a general rule or law; and (3) the derivation of further conclusions from the set of

41 Reid was continually claiming that Newton was carrying on Bacon's work. In his *Intellectual Powers* (p. 436) he asserted that "Lord Bacon first delineated the only solid foundation on which natural philosophy can be built; and Sir Isaac Newton reduced the principles laid down by Bacon into three or four axioms which he calls *regulae philosophandi*." In his *Brief Account of Aristotle's Logic* (*Works*, II, 712), he insisted that Newton "in the third book of his 'Principia' and in his 'Optics', had the rules of the *Novum Organum* constantly in his eye." Or, elsewhere, "… the best models of inductive reasoning that have yet appeared, which I take to be the third book of the *Principia* and the *Optics* of Newton, were drawn from Bacon's rules" (*Human Mind*, p. 200).
42 For a detailed discussion of Baconian induction, see M. Hesse's "Francis Bacon" in D. J. O'Connor's *Critical History of Western Philosophy* (London, 1964).
43 See (5) in the previous sec. of this paper.
44 It was a common eighteenth-century mistake to write about Newton as if he invariably kept the *Novum Organum* at his finger-tips. For an early and influential example of this tendency, see the Introduction to Pemberton's *View of Sir Isaac Newton's Philosophy*. It is perhaps significant that among Reid's surviving manuscripts is a *Précis* of Pemberton's *View*.

general rules.[45] These three steps embody, so far as Reid is concerned, the essence of Newton's basic doctrines;[46] and Reid candidly concedes that this is "the view of natural philosophy which I have learned from Newton."[47] The crucial point, of course, is the second step and Reid is as vague on this score as most of his fellow inductivists have been.[48] He does not, by any means, believe that we can legitimately generalize every set of similar observations. Like Bacon, he insists that the amount of data should be large and that our generalizations must be gradual. Indeed, he argues that the only real difference between genuine science and pseudo-science is that in the former our observations are more numerous and our generalizations less hasty: "Omens, portents, good and bad luck, palmistry, astrology, all the numerous arts of divination and interpreting dreams, false hypotheses and systems, and true principles in the philosophy of nature are all built upon the same foundation in the human constitution, and are distinguished only according as we conclude rashly from too few instances, or cautiously from a sufficient induction" (*Human Mind*, p. 113).

So far as one can tell from Reid's text, he usually uses induction in the straightforward sense of generalization from particulars to universals. Whatever latent properties are found to belong to a few individuals of a particular type are presumed to belong to all instances of that type. This kind of induction, from particular facts to general conclusions, is "the master-key to the knowledge of Nature, without which we could form no general conclusions ..." (*Intellectual Powers*, p. 402). All we can know in natural science is what we can learn by induction: "In the solution of natural phaenomena, all the length that the human faculties can carry us, is

45 "The true method of philosophizing is this: From real facts, ascertained by observation and experiments, to collect by just induction the laws of Nature, and to apply the laws so discovered, to account for the phenomena of Nature" (*Intellectual Powers*, pp. 271ff).
46 "The whole object of natural philosophy, as Newton expressly teaches, is reducible to these two heads: first, by just induction from experiment and observation, to discover the laws of nature; and then, to apply those laws to the solution of the phaenomena of nature. This was all this great philosopher attempted, and all that he thought attainable." (*Active Powers*, p. 529)
47 Reid to Kames, 16 December 1780, *Works*, I, 57; cf. p. 59.
48 Even Dugald Stewart, one of Reid's most enthusiastic admirers, admits that Reid was less candid than he might have been about the sort of inductions he endorsed. In an account of Reid's life written in 1803, Stewart noted that: "it were perhaps to be wished that he [Reid] had taken a little more pains to illustrate the fundamental rules of that [inductive] logic the value of which he estimated so highly ..." (in Reid, *Works*, I, 11). For an interesting contemporary critique of Reid's theory of induction, see Joseph Priestley's *Examination of Dr. Reid's Enquiry* (London, 1774), pp. 110ff.

only this, that, from particular phaenomena, we may by induction, trace out general phaenomena, of which all the particular ones are necessary consequences."[49] But Reid never suggests any criteria for distinguishing between what he considers a *just* or *sufficient* induction and a premature generalization. On the other hand, he would probably have defended himself against the charge that he was needlessly vague on the meaning of induction by pointing out that Bacon and Newton had already described the nature and conditions of inductive inference and that he himself simply acquiesced in their analysis. Thus, of Bacon, he writes: "The rules of inductive reasoning, or of a just interpretation of Nature, have been, with wonderful sagacity, delineated by the great genius of Lord Bacon: so that his *Novum Organum* may be justly called 'A Grammar of the Language of Nature'" (*Human Mind*, p. 200). Again he observes: "Lord Bacon first delineated the strict and severe method of induction; since his time it has been applied with very happy success in some parts of natural philosophy and hardly in anything else."[50]

Notwithstanding his high regard for Bacon, Reid insisted that it was Newton's rules of philosophizing which codified and embodied Bacon's inductive principles and it was to them that Reid invariably turned when dealing with questions of scientific method.[51] Newton's *regulae*, he maintains, "are maxims of common sense, and are practised everyday in common life; and he who philosophizes by other rules, either concerning the material system or concerning the mind, mistakes his aim" (*Human Mind*, p. 97). Indeed, all of Reid's writings, both published and unpublished, are teeming with laudatory references to Newton's rules of philosophizing; and in this case, Reid's deferential lip-service, which is misleading when paid to Bacon,

49 *Human Mind*, p. 163. Elsewhere he asserts that "all our curious theories ... so far as they go beyond a just induction from facts, are vanity and folly ..." (*ibid.*, pp. 97–98). Reid sees the "slow and patient method of induction" as "the only way to obtain any knowledge of nature's work" (*Intellectual Powers*, p. 472). Again, he suggests that the discovery of *inductive* laws "is all that true philosophy aims at, and all that it can ever reach" (*Human Mind*, p. 157).

50 *Human Mind*, p. 202. Reid was convinced that Bacon was the unquestioned founder of inductive logic. In his *Brief Account of Aristotle's Logic*, he wrote: "After men had laboured in the search of truth near two thousand years by the help of syllogisms, Lord Bacon proposed the method of induction, as a more effectual engine for that purpose. ... His *Novum Organum* ought therefore to be held as a most important addition to the ancient logic. Those who understand it ... will learn to hold in due contempt all hypotheses and theories." (Pp. 711–12)

51 "Since Sir Isaac Newton laid down the rules of philosophizing, in our inquiries into Nature, many philosophers have deviated from them in practice; perhaps few paid that regard to them which they deserve" (*Intellectual Powers*, p. 251).

is indicative of a profound debt on Reid's part to those four propositions at the beginning of the third book of the *Principia*. He called them "the only solid foundation on which natural philosophy can be built" (*Intellectual Powers*, p. 436), and argued that Newton's physics "would never be refuted because it was based on these self-evident principles" (*ibid*). There is a particularly interesting fascicule among Reid's MSS. which illustrates his high regard for the *regulae*. It is titled "Of the Order in which Natural Philosophy Ought to Be Taught." Of the nine headings in his outline, the second is: "Laws of Philosophizing from S^r. Is. Newton's Princ. Lib. 3."[52] Again, in his lecture notes on pneumatology (*c.* 1768–69), he calls the *regulae* "the axioms upon which men reason in physics."[53] In an unpublished draft version of the *Essays on the Intellectual Powers of Man*, he writes: "There are also first principles in physicks or natural philosophy. Sir Isaac Newton has laid down some of the most important of these in the third book of his *Principia* under the name of axioms or laws of philosophizing, & by this means has given a stability to that science which it had not before."[54]

Just as the rules of the syllogism govern deductive reasoning, so must Newton's *regulae* be the criteria for assessing the validity of all empirical or inductive reasoning.[55] Although Reid concedes that the *regulae* are not, as the laws of syllogistic are, necessarily true, he argues that they are nonetheless so obvious to men of good sense that they can be used legitimately as canons for all scientific and philosophical research.[56] Besides copious

---

52 Birkwood Collection, box 2131.7, parcel 2. The total list of entries is as follows:
   1. "Definition of body & explication ... of its primary qualities"; 2. "Laws of philosophizing from S^r. Is. Newton's Princ. Lib. 3"; 3. "Def. [initions] from same Lib. 1"; 4. "Three Laws of Nature ..."; 5. "Gravity ..."; 6. "Attraction of Cohesion"; 7. "Corpuscular attraction"; 8. "Magnetism"; 9. "Electricity." The copyright on this and all subsequent material quoted from the Birkwood Collection belongs to the Library of King's College, Aberdeen. The author is grateful to Mr. A. T. W. Liddell of the University of Reading for his valuable assistance in connection with Reid's papers and to King's College for permission to quote from those papers.
53 Birkwood Collection, box 2131.5 (8), f. 37.
54 *Ibid.*, box 2131.6 (II) (53).
55 In his unpublished "Lectures on Natural Philosophy" (1758), in the Library of the University of Aberdeen, Reid calls the *regulae* "the rules for reasoning by induction" (p. 7).
56 "Sir Isaac Newton, the greatest of natural philosophers, has given an example well worthy of imitation, by laying down the common principles or axioms, on which the reasonings in natural philosophy are built. ... [the *Regulae*] are principles which, though they have not the same kind of evidence that mathematical axioms have; yet have such evidence that every man of common understanding readily assents to them ..." (*Intellectual Powers*, p. 231).

allusions to Newton's *regulae*, Reid also adopts the analysis-synthesis language of Newton's optical queries when discussing questions of scientific method. In an almost literal transcription of a section from Query XXXI, Reid writes to Kames:

Our senses testify particular facts only: from these we collect by induction, general facts, which we call laws of nature or natural causes. Thus, ascending by a just and copious induction, from what is less to what is more general, we discover as far as we are able, natural causes or laws of nature. This is the analytic part of natural philosophy. The synthetical part takes for granted, as principles, the causes discovered by induction, and from these explains or accounts for the phaenomena which result from them. This analysis and synthesis make up the whole theory of natural philosophy ... From this view of natural philosophy, which I have learned from Newton, your Lordship will perceive that no man who understands it will pretend to demonstrate any of its principles. ...[57]

Despite his high regard for induction as a method, Reid – again like Newton – was quite prepared to admit that it was fallible.[58] No matter how cautious our inductions and regardless of how extensive our evidence, we may discover that some of the propositions we think to be natural laws are in fact false.[59] However keenly Reid might have wanted to establish Newton's *regulae* as indubitable first principles, no post-Humean philosophers could altogether neglect the doubts that the *Enquiry* and the *Treatise* had cast on the legitimacy of induction and the assumption of the uniformity of nature. Indeed, Hume's analysis seemed to undermine both the second[60]

57 Sixteen December 1780, *Works*, I, 57. Compare this with Newton's observation that: "As in Mathematics, so in Natural Philosophy, the Investigation of difficult Things by the Method of Analysis, ought ever to precede the Method of Composition. This Analysis consists in making Experiments and Observations, and in drawing general Conclusions from them by Induction. ... By this way of Analysis we may proceed from Compounds to Ingredients, and from Motions to the Forces producing them; and in general from Effects to their Causes, and from particular Causes to more general ones, till the Argument end in the most general. This is the Method of Analysis: And the Synthesis consists in assuming the Causes discover'd and establish'd as Principles, and by them explaining the Phaenomena proceeding from them, and proving the Explanations." (*Opticks*, ed. Cohen [New York, 1952], pp. 404–5)

58 Cf. Newton's Regula IV where he concedes that "propositions inferred by general induction from phenomena ... may either be made more accurate, or liable to exceptions [i.e. refuted]."

59 "There must be many accidental conjunctions of things, as well as natural connections; and the former are apt to be mistaken for the latter. ... Philosophers, and men of science, are not exempted from such mistakes." (*Human Mind*, p. 197) The evidence that scientific laws "have no exceptions, as well as the evidence that they will be the same in time to come as they have been in time past, can never be demonstrative" (*Intellectual Powers*, p. 484). Cf. *ibid.*, p. 272.

60 The second rule was this: "And so to natural effects of the same kind are assigned the same causes, as far as they can be."

and the third[61] rules of philosophizing. Reid saw it as one of his tasks to defend those *regulae* (which were, after all, "the foundations of the philosophy of common sense") from Hume's onslaughts.

Hume had argued that our belief in the continuance of nature's laws could not be derived from reason, that we could neither know nor even rationally expect that the future will resemble the past. In his view, our confidence in the uniformity of nature was merely a belief or expectation, to be distinguished sharply from perception, memory, and imagination. Hume distinguished those four in terms of the vivacity or faintness of the associated idea. Suppose, for instance, that the idea is one of a sunrise. A perception of a sunrise here and now is very vivid; a memory of a sunrise is fainter; a belief that the sun will rise tomorrow is fainter still; and our imagining a sunrise is so faint and lack-lustre as to carry no conviction of its truth at all. This attempt to distinguish perception, memory, prophecy or prediction, and imagination solely in terms of the vividness of the accompanying ideas is rejected by Reid. He points out that if one takes a memory of yesterday's sunrise and slightly fades its vivacity, one obtains, not an idea of a future sunrise, but an idea of a sunrise in the more distant, but remembered, past. Surely, he argues, it is absurd to suggest that "there is a certain period of this declining vivacity, when, as if it had met an elastic obstacle in its motion backward, it suddenly rebounds from the past to the future, without taking the present in its way" (*Human Mind*, p. 198).

Notwithstanding Reid's rejection of Hume's distinction between ideas of past, present, and future in terms of their vivacity, he accepts Hume's thesis that our belief in the uniformity of nature is instinctive and non-rational. But on Reid's view, it is instinctive not by virtue of the habitual associations of experience but because of an innate disposition in man's nature, which Reid calls *the inductive principle*:

... our belief in the continuance of nature's laws is not derived from reason. It is an instinctive prescience of the operations of nature, very like to that prescience of human actions which makes us rely upon the testimony of our fellow creatures ...

Upon this principle of our constitution, not only acquired perception but also inductive reasoning, and all our reasoning from analogy, is grounded; and, therefore, for want of another name, we shall beg leave to call it the *inductive principle*. (*Human Mind*, p. 199)

61 Rule III began as follows: "The qualities of bodies which admit neither intension nor remission, and which belong to all bodies on which one can make experiments, are to be taken as the qualities of all bodies whatsoever."

The disposition to believe in the uniformity of nature is innate and not, as Hume suggested, a habit acquired from experience. "Prior to all reasoning," Reid insists, "we have, *by our constitution*, an anticipation that there is a fixed and steady course of nature ..." (*ibid.*; my italics). A young child does not have to be burned more than once before he keeps a healthy distance from the fire. Indeed, experience, far from giving rise to the inductive principle, as Hume suggests, tends to circumscribe it and makes us more critical and restrained in following its dictates: "This [inductive] principle, like that of credulity, is unlimited in infancy, and [becomes] gradually restrained and regulated as we grow up" (*ibid.*). The important point, however, is that man's mind is structured in such a way that he inevitably presupposes uniformity in nature: "We are so made that, when two things are found to be conjoined in certain circumstances, we are prone to believe that they are connected in nature, and will always be found together in like circumstances. The belief which we are led into in such cases is not the effect of reasoning, nor does it arise from intuitive evidence in the thing believed; it is, as I apprehend, the immediate effect of our constitution." (*Intellectual Powers*, p. 332; cf. p. 451)

To ask, as Hume did, about the justification for our belief in the uniformity of nature, is to misconceive the nature of the inductive principle. It is simply instinctive, constitutional, and innate; like Dr. Johnson, Reid feels that we can no more justify it than we can rid ourselves of it. Reid sees the inductive principle, construed as a disposition to belief, as the ground for, and the justification of, Newton's second *Regula*: "It is from the force of this principle that we immediately assent to that axiom upon which all of ɔur knowledge is built. That effects of the same kind must have the same cause. ..."[62]

It is true that we can have no conception of the uniformity of nature prior to our having experiences or sensations, and in this sense experience is a necessary condition for our belief in the uniformity of nature. But – and here Reid's reaction to Hume resembles Kant's – our belief in the uniformity of nature and in the causal axiom *is not derived from experience*.[63] Without the

---

62 *Human Mind*, p. 199. This axiom is an exact translation of Newton's remark in the second *regula* to the effect that "Effectuum naturalium ejusdem generis easdem esse causas." Elsewhere, Reid remarks that the second rule "has the most genuine marks of a first principle" (*Intellectual Powers*, p. 451).

63 This interesting similarity must be qualified by noting that what Kant sees as necessary categories for perception, Reid interprets as inborn but nonetheless necessary dispositions. In both cases, causal relations are subjective in their genesis rather than objective.

inductive principle, we could learn nothing from nature because generalization would be impossible[64] and science, either natural or mental, would be unthinkable.[65]

Reid not only maintains that a belief in the uniformity of nature is perfectly natural and inevitable, he also insists that nature itself is uniform and that every change in the material system is strictly governed by immutable laws.[66] He claims that God is the author of all things and that, in his wisdom, he made a universe governed by fixed laws. We have no way of knowing with certainty whether the propositions we think to be laws are in fact the true laws of the universe, and that is why our inductions must be cautious and our conclusions always subject to modification. However, man's fallibility is certainly no sign that the universe is governed by chance and Reid has no qualms about stating categorically that all physical events are subject to scientific laws. None of Reid's arguments really constitute a satisfactory answer to Hume's doubts, and one is almost inclined to say that he simply took the propositions which Hume found most dubious (e.g. "nature is uniform") and asserted them as first principles or as matters of faith. Even so, there is a sense in which his insistence that our causal prejudices are *a priori* and dispositional is a positive step beyond Hume.

Causes and Laws. Newton was less explicit on the meaning of causality than on many other metascientific issues. Reid's analysis of causation was probably closer in spirit to Newton's position – and more far-reaching in its effects – than either his opposition to hypotheses or his inductivism. Newton was in rather a quandary about causal questions. He maintained that science was concerned with discovering causes (which he usually assimilated to forces) yet he did not believe that these were, in Aristotle's language, efficient causes. On his view, matter was passive and inert and had no vital powers *per se*; thus it was incapable of being the efficient cause of anything. It was God who functioned as the efficient cause of motion and change. Accordingly, when Newton spoke of physical causes of certain effects, he did not generally mean agents or efficient causes, but simply the phenomena invariably preceding those effects. "Finding a cause for an

---

64 "Take away the light of this inductive principle, and experience is as blind as a mole; she may, indeed, feel what is present, and what immediately touches her; but she sees nothing that is either before or behind, upon the right hand or upon the left, future or past" (*Human Mind*, p. 200).
65 "A natural philosopher can prove nothing, unless it is taken for granted that the course of nature is steady and uniform" (*ibid.*, p. 130; cf. *ibid.*, p. 198).
66 "The laws of nature are the rules by which the supreme Being governs the world. ..."

effect" means, for Newton, finding some event from which, in conjunction with our inductive theories, we can deduce the occurrence of the effect.

On the other hand, Newton sometimes confuses "cause" in this weaker, deductive sense with the stronger notion of an efficient cause with active, vital powers, rather like Aristotle's entelechy. This confusion is especially clear when he talks of forces which he sometimes conceives as powers and real causal agents, and other times treats as dynamic variables without causal efficacy.

Reid attempts to do justice to both these concepts of causality, while distinguishing between them, and their respective domains, more clearly than Newton had done. Reid argued that science is not, and cannot be, concerned with efficient causes. The scientist deals solely with the discovery of scientific laws and in so far as the term "cause" occurs in natural philosophy, it denotes not agents or powers but merely the antecedent event in a scientific law or the scientific law itself: "Natural philosophers, who think accurately, have a precise meaning to the terms that they use in the science, and when they pretend to show the cause of any phaenomenon of nature, they mean by the cause, a law of nature of which that phenomenon is a necessary consequence."[67] Elsewhere, he says that:

By the cause [in the scientific sense] of a phenomenon, nothing is meant but the law of nature, of which that phenomenon is an instance, or a necessary consequence ... such laws cannot be the efficient cause of anything. They are only the rule according to which the efficient cause operates. ... Efficient causes, properly so called, are not within the sphere of natural philosophy. Its business is, from particular facts in the material world, to collect, by just induction, the laws that are general, and from these the more general, as far as we can go. And when this is done, natural philosophy has no more to do.[68]

It is obvious from these passages that Reid's notion of a (scientific) cause is inexorably bound up with the notion of a scientific law.[69] Causes, on his view, were either the laws themselves or else the events described in the

---

67 *Active Powers*, p. 527. Strictly speaking, of course, no event or "phenomenon" is a necessary consequence of a law since laws are conditional "if-then" statements. Reid, however, was perfectly aware that we need not only a law but also a statement instantiating the antecedent in the law before we can deduce a description of an event. His looser and less technical language here, therefore, is not indicative of a logical solecism on his part.

68 Reid to Kames, 16 December 1780, *Works*, I, 57–58.

69 As early as his unpublished "Lectures on Natural Philosophy" (1758), Reid was making such an identification: "When we can show that any phaenomenon of nature is a necessary consequence of some known law of nature, this is called *accounting* for that phaenomenon, *solving* it, or *showing the* cause of it ..." (p. 5).

antecedent of laws. (He suggests that both these meanings are sanctioned by the way in which scientists use the term "cause.")[70] Thus, the search for causes reduces to the search for laws and that search is the "*ne plus ultra* in natural philosophy."[71] Just as the cause of an event is either a law from which the event can be deduced or another event which invariably precedes it,[72] so the *cause of a law* is a more general law from which that law can be deduced.[73] To speak of a causal law is, for Reid, redundant since laws are, by definition, causes. He often describes laws as "general facts" (see esp. *Human Mind*, p. 159), and he sees no logical or epistemological difference between particular facts and general facts; both are true propositions about the physical world obtained from experimental evidence.

Even so, Reid's insistence that scientific causes are not efficient ones does not persuade him, as it did Hume, that all talk of efficient causes is meaningless. He maintains that there are real and proper efficient causes, although it is only the metaphysician and not the natural philosopher who can discover and study them.[74] Natural science can neither confirm nor refute a claim of the form "A is the efficient cause of B,"[75] and so the scientist must remain agnostic on the question of efficient causality. Reid's notion of an efficient cause is the classical one: "In the strict and proper sense, I take an efficient cause to be a being who had power to produce the effect, and exerted that power for that purpose."[76]

It is in this sense that men are said to be the efficient causes of their actions; and it is in this same sense that Reid speaks of God as being the efficient cause, either directly or indirectly, of all change in the physical world. Reid suggests that this distinction between scientific causes and metaphysical causes was first perceived by Newton, who "has taught us to acquiesce in a

---

70 "A law of nature is the *cause* of a phenomenon in physicks, or, perhaps, the *cause* is another phenomenon which always goes before it" (Reid to Gregory, n.d., *Works*, I, 75).
71 Reid to Gregory, 30 July 1789, *ibid.*, p. 73.
72 "A cause . . . means only something which, by the laws of nature, the effect always follows" (Reid to Gregory, 23 September 1785, *ibid.*, p. 67).
73 "... a natural philosopher may search after the cause of a law of nature; but this means no more than searching for a more general law, which includes that particular law, and perhaps many others under it" (Reid to Kames, 16 December 1780, *ibid.*, pp. 57–58).
74 Reid says of the search for efficient causes that "these are very noble and important inquiries, but they do not belong to natural philosophy; nor can we proceed in them in the way of experiment and induction, the only instruments the natural philosopher uses in his researches" (Reid to Kames, 16 December 1780, *ibid.*, p. 58).
75 Cf. *ibid.*, p. 59.
76 Reid to Gregory, 14 June 1785, *ibid.*, p. 65.

law of nature, according to which the effect is produced, as the utmost that natural philosophy can reach, leaving what can be known of the agent or efficient cause to metaphysicks or natural theology. This I look upon as one of the great discoveries of Newton. ..."[77] Although Reid distinguishes between the domains of scientific and efficient causes, he does not believe that the two are unrelated. On the contrary, a scientific cause (i.e. a law) is "only the rule according to which the efficient cause operates."[78]

Reid is prepared to admit Hume's argument about constant conjunction and causality so far as scientific causes are concerned;[79] but he denies that efficient causality can be reduced to constant conjunction. "No reasoning," he says, "is more fallacious than this; that, because two things are constantly conjoined, therefore one must be the [efficient] cause of the other. Day and night have been joined in a constant succession since the beginning of the world; but who is so foolish as to conclude from this that day is the cause of night, or night the cause of the following day?" (*Intellectual Powers*, p. 253) He offers other arguments as well against the thesis that constant conjunction is definitionally equivalent to efficient causality. For instance, he points out that efficient causes are not always exerting their power even when they are capable of doing so. Hence there are times when an efficient cause will exist but will have no effect and in that case there would be no constant conjunction between cause and effect.

As we have already seen, Reid disagrees with Hume both about the genesis of the notion of causality and about its epistemic characteristics. On Reid's view, it is the inborn inductive principle that gives rise to our conception of causation. We could never get the idea of cause from experience, for all we experience are sequences of events: "A train of events following one another ever so regularly could never lead us to the notion of a cause, if we had not, from our constitution, a conviction of the necessity of a cause to every event" (*Active Powers*, p. 523). There is another important reason why we cannot derive the concept of causality from experience; namely, the fact

---

77 Reid to Gregory, n.d., *ibid.*, p. 76. Bacon, on the other hand, was "less enlightened on this point" (*ibid.*), believing that science could discover the *latens processus* by which natural causes really produce their effects.

78 Reid to Kames, 16 December 1780, *ibid.*, p. 57.

79 "What D. Hume says of causes, in general, is very just when applied to physical causes, that a constant conjunction with effect is essential to such causes, and implied in the very conception of them" (Reid to Gregory, March 1786 (?), *ibid.*, p. 67).

  In another letter to Gregory, he observes: "Modern philosophers know that we have no ground to ascribe efficiency to natural causes, or even necessary connection with the effect. But we can still call them causes, including nothing under the name but priority and constant conjunction." (N.d., *ibid.*, p. 76.)

that the causal axiom (i.e., that every event must have a cause) *is a necessary truth*. At the very most, all experience can do is to confirm that observed events do have causes; it cannot show that they *must* have causes. Moreover, quite apart from its necessity, the causal axiom is too *universal* to be derived from experience (*Intellectual Powers*, pp. 457ff). We can only assign causes to a small fraction of the events we perceive every day and there is no inductive rule which would justify our inferring a universal statement from evidence of that kind.[80]

On Reid's view, we get the idea of an efficient cause by virtue of two innate feelings: one, of the uniformity of nature; the other, of our apparent control over our own actions. The former, based on the inductive principle, is all we need to understand scientific causes; we need the latter as well if we are to understand efficient causes.

Conclusion

In discussing the salient features of Reid's philosophy of science, I hope I have been able to convey some idea of the profound and fundamental Newtonian influences to be found in his work. Unlike the empiricists, who had neither the scientific background nor the philosophical biases necessary for a sympathetic reading of Newton, Reid was able to draw equally on the insights of the empiricists and the inductivists and to fuse the two, thereby giving rise to the empiricist-inductivist tradition that played so large a role in nineteenth-century philosophy of science.

80 It was precisely because of the necessity and universality of causal laws that William Whewell was later to insist that they had non-experiential elements. See his *Collected Works*, ed. G. Buchdahl & L. L. Laudan (London, 1967), vi, 451–52.

VII
Whewell on Newton's Rules of Philosophizing

ROBERT E. BUTTS

Throughout his scientific and philosophical career William Whewell had a deep concern for methodological issues. His own positive methodological theories were developed in the three editions of *Philosophy of the Inductive Sciences*.[1] Also relatively well known is his exchange with Mill on a large range of topics touching on induction.[2] But what is perhaps not so well known about Whewell's interest in methodology is that it was a partly practical, not merely philosophical, interest. His search for methods showed an abiding concern for discovering the best ways of accumulating scientific knowledge; he wished to hand on to his followers a finished method no longer in need of philosophical justification. In addition, he wished to discover the method of teaching science and mathematics that would best further the actual pursuit of scientific knowledge. Both motives appear early in his writings, for example, in *The Mechanical Euclid* of 1837.[3] This does not mean that Whewell was unaware of the basic philosophical questions underlying acceptance of this or that method. His writings give ample indication that such questions in philosophy of science were of great importance to him.

I mention these facts about Whewell only for the sake of perspective. Nowadays philosophers interested in methodology concern themselves mainly with the so-called logic of scientific systems. Given a scientific system in a relatively finished state, they show us how it fits together, and where the fit is easy, where strained. Today hardly anyone is seeking methods that

1 William Whewell, *The Philosophy of the Inductive Sciences*, 1st ed., 2 vols. (London, 1840); 2nd ed., 2 vols. (London, 1847), abbreviated to *Inductive Sciences*; 3rd ed. appeared as *The History of Scientific Ideas*, 2 vols. (London, 1858); *Novum Organon Renovatum* (London, 1858); and *On the Philosophy of Discovery* (London, 1860), abbreviated to *Discovery*.
2 William Whewell, *Discovery*, ch. xxii; John Stuart Mill, *A System of Logic* (London, 1843), Book ii, chs. v, vi, Book iii, ch. ii.
3 William Whewell, *The Mechanical Euclid* (Cambridge, 1837), Appendix, "Remarks on Mathematical Reasoning and on the Logic of Induction," pp. 143–82.

someone will actually apply either in doing or in teaching science. It is perhaps unwise to hazard a guess why this is so. Perhaps in Whewell's day
science stood more in need of defence than it does today. Perhaps, too, the
transition in a great university like Cambridge from a classical curriculum
to one that includes experimental science and mathematics was a harder and
more complicated transition than we realize.[4]

Whewell's twofold epistemological and practical interest in methodology
comes across quite clearly in his discussion of other philosophers and
scientists. We see it in his evaluation of Mill and Comte and in his critique
of Bacon.[5] We see it in his debate with Hamilton on the question of whether
logic or mathematics is the best tool for teaching students to reason capably.[6]
But perhaps the most interesting instance is Whewell's extended discussion
of Newton's Rules of Philosophizing,[7] a discussion that seeks an interpretation of the four rules that will allow for each an epistemologically justified
status and a fruitful application.

Whewell's interest in Newton's rules is neither idle nor merely historical.
He had a great reverence for Newton's positive science, and thought
that his general methodology was in the main correct (184). But he was not
mainly concerned to show how Newton himself understood the rules, nor
did he undertake a consideration of how others before him had construed
them. He was interested in seeing whether Newton's rules could be assimilated to his (Whewell's) own methodology.

At the outset of his discussion, Whewell does admit that the rules provide
adequate safeguards to the reasoning required in order to establish the
hypothesis of universal gravitation. Indeed, he thought that Newton intentionally adapted them to this case.

Thus the first Rule is designed to strengthen the inference of gravitation from the
celestial phenomena, by describing it as a *vera causa*, a true cause; the second Rule

4 Whewell was active in university reform throughout his life at Cambridge. He was
instrumental in introducing massive changes in the teaching of science and mathematics, and he introduced the first programme in moral science (philosophy). For
details of his scientific and philosophical life, see Isaac Todhunter, *William Whewell,
D.D.*, 2 vols. (London, 1876). His academic and personal life is discussed in Mrs. Stair
Douglas, *The Life of William Whewell* (London, 1881).
5 Whewell, *On the Philosophy of Discovery*, chs. XXII, XV, XVI, XXI.
6 William Whewell, *Thoughts on the Study of Mathematics as a Part of a Liberal Education* (Cambridge, 1835). William Hamilton, review of Whewell's *Thoughts on the
Study of Mathematics, Edinburgh Review*, no. 126 (Jan. 1836), 409–55; Whewell, reply
to Hamilton, *ibid.*, no. 127 (April 1836), 270–72; Hamilton, reply to Whewell, *ibid.*,
272–75.
7 Whewell, *On the Philosophy of Discovery*, ch. XVIII. All numbers in parentheses in the
text of the paper refer to pages in this ch. of *Philosophy of Discovery*.

countenances the doctrine that the planetary motions are governed by mechanical forces, as terrestrial motions are; the third rule appears intended to justify the assertion of gravitation, as a *universal* quality of bodies; and the fourth contains, along with a general declaration of the authority of induction, the author's usual protest against hypotheses, levelled at the Cartesian hypotheses especially. (185–86)

In addition, Whewell concedes that rules receive a kind of pragmatic justification by being so constructed as to authorize inferences actually made in scientific reasoning (191). But he also realizes that unless the domain of application of inference rules can be extended beyond the original cases, the rules lose both general applicability and meaningfulness. Thus his general charge against Newton's own formulation of his rules is that they appear loose, ambiguous, or inapplicable (as simple truisms are inapplicable), if applied to any general contexts of reasoning *not* having to do with the inference to universal gravitation. The task, then, is to elaborate the rules so that they will have that general application beyond the original cases of inference that Newton's great scientific authority claimed for them. Newton's rules are:

Rule I We are not to admit other causes of natural things than such as both are true, and suffice for explaining their phenomena.

Rule II Natural effects of the same kind are to be referred to the same causes, as far as can be done.

Rule III The qualities of bodies which cannot be increased or diminished in intensity, and which belong to all bodies in which we can institute experiments, are to be held for qualities of all bodies whatever.

Rule IV In experimental philosophy, propositions collected from phenomena by induction, are to be held as true either accurately or approximately, notwithstanding contrary hypotheses; till other phenomena occur by which they may be rendered either more accurate or liable to exception.

In his discussion of Newton's first rule, Whewell proposes four interpretations, the first three of which are quickly eliminated in favour of the fourth. For ease in reference, I set down the interpretations here in order:

(1) "... in attempting to account for any class of phenomena, we must assume such causes only, as *from other considerations*, we know to exist" (186).

(2) In any given case, a true cause is that with which all men are *familiar*;

thus, "... the causes by which science explains the facts which she notes and measures and analyses, shall be causes which men, without any special study, have already come to believe in, from the effects which they casually see around them ..." (187–88).

(3) In attempting to account for any class of phenomena, we must assume "... only causes *of such kinds* as we have already satisfied ourselves do exist in nature" (188).

(4) "... we may, provisorily, assume such hypothetical cause as will account for any given class of natural phenomena; but ... when two different classes of facts lead us to the same hypothesis, we may hold it to be a *true cause*" (192).

Whewell disposes of interpretations (1) and (2) in short order. Both depend upon appeal to causes with which we are already familiar; and if each is taken strictly, it forbids us to look for new causes. Thus Whewell says of interpretation (1) that it is "... an injurious limitation on the field of in-duction ... if we follow this rule, how shall we ever become acquainted with any new cause?" (186) The rule as interpreted in (1), therefore, is too narrow and promises an early cessation of progress in scientific inquiry.

Appeal to familiar causes in sense (2) restricts the application of the rule just as much as under interpretation (1). In addition, the second interpre-tation has the enormous disadvantage of making adequate explanation in science depend in essential ways upon what the common understanding of untrained men takes to be causally efficacious. Science may be, as some contend, an extension of common sense; but clearly science cannot be held epistemologically to depend upon the pronouncements of common sense for the establishment of the adequacy of its conclusions. Whewell offers the example of Aepinus' hypothesis of repulsion of electrical particles to account for various electrical phenomena as a substitute for the vulgar belief in the "true cause" thought to be electrical atmospheres. The former, unlike the latter, advanced the science of electricity.

Since he was discussing a rule that licensed Newton's own inference to universal gravitation, Whewell might have chosen a more apt example, namely the Aristotelian and mediaeval account of gravity in terms of weight and natural place, an account in some ways much closer to understanding via familiar causes than Newton's inverse-square law. One could refer to the mediaeval prejudice in favour of two kinds of motions, the celestial and the terrestrial, differing in part according to the weight of the objects involved, celestial bodies being lighter (like balloons?). The grip of the example comes precisely at the point where one realizes that Newton's inference to universal gravitation, though it appeals to the same causal forces as operating in both celestial and terrestrial regions (and thus presumably establishes mechanical forms of explanation as the preferred ones), is simply not an inference based upon familiar causes in the Aristotelian-mediaeval sense. It may be, of course, that Galilean forms of explanation of terrestrial motion in mechanical terms provide a "familiar" set of terms of reference to apply to explanation of the motions of celestial bodies, but it should be realized that even these Galilean explanations entail observable consequences that are commonsensically counter-intuitive and thus require experimental "fabrication" of circumstances in which the relevant observations may be made, *independently of what is seen to occur* as interpreted in the common idiom.

For example, pennies and feathers do not fall side-by-side in "familiar" circumstances; they do so fall in an evacuated vacuum tube. But just consider how exaggeratedly counter-intuitive is a vacuum tube! And at least at some periods in the history of science (the seventeenth century being one such) there appeared to be a choice between certifying scientific inferences by reference to what is familiar experience and what is experience manufactured in laboratories. At the very least, then, if one is to interpret Newton's first rule in sense (2), one must regard the meaning of "familiar" as being very different from what is intended when "familiar" is used in ordinary contexts free of scientific bias of any sort.[8]

Nevertheless, and uncharacteristically, Whewell does miss an important point in his discussion of interpretations (1) and (2). It is surely possible to distinguish two different senses in which Newton's first rule (and the same is true of the other three) may be regarded as a *rule*. Throughout his criticisms of Newton's rules, Whewell labours the point that, taken together, they license the inductive inference to universal gravitation. He then questions the universality of these rules as *inference* rules; the question is: given that a certain induction has been made and validated under these rules, will they underwrite the truth of other inductive conclusions? But the rules can be regarded in another way. They can be taken as maxims of *discovery*. (In future I shall make easy reference to inference rules as I-rules, and to discovery rules as D-rules.) In this second sense, the D-rules would tell us what

8 Unfortunately, Whewell unfairly prejudices the case by construing "familiar" as "what is familiar to everyone prior to receipt of any scientific training." The Master of Trinity College bristled at the suggestion that science took its start in, and accommodated itself to, ordinary experience. But clearly this view of science can by no stretch of philosophical polemic be applied to Newton.

general features of things and theories to look for as aids in discovering new truths. Nowadays the so-called "logic" of discovery is a taboo subject (despite the massive efforts of the late N. R. Hanson to exhibit something useful about the "logical" structure of analogy as it works in cases of sceintific discovery). However, Whewell wanted to exempt his own theory of induction from ordinary logic, and in his exchange with De Morgan on the topic suggested that he might have called his induction "Discoverer's induction." So one might have expected him to be charitable in his reading of Newton's rules, and to have realized that if Rule I is understood as a D-rule, something can be said for it, even under interpretations (1) and (2).[9]

Clearly Rule I will not work as an I-rule under interpretations (1) and (2); the appeal to familiarity is not logically constraining. But as a D-rule, Rule I can be regarded as urging us to look for forms of explanation and theoretical entities of a kind that have been shown to be successful in former cases of discovery. If a certain kind of geometrical conceptualization works well in describing celestial phenomena, why not at least try it in attempting to describe motions of terrestrial bodies? Again, Galileo seems to have had a genuine choice between continuing the dissemination of the "familiar" Aristotelian celestial-terrestrial distinction, and appealing to the not-so-familiar, but apparently successful, Keplerian mathematization of motions of heavenly bodies. Of course D-rules, like I-rules but in other respects, are reactionary. Continued application along certain lines tends to stultify progress. But the concept of a D-rule does help to focus attention on the genuine problem. It is not a question of choosing between this-or-that familiar aspect of theory or known fact, but of choosing between whole conceptual frameworks containing substantive factual claims and various categories of law forms. In this sense there are no helpful D-rules, and in this sense it is fruitless to talk about the "logic" of discovery. To set out to discover is not to

9 The exchange between Whewell and De Morgan on the so-called logic of induction is fascinating for what it brings out about Whewell's own confusions. He invented a heuristic device which he called an "inductive table," the point of which was to display formally the validity of inductive inferences. At the same time, however, he insisted that induction involved non-logical components. De Morgan bemoaned Whewell's confused and stretched use of the term "logic" in this context, insisting that discovery and inference are two different things. In a letter Whewell replied, "... I do not wonder at your denying these devices [the inductive tables] a place in Logic; and you will think me heretical and profane, if I say, *so much the worse for Logic*" (Isaac Todhunter, above, n. 4, II, 417). I discuss these features of Whewell's theory of induction at length in the Introduction (IV. Whewell's Theory of Induction) to Robert E. Butts, ed., *William Whewell's Theory of Scientific Method* (University of Pittsburgh Press, 1968).

adopt this or that set of D-rules; it is to be ready to construe theories and facts in certain forms taken to be philosophically defensible, if not at present philosophically defended.

Thus we might suggest that lurking just under the surface of Newton's Rule I (interpreted in forms (1) and (2)) is a whole set of commitments to ways of doing science (including ways of recognizing allowable theoretical entities). To spell out the details of the members of the set would require an exploration of Newton's entire philosophy of science, a task outside our present interest. Suffice it to say that Rule I regarded as a D-rule brings out this fascinating hypothesis concerning the deeper philosophical motives of Rule I; reading it as an I-rule pure and simple results in the methodological platitude that familiarity has no logical status in canons of validity.

Similar comments seem dictated in discussing Whewell's third interpretation of Rule I, namely, we are to introduce into our explanations only causes of *such kinds* as have already proved successful in accounting for other phenomena. Here again Whewell has an easy time dismissing Rule I under interpretation (3) as an I-rule. For the effect of applying it as an I-rule would be nugatory; it prohibits the introduction of no hypotheses at all, unless other restrictions as to allowable hypotheses are introduced. Here, Whewell was within an ace of recognizing the distinction between I and D rules. For he points out that (regarded as an I-rule) Rule I would allow us to introduce the Cartesian hypothesis of the vortices (or at least would not prohibit us from introducing it), whereas Newton surely wanted the rule to condemn this and other speculative hypotheses (189). Had he suggested that we regard the rule as a D-rule, Whewell would have seen that Descartes' permitted theoretical entities are ruled out by it, but only in the much more interesting sense that Newton's whole philosophical framework argues against the substance and form of Cartesian explanation. Why is Cartesian explanation not an allowable *kind* of explanation? Surely no rule can decide *that* question; it is a question that only metaphysical argument or the search for a scientific meaning criterion can hope to answer. Newton's Rule I not only applauds a certain way of doing science, it also speaks against a certain cluster of metaphysical propositions.[10]

---

10 This point seems heavily confirmed by passages in Cotes' Preface to the second edition of the *Principia* in which he actually cites details of Newton's metaphysics and the opposing metaphysics of the Cartesians. The following two passages will have to suffice as evidence:

"[Newtonians want] ... to follow causes proved by phenomena, rather than causes

Whewell's quest for an interpretation that will turn Rule I into a valid inference rule ends with interpretation (4). To get this interpretation, Whewell suggests that we discount what others might take to be true causes, and concentrate attention on causes that "... are justly and rigorously inferred" (189). Thus gravity is a true cause because the downward pressures and downward motions of bodies near the surface of the earth "... lead us, by the plainest and strictest induction, to the assertion of such a force" (190). However, Whewell points out, this will mean that terrestrial gravitation is inferred in the same manner as is celestial gravitation, and the cause is not more entitled to be called "true" because it is inferred from celestial data than from terrestrial ones. "We thus obtain an intelligible and tenable explanation of a *vera causa*; but then, by this explanation, its *verity* ceases to be distinguishable from its other condition, that it 'suffices for the explanation of the phenomena'" (190). We assume (hypothetically) the existence of universal gravitation. On the assumption we are able to explain the fall of a stone, the motions of heavenly bodies, the apparent idiosyncrasies of the tides. The explanations, of course, are only counted as adequate if the predictions of the theory are confirmed in experimental and observational contexts. If such confirmation is forthcoming, then the supposed causes (explanatory principles) exist, have ontological status.

Whewell's suggestion is ingenious, and, in the nineteenth century, must have counted as a staggering new insight. There appear to be two ways in which we can certify the existence of a presumed scientific entity (cause). Either we have an independent encounter with it (making it "familiar" via experience, revelation, metaphysical intuition, or some other source); or we accept its ontological status because the theoretical system that hypothesizes its existence turns out, on experiment and observation, to be confirmed by the data. Whewell's suggestion, then, appears to amount to saying that we should absorb ontological questions about true (actually existing) causes

only imagined, and not yet proved. The business of true philosophy is to derive the natures of things from causes truly existent. ..."

"Therefore if it be made clear that the attraction of all bodies is a property actually existing *in rerum natura*, and if it be also shewn how the motions of the celestial bodies may be solved by that property, it would be very impertinent for any one to object that these motions ought to be accounted for by vortices. ... Those rather have recourse to occult causes who set imaginary vortices, of a matter entirely fictitious, and imperceptible to our senses, to direct these motions."

Roger Cotes, Preface to the second ed. of the *Principia*, in Sir Isaac Newton, *The Mathematical Principles of Natural Philosophy*, trans. Andrew Motte and William Davis, 3 vols. (London, 1819), I, xxiv, xxiii.

into systematic questions about the adequacy of explanations given in the context of well-formulated hypothetico-deductive theories. To be a true (existent) cause is then equivalent to being a theoretical entity ingredient (via observation predicates) in a theory that is highly confirmed, and hence explains, the phenomena it was introduced to explain. We abandon the search for true causes (and surely Whewell has at least cast doubt upon the status of this enterprise), and begin to talk about the adequacy of explanations, or the success of theories.

Having moved from ontological talk about entities ("causes") to systematic talk about explanations, Whewell was willing, largely on the basis of his own elaborate theory of scientific method, to go the whole way and to regard Rule I (under interpretation (4)) as an I-rule permitting a distinction between the adequacy of competing systems. In so doing, he injected one of the most distinctive features of his own methodology into his reading of interpretation (4).[11] Whewell was aware of the notorious circularity evident in introducing a single hypothesis to explain a given body of data. If the theory is formulated with care (preferably in deductive form), the data that confirm the hypothesis are precisely those it was introduced to explain. This logical symmetry between explanation and confirmation has often been noted. The problem is that systems thus constructed tend to be self-satisfying with respect to truth, precisely since the allowable decisive observations are just those logically generated by the hypothesis itself.[12] Whewell, and other

---

11 Ralph M. Blake, "Isaac Newton and the Hypothetico-Deductive Method," in *Theories of Scientific Method: The Renaissance through the Nineteenth Century*, ed. Edward H. Madden (Seattle, 1960), p. 134, writes: "It may well be doubted ... whether ... [Whewell's] interpretation does not exhibit more ingenuity in telling us what Newton *should* have meant by his statements, than success in informing us what he actually *did* have in mind when he wrote them." Blake's comment is fair, but it should be kept in mind that Whewell is not writing as a historian of philosophy of science, he is writing as a philosopher deliberately endeavouring to extract illumination from Newton's rules. This philosopher's use of historical materials frequently infuriates historians; but it is a defensible kind of philosophizing, and one at which Whewell was a master. Indeed, as I am endeavouring to show in this paper, Whewell's philosophical analysis of the rules *does* bring out the background of Newton's understanding of them. Thus philosophy and history *can* converge on a single point, and my account may be taken as a sample of just this phenomenon. Beyond this, it would take an extended essay in historiography to generalize from the sample.

12 In a number of works, Paul K. Feyerabend has exposed this feature of scientific systems, and has endeavoured to provide a philosophical solution of the problem of deciding between competing scientific systems. Whewell, it seems to me, anticipates a number of Feyerabend's problems, and suggests some roughly similar lines of solution. In other respects, however, Whewell's theory is a good example of the scientific conservatism that Feyerabend is combating. See Paul K. Feyerabend, "Problems of Empiricism," in Robert G. Colodny, ed., *Beyond the Edge of Certainty* (Englewood

methodologists, have sought to save deductively formulated systems from this circularity by requiring that a given hypothesis explain *more than* it was introduced to explain (forgetting, all the while, that any data, even novel ones, explained by the hypothesis will have to be deductive consequences of it, thus yielding the very same problem over and over again). In any case, Whewell now proposes to bolster interpretation (4) by linking it with his own concept of "consilience of inductions."

This concept of the consilience of inductions is central to Whewell's own theory of induction. He was fond of repeating in many of his works that no theory in the history of science that has passed the consilience test has later proven to be false. The claim may be a bit extravagant, but the concept is well worth looking at in some detail. Following a discussion of the kind of evidence that stands in favour of an hypothesis when its deductive consequences are all of the same kind, Whewell writes:

But the evidence in favour of our induction is of a much higher and more forcible character when it enables us to explain and determine cases of a *kind different* from those which were contemplated in the formation of the hypothesis. The instances in which this has occurred, indeed, impress us with a conviction that the truth of our hypothesis is certain. No accident could give rise to such an extraordinary coincidence. No false supposition could, after being adjusted to one class of phenomena, exactly represent a different class, where the agreement was unforeseen and uncontemplated. That rules springing from remote and unconnected quarters should thus leap to the same point, can only arise from *that* being the point where truth resides. (*Novum Organon Renovatum*, pp. 87 88)

Thus, when one hypothesis explains many different types of data (without, of course, being supplemented *ad hoc* by the addition of other hypotheses), we have Whewell's consilience of inductions. Clearly, there are logical problems involved in taking Whewell's consilience concept as a test of the truth of an hypothesis. The confirmation-explanation circle is not broken out of by merely adding new sets of data that a given hypothesis will explain; the addition of many apparently successful explanation-confirmation chains will only compound the logical problem, although our *psychological* conviction in the truth of the hypothesis might thereby be greatly reinforced.

Whewell's system has an answer to this implicit charge of question-begging.

Cliffs, New Jersey, 1965), pp. 145–260. See also Robert E. Butts, "Feyerabend and the Pragmatic Theory of Observation," *Philosophy of Science*, XXXIII, 4 (Dec. 1966), 383–94.

For Whewell (and in this he has many supporters among contemporary philosophers of science) accepts the explanation-confirmation symmetry as generating no special logical problems, and then goes on to account for the structure of inductive logic differently. Briefly, the test of inductive truth, if there is any at all, is bound up with considerations of the *simplicity* of a complete scientific theory. Those systems whose basic concepts are, broadly speaking, the most inclusive (and hence the most simple in the sense of being able to generate many predictions), are those most likely to be true. It is plain what role consilience of inductions would have in such a scheme. The more a system tends toward consilience of its many explanation-confirmation chains, the more it tends to have increasingly powerful predicates. The rest of the story can only be told by examining Whewell's theory of induction in greater detail, a task beyond the limits of the present paper.[13]

We need only see how Whewell applies the consilience concept to his fourth interpretation of Rule I. Two quotations should make the point clear.

When the explanation of two kinds of phenomena, distinct, and not apparently connected, leads to the same cause, such a coincidence does give a reality to the cause, which it has not while it merely accounts for those appearances which suggested the supposition. (190)
When such a convergence of two trains of induction points to the same spot, we can no longer suspect that we are wrong. Such an accumulation of proof really persuades us that we have to do with a *vera causa*. (191)

The concept of consilience, as these quotations show, supplies the nerve of the argument that the ontology of causes is to be construed from now on in terms having to do with the success of explanatory systems. Under interpretation (4), Newton's Rule I conveys methodological plausibility to those hypotheses which, like the hypothesis of universal gravitation, are ingredient in systems with high indices of simplicity. Notice, however, that Rule I is now an I-rule in a much modified sense. Rule I does not license particular inductive inferences. It does two other things. First, it implicitly defines "true cause" in terms of successful explanatory systems. Second, it recommends appeal to simplicity as the decisive appeal when choosing between two or more hypotheses. Whewell did regard Newton's system as simpler than its competitors, and thought that he could give an account of the inductive strength (in Whewell's sense of this term) of the Newtonian system that would make Rule I, under interpretation (4), stand as a legitimate I-rule.

13 See the Introduction to my *William Whewell's Theory of Scientific Method* cited in n. 9 above.

Whewell's remarks on Newton's second rule (effects of the same kind are to be assigned to the same causes, in so far as is possible) are brief. He points out first that all scientific systems attempt to conform to this rule. Furthermore, the rule itself introduces a problem that it does not give us the materials for solving, namely, the question: when are events (or effects) of the *same* kind? The problem, thought Whewell, is the one of determining a scientifically respectable criterion of resemblance or sameness. It is not the question of sameness of meaning, nor of perceptual recognition of visual resemblances. Rather, Whewell seems to want to absorb the question into one about ascertaining whether or not an hypothesis introduces entities that fit a certain physical *model*. This seems implicit in the following statement: "Are the motions of the planets of the same kind with the motion of a body moving freely in a curvilinear path, or do they not rather resemble the motion of a floating body swept round by a whirling current? The Newtonian and the Cartesian answered this question differently. How then can we apply this Rule with any advantage?" (193) Whewell's reply to the question is that we cannot apply the rule without in fact doing the science required to settle the issue as between the two competing hypotheses. This involves, among other things, trying to obtain a clear idea of what the hypotheses entail, and then reasoning rigorously to these consequences. "Thus it does not appear that this Rule of Newton can be interpreted in any distinct and positive manner, otherwise than as enjoining that, in the task of induction, we employ clear ideas, rigorous reasoning, and close and fair comparison of the results of the hypothesis with the facts" (194).

Whewell makes no effort to reformulate Rule II as a valid I-rule. Instead, he simply concludes that the rule gives us no inference criteria at all; the rule turns out, instead, to be merely a prudential maxim admonishing us to do science with care and rigour. Here again, Whewell might have gotten a more charitable reading of Rule II had he thought of it as a D-rule. In D-rule form, it would be taken as saying something like "in framing hypotheses, link them to those models that already embody well-understood regularities; seek analogies between the form of the phenomena to be explained, and the form of phenomena for which we already have a law." Of course, such a D-rule might turn out to be as vacuous as Rule II regarded as a prudential maxim. How else, after all, *would* one proceed in framing hypotheses?

Newton's third rule (qualities of bodies observed without exception are to be taken as universal properties of all bodies) is rejected by Whewell on two counts, one logical and the other epistemological. The logical point is simply that we cannot *legislate* universality of physical properties. However it is that we determine that some property of bodies is universal (and Whewell has some fascinating things to say on this topic), we cannot decide the matter in individual cases by invoking a rule. To attempt to do so would be seriously to prejudice the future course of scientific inquiry, for we might foreclose a certain line of more basic inquiry, having legalized a certain property as universal. We might seek to turn aside the obvious force of Whewell's objection by adding a final clause to the rule, to wit, "until further notice." But the move would be unsuccessful. So to qualify the rule would be merely to reaffirm our limited confidence in induction; but the qualification would wipe out any intelligible sense of "universal." This suggestion leads to Whewell's second, much more damaging, criticism of Rule III.

The problem is just this: can induction or observation alone decide the universality of a given physical property? The question arises because in Newton's formulation of Rule III we are clearly invited to bestow legal universality upon properties of bodies observed in experimental contexts. And the question, however one decides it, is probably the most basic one in philosophy of science – what is the logical and epistemological status of natural laws? The Newtonian view, which Whewell rejects, is that universality of properties is seen to apply in some cases because of what we observe. It is central to Whewell's philosophy of science that we recognize that observation, even experimentally regularized observation, can confer on propositions about fact only a probable universality. No set of observations, however large, can conclusively establish sufficient universality of properties, so that no amount of observational evidence will ever yield *necessary* propositions. Whewell's complex theory of necessity need not be gone into here in great detail.[14] Perhaps it will be enough to point out that for Whewell the necessity of a proposition can only be seen as a function of the concepts or ideas involved in it. The test of necessity is intuition. A proposition is necessary if we cannot distinctly conceive its contrary. Thus, whereas appeal to experience might establish limited universality, it can never prove a proposition to be necessary. The proposition expressing universal gravi-

14 Whewell discusses the role of ideas and necessary truth in science in many of his works. The fullest discussions are in *The Philosophy of the Inductive Sciences*, 1st and 2nd eds., pt. 1, and in *The History of Scientific Ideas*. See Robert E. Butts, "Necessary Truth in Whewell's Theory of Science," *American Philosophical Quarterly*, II, 3 (July 1965), 1–21; Robert E. Butts, "On Walsh's Reading of Whewell's View of Necessity," *Philosophy of Science*, XXXII, 2 (April 1965), 175–81; and Harold T. Walsh, "Whewell on Necessity," *Philosophy of Science*, XXIX, 2 (April 1962), 139–45.

tation cannot be taken as universal in the strong sense (necessary) on the strength of any observations, however numerous.

Whewell believed that scientific inquiry did yield necessary truths, and that part of the process involved induction (but not simple induction by enumeration). But the inductive observations do not prove necessity (only certain relations between ideas can do this), and hence Newton's Rule III in inductive form will not suffice. So Whewell concludes: "... The reason given for the Third Rule of Newton involves a mistake respecting the nature and authority of experience. And the Rule itself cannot be applied without attempting to decide, by the casual limits of observation, questions which necessarily depend upon the relations of ideas" (196). Whatever the limitations of Whewell's own view of necessity might be (and I think they are considerable), I think his criticism of Newtonianism on this point is fair and well taken. Unless we are to settle for a characterization of natural laws that analyses them as mere descriptions of what has occurred, we must turn to something other than experience to account for the strong universality of these laws. If, along with a number of contemporary philosophers of science, we conceive laws as having counter-factual import (telling us not only what did happen, but also what would have happened if), then we must look beyond the narrow evidence that we take as confirming the laws. We may look elsewhere than Whewell's test by intuition, but surely he is right in insisting that we look elsewhere. Rule III may be applicable as an inductive inference rule, but it is not powerful enough to guarantee lawfulness to any proposition.

Whewell also contends that Newtonians give too much authority to experience in their way of regarding the fourth rule ("Propositions collected from phenomena by induction, shall be held to be true, notwithstanding contrary hypotheses; but shall be liable to be rendered more accurate, or to have their exceptions pointed out, by additional study of phenomena"). This rule certainly expresses Newton's confidence in induction, and once again reinforces his objection to merely speculative hypotheses. Whewell applauds Newton's insistence that inductive generalizations be constantly reapplied to test their accuracy and to find their exceptions, if any. But, for Whewell, deciding questions of accuracy and exception is not a matter of consulting experience to see what it says. Whewell refuses to read Rule IV as intending that we hold inductive conclusions to be merely tentative, awaiting the results of future experience to either weaken or strengthen our confidence in them. On Whewell's view there is a point at which the confidence in an induction reaches certainty (presumably at that point at which it is impossible for us to see the data explained in any other way). Beyond that point, no complete falsification of the proposition is possible, though we may come to understand that there are exceptions and that greater accuracy can be achieved in the statement and application of the law. So again, it is not experience that proves exceptions and gives greater accuracy; it is our adjustment of the concepts involved in the law as we apply it in more and different situations.

The point at issue in Whewell's commentary on Rules III and IV is in effect the whole question of the nature and status of induction. Both Whewell and Newton had an unwavering confidence in the powers of induction, but each had a different view of induction. For Newton (at least as Whewell read him) induction is collection of laws from phenomena; for Whewell induction only inessentially involves collection of data, what it involves essentially is the imposition of a new idea on the data.[15] For Newton, on this reading, Rules III and IV could only obtain their credentials from experience; for Whewell, only appeal to ideas and ways of manipulating them could credit the rules. However, if Whewell is right in his way of reading Rule IV (as meaning that Newton was not suggesting that we hold inductive conclusions only tentatively), then the two theories of scientific method have a curious common point, and one that seems to give Whewell the edge in his assessment of Newton's rules.

15 One can probably make out a fair case for reading Newton Whewell's way. However, a consideration of just what Newton (and Newtonians) meant by "phenomena" shows that Whewell's view is greatly over-simplified. Indeed, Feyerabend has interpreted Newton's phenomena (and the phrase "derived from the phenomena") in a way that makes the Newtonian view almost compatible with Whewell's own theory of induction. He writes:

Newton's "phenomena," which are the elements of the new "experience," are not everyday facts pure and simple; nor are they an experience that has been cleared from prejudicial elements and left that way. They are rather an intimate *synthesis of laws*, possessing instances in the domain of the senses and certain mathematical ideas. ... Actual experiment, which always depends on a large variety of irrelevant variables, may therefore *illustrate* the phenomenon; it cannot *establish* it. ... Describing a phenomenon means stating a law. It is therefore not at all surprising that one can now obtain laws by a derivation "from the phenomena." Nor is it surprising that many of the laws obtained are regarded as irrevocable. After all, they are based upon premises that are part of "experience" and that are therefore beyond reproach. (P. K. Feyerabend, above, n. 12, pp. 159–60)

On this reading of Newton – which has much merit – Newton's concept of phenomenon combines the two elements that Whewell insisted upon, ideas and sensations. The interpretation also implies that Newton's system was committed to the explanation-confirmation symmetry that Whewell thought so important. See also Feyerabend's paper in the present volume.

I have in mind the following crucial point. If Newton (and Whewell's reading of Rule IV gives credence to the view) thought as Whewell did, that inductive conclusions can at some point be taken once and for all to be true, then future experience alone could not render the conclusion more accurate and show its exceptions, if any. There is a fundamental epistemological difference between holding a proposition describing experience to be true, but liable to more accurate formulation and to exceptions, and holding such a proposition tentatively to be true, but liable to falsification on the basis of future observations. If future experiences foster the latter kind of liability, then experience has the authority to overthrow inductive beliefs, in which case Rules III and IV become not only inapplicable, but meaningless prejudices. On the other hand, if Whewell is right in reading his own methodological conservatism into Newton's Rules III and IV, he would seem quite justified in suggesting that a more elaborate analysis of the conceptual trappings of induction and law is epistemologically demanded. *Falsification* of a law must surely come from observation of the falsifying experience; *refinement* of a law (either in the direction of greater accuracy or of increasing its systematic power to handle exceptions) already presupposes that the law is true; so systematic conceptual decisions take over the job, not experience.[16]

After all this, what positive gain has been derived from Whewell's discussion of Newton's rules? Add up the results: Rule I must be radically reinterpreted so that talk about true causes is replaced by talk about general features of acceptable explanatory theories. Rule II must be dropped altogether as vacuous. Rules III and IV presuppose an inadequate theory of induction and an equally inadequate epistemological appeal to experience. There are several important consequences of these results. First, as we suspected all along, the four rules will not serve as D-rules designed to aid future scientific inquiry. Second, the rules – except for the reformulated Rule I – are not valid as I-rules. They will not serve to underwrite the validity of inductive inferences. Even Rule I under interpretation (4) will not do this, for under this interpretation it ceases to be an I-rule giving credentials to

16 For an illuminating discussion of the difference between regarding a law (or a system of laws) as subject to further refinement, but not to further confirmation (or possible disconfirmation), see Thomas S. Kuhn, *The Structure of Scientific Revolutions* (Chicago, London, 1965), 4th impression, chs. II–V. His concepts of "normal science" and "scientific paradigm" seem to me partially to capture what Whewell had in mind. In his paper in this volume (secs. 11, 12, nn. 9, 16, 33) Feyerabend interprets Rule IV in the same way as does Whewell. Of course Whewell, unlike Feyerabend, agrees with the main features of the hypothetico-deductive method.

particular inductive inferences, and introduces instead a general criterion for assessing whole theories. There is an important corollary to this second point. If the rules are not generally valid as ɪ-rules, then they are not valid either as the rules guaranteeing the correctness of Newton's inference to universal gravitation. It would seem conceptually muddled to hold that a rule is satisfactory as a rule if all that it can do is license one case. Just as we expect a valid deductive rule to license all inferences of a certain form, so we would expect an inductive ɪ-rule to license all inductive inferences of a certain form. Whewell has certainly shown that the rules cannot carry this heavy burden.

In some ways, the most important consequence of Whewell's analysis of the rules is the following. In the significant cases (discussion of Rules ɪ, ɪɪɪ, and ɪv) Whewell shows with great insight and clarity that what is at issue is not the satisfactoriness of a rule, but a whole set of connected philosophical commitments. On Whewell's reading of Newton, the great physicist was committed – and his rules are expressions of these commitments – to at least the following set of philosophical propositions: (1) There is a difference between a cause *quâ* entity, and a scientific system giving causal explanations. Hence we ought to be able to give the metaphysics of causes (after all, they are at base all particles) independently of the logic of scientific systems. (2) The evidence for the empirical universality (counter-factual import) of generalizations over matters of fact is observation (experience). (3) One allowable form of induction is "collection" (simple enumeration?). (4) It is experience that dictates refinements in laws already taken to be conclusively established by induction. And so on. It is plain that Whewell regards the rules as revealing these more far-reaching philosophical opinions of Newton. The consequence is that he views Newton as having been a fairly narrow empiricist and inductivist who emphasized the metaphysics of observables, and induction as mere conceptual reproduction of what has been seen; and played down all conceptual or theoretical aspects of science, for example, hypothesizing, theory construction and assessment, the role of concepts in the formalism of a system. Whewell, of course, is probably the most determined opponent of this kind of philosophy of science in the history of the subject. Whewell's Newton is doubtless an over-simplification; generations of Newton scholars have sought to show that Newton was no narrow inductivist like Mill. But then he did not set out to capture the "real" Newton; he set out to learn something by analysis of the rules. And what he learned is that a philosophical controversy rages in the background of the rules, and that he had to take sides in the controversy. What he gives *us* is a fascinating capsule view of the clash between two important general philosophies of science.

VIII
Classical Empiricism*

PAUL K. FEYERABEND

I

In the present paper I want to describe certain features of post-Galilean, or "classical," science that deserve greater attention than has been given them so far. These features are summarized in the following three points:

i. The *practice* of post-Galilean science is *critical* in the sense that it allows for the revision of any part of it, however fundamental and however close to "experience." Resistance must of course occasionally be overcome, but the resistance is never strong enough to *stabilize completely* some particular piece of knowledge.

ii. This critical practice is accompanied by a *dogmatic ideology*. The ideology admits that science may contain hypothetical parts. But it is emphasized that such parts are preliminary, that they will either disappear as the result of further research, or will turn into trustworthy theories. Moreover, it is assumed that all theories rest on one and the same stable foundation, *experience*. It is experience which supports, and gives content to our ideas without itself being in need of support and interpretation.

iii. Thus on the one hand we have the assumption of a stable foundation, while on the other hand we are engaged in an activity that prevents such a foundation from ever coming into existence. Now the peculiarity of post-Galilean "classical" science I want to describe consists in the manner in which this abyss between ideology and practice is bridged: first, experience is identified as that part of a newly conceived hypothesis that can most readily be illustrated by simple and eye-catching procedures. Secondly, the experience so defined is made solid by the success of the hypothesis it illustrates (which success may have been brought about with the help of *ad hoc* assumptions) as well as by the vividness of the illustrating examples. Thirdly, it is given the appearance of *stability* through a method of interpretation that aims at, and succeeds in, concealing all change. The aim is reached by

* For support of research the author is indebted to the National Science Foundation.

concentrating on the illustrations themselves rather than on the role they play in a particular theory (the same picture, after all, can illustrate very different things). I use the term "classical empiricism" to describe this fascinating, tortuous, schizophrenic combination of a conservative ideology and a progressive practice. The most outstanding practitioner of classical empiricism is Newton.

II

Classical empiricism differs both from the empiricism of Aristotle and from that of Bacon.

The demand that we base knowledge upon experience makes excellent sense in the Aristotelian philosophy where experience is defined as the sum total of what is observed under normal circumstances (bright daylight; senses in good order; undisturbed and alert observer) and what is then described in some ordinary idiom that is understood by all.[1] Aristotelian empiricism, as a matter of fact, is the only empiricism that is both clear – one knows what kind of thing experience is supposed to be – and rational – one can give reasons why experience is stable and why it serves so well as a foundation of knowledge.

For example, one can say that experience is stable because human nature (under normal conditions) is stable. Even a slave perceives the world as his master does. Or one can say that experience is trustworthy because normal man (man without instruments to becloud his senses and special doctrines to becloud his mind) and the universe are adapted to each other; they are in harmony.

This rational context that enables us to understand the Aristotelian doctrine and that also provides a starting-point of discussion is eliminated by the Enlightenment of the sixteenth and seventeenth centuries.

III

It is characteristic of this enlightenment that it constantly mentions new and undiluted foundations of knowledge and of the faith while at the same time making it impossible ever to *identify* these foundations and to build on them. (This corresponds to items ii and i of sec. I.)

1 G. E. L. Owen, "ΤΙΘΕΝΑΙ ΤΑ ΦΑΙΝΟΜΕΝΑ," *Aristotle et les problèmes de la méthode* (Louvain, 1961), pp. 83–103. Reprinted in *Aristotle*, ed. Moravcsik (New York, 1967), pp. 167–90. See also Aristotle, *De Anima, De Sensu, Anal. Post.*, and parts of *De Part. Anim.*

Thus Luther and Calvin (1) declare Holy Scripture to be the foundation of all religion. This is the new Protestant Rule of Faith from which everything else is supposed to proceed. But we are also urged (2) to put aside, and never to use, what cannot be justified by this rule. Now this second step clearly voids the first, or, to express it differently, the Protestant rule of faith as expressed in (1) and restricted in (2) is *logically vacuous*. The argument, briefly, is as follows.[2]

2 (a) For the Protestant rule of faith see Martin Luther, *The Babylonian Captivity of the Church*, in Henry Bettenson, ed., *Documents of the Christian Church* (Oxford, 1947), p. 280: "For what is asserted without the authority of Scripture and of proven revelation may be held as an opinion, but there is no obligation to believe in it." For an interesting addition see the following report of Luther's encounter with Nicholas Storch (falsely called "Mark" in the report) as quoted in Preserved Smith, *Life and Letters of Martin Luther* (Boston, 1911), p. 150: "In 1522 Mark Storch came to me with sweet seductive words to lay his doctrines before me. As he presumed to teach things not in Scripture I said to him: 'I will not agree with that part of your doctrine unsupported by Scripture *unless you work miracles to prove it*! ... He said: 'You shall see miracles in seven years.' ..." (My italics)

Despite his insistence upon foundations and upon the purity of faith and despite his frequent violence in writing, Luther seems to have objected consistently to the use of force; he was also quite tolerant towards deviations for which a good reason could be given. "I have gathered from the writings of these people," he writes to Frederick of Saxony (letter of July 1524, quoted from Smith, p. 151) discussing the action of some contemporary revolutionaries, "that this same spirit will not be satisfied to make converts by word only, but intends to betake himself to arms and set himself with power against the government, and forthwith to raise riot. Here Satan lets the cat out of the bag. What will this spirit do when he has won the support of the mob? Truly here at Wittenberg I have heard from the same spirit that this business must be carried through with the sword. ... It is a bad spirit which shows no other fruit than burning churches, cloisters, and images, for the worst rascals on earth can do as much. ... It is [also] a bad spirit which dares not give an answer. ... For I, poor, miserable man, did not so act in my doctrine. ... I went to Leipzig to debate before a hostile audience. ... If they will do more than propagate their doctrines by word, if they attempt force, your Graces should say: we gladly allow any one to teach by the word, that the right doctrine may be preserved; but draw not the sword, which is ours ... they are not Christians who would go beyond the word and appeal to force, even if they boast that they are full of holy spirits." In his work *Against the Heavenly Prophets of Images and the Sacrament*, the first part of which appeared late in December 1524, he defends pictures "as a help to the faith of the ignorant" (Smith, p. 156). "These prophets," he continues, criticizing such radicals as Carlstedt, Muenzer, and Storch, "teach that the reform of Christendom should start with a slaughter of the godless, that they themselves may be lords of the earth ... [But] those who preach murder can have no other origin than the devil himself." "On August 22, 1524," writes Smith (p. 154) describing a meeting between Luther and Carlstedt, "the two had a conference in Jena and parted with a friendly agreement to differ. 'The more ably you attack me', said Luther, 'the better I shall like it' and gave his old colleague a gold gulden as a sign that he was free to advance what opinions he liked so long as they were supported by argument only and not by violence." Even after Carlstedt had preached sedition, and spread death and destruction, Luther would still give him shelter and write to the Elector in his defence. There were many admirable qualities in Luther and he was strong enough to withstand the consequences of his own

(a) The rule does not provide any means of *identifying* scripture (no version of scripture contains a passage to the effect that "the preceding ... and the following ... pages are Scripture"). We are told what the basis of the right faith ought to be; but we do not receive any indication of how we can find this basis among the many books and tales in existence.

(b) Given scripture we do not know how to *interpret* it (no version of scripture contains a grammar and a dictionary of the language in which it is written. Such a grammar and such a dictionary are of course available, and often unnecessary; for example, they are unnecessary when we understand the language of the bible. But then our traditional understanding of a particular language is added to scripture whereas the rule of faith, and especially the second principle enounced above, wants scripture to be the only authority. We see how much more reasonable, *and human*, the Roman position had been).

(c) Given scripture and a certain reading of it we have no means of *deriving consequences* (no version of scripture contains a logic or a more general system for the production of statements on the basis of other statements). Even if we recognize the basis of our faith, and even if we know how to interpret it, still we have no means of going beyond it, not in the simplest matter. For example, we cannot apply it to contemporary problems.

mischievous rule of faith. But irrational rules share with the institution of tyranny this one disadvantage: they may work wonders in the hands of men strong enough to go their own ways; but they create havoc in the hands of almost everyone else. This becomes clear at once when turning to Calvin.

Calvin showed much less tolerance (example: the execution of Servetus). He was much clearer, much more consistent, and therefore much more terrible in his unflinching pursuit of what he thought to be the proper faith. (This, by the way, is one of the reasons why I would prefer lukewarm defenders of inconsistent doctrines to serious exponents of clear, precise, and, above all consistent, views.) The reader interested in Calvin's formulation of the rule of faith should turn to ch. vii of the *Institutes of the Christian Faith* in J. T. McNeill, ed., *On the Christian Faith* (Indianapolis, 1958), pp. 19ff, as well as to R. H. Popkin, *The History of Skepticism from Erasmus to Descartes* (New York, 1964). Professor Popkin's book has been a great help to me, both in a course which I gave in summer 1966 at the University of California in Berkeley (and which led me away from the philosophy of science into church history) and in the preparation of the present paper.

Both Luther and Calvin are anticipated by (and consciously follow) St. Paul, who writes (Colossians ii): "Beware lest any man spoil you through philosophy and vain deceit derived from the *traditions* of men, conforming to the rudiments of the world, and not to Christ."

(b) The argument in the text below is due to the Jesuit father François Véron of La Flèche, where Descartes received his early education. It is summarized in Popkin, pp. 72ff, where the reader will also find an excellent description of Véron's method and of his impact. The argument anticipates and excels in clarity and conciseness all the subsequent criticisms of fundamental doctrines up to and including Wittgenstein.

IV

Now it is interesting to see that these objections, which were first put forth by a Jesuit Father (see n. 2 (b)) and which have never been superseded in clarity and conciseness, apply point for point to the Baconian philosophy, the second great fundamentalist doctrine of the seventeenth century.

The "rule of faith" of Baconian science is experience. Again this rule does not allow us (a) to *identify* experience (see the corresponding letters in the preceding section). Just as it was taken for granted by the defenders of the new faith that scripture was known to everyone, in the very same manner the identity of experience is now assumed to be known without the shadow of a doubt. This was permissible as long as one defined experience in the Aristotelian manner, comprising all those things and processes which are noticed under normal circumstances, with one's senses in good order, and which are then described in some ordinary idiom; that is, as long as one could make use of some *tradition* (cf. above, sec. II). However, just such a use of tradition (or of preconceived opinion as tradition was soon called) is to be avoided. This is the essence of the Baconian creed. But with it the only means of identifying experience in a rational manner disappears also. The first objection of the previous section applies.

Nor are we able (b) to determine what experience tells us. Experience, taken by itself, is mute. It does not provide any means of establishing a connection with a language unless one already includes in it some elementary linguistic rules, that is unless one again refers to tradition. Wittgenstein has seen this point and has expressed it more or less clearly. He has seen that whenever we observe and report observations we make use of traditional elements ("forms of life"). However, he has failed to indicate how traditions can be improved and has even created the impression that such improvement is impossible.[3]

Finally (c), there is no way of obtaining the complex theories which were soon used to support the empiricist creed (and which in turn received support from it) even if one makes the additional assumptions that experimental statements are singular statements and that means of deduction are readily available. This point was made most forcefully by Berkeley (*Principles of Human Knowledge*, sec. 107), and by Hume.

3 For this point compare sec. xv of my "Problems of Empiricism," in Robert G. Colodny, ed., *Beyond the Edge of Certainty* (Englewood Cliffs, New Jersey, 1965).

It is rather interesting to examine the similarities between the theories of Protestantism and of Baconian empiricism. These similarities are expressed not only in the structure of the respective doctrines, but even in the phrases which are used to direct attention to the respective bases (scripture, experience): reverence is demanded of both of them, success and a clear view of an all-embracing entity (God; nature) are promised in both cases, and in almost the same exalted terms.[4] A detailed description of such phenomena is a challenging task for the historian of ideas.

Now what interests us in the present paper is not only the (Protestant; Baconian) ideology, but also the way in which this ideology is applied in practice. It is the practical application of the (Protestant and Empiricist) rule of faith that will return us to item iii sec. I and serve as an introduction into Newton's philosophy. In a nutshell this practical application can be described by saying that the rule of faith *although logically vacuous, is by no means psychologically vacuous*. We first illustrate this feature in the case of Protestantism, especially of the Calvinist variety.

V

To do this we must remind ourselves that the rule is not introduced in a vacuum. It is introduced, and taught, in a community (such as the community of Calvinists in Geneva in the sixteenth century) which is already committed to a certain doctrine. Children are educated by Calvinist parents in Calvinist schools where religious instruction plays a fundamental role and pervades all subjects; they are encouraged when they say the "right things," punished when they "do wrong." From their most tender years they are part of a life all aspects of which are guided by religious considerations. The language they learn is permeated with religious sentiment and is structured accordingly. Bible passages ring in their ears, for they are read and pronounced on every and any occasion. Their knowledge of the bible is constantly tested by examinations at school and in conversations with others; and mistakes, that is deviations from the accepted point of view, from the "party line," are corrected at once. Having been prepared in this

---

4 "We have now treated of each kind of idols, and their qualities, all of which must be abjured and renounced with firm and solemn resolution, and the understanding must be completely freed and cleared of them, so that the access to the kingdom of man, which is founded on the sciences, may resemble that to the kingdom of heaven, where no admission is conceded except to children" (Francis Bacon, *Novum Organum*, Aphorism lxviii).

fashion they will of course interpret scripture, that is the books used in the community, as everyone else does, and they will not at all be aware of the logical gap that separates this common faith from the "word of God" as defined by the rule. The believers will simply perceive in the lines of scripture the very same God they have been taught to revere. Now the rule of faith, which in Calvin's version refers to an "intuitive perception of God himself" (cf. n. 2 (a)) is wide and indefinite enough to allow this act of recognition to become a foundation of the faith. On the other hand, the indoctrination is specific enough to identify this act as the sole foundation of the faith. Thus the *psychological* result of indoctrination becomes the *theological* basis of the doctrine taught[5] and further strengthens belief in it (cf. iii/3 of sec. i).

5 This is a very familiar procedure. It occurs, in various forms, at almost every stage of the history of the Church (of science, of law, and what have you). Thus the selection of the canon was determined by the doctrines held at the time. Alfred Wikenhaeuser, in his *Einleitung in das Neue Testament* (Herder, 1961), p. 57, describes the situation by saying that "the text of the New Testament has been preserved not critically, but dogmatically," which means, when put into plain English, that the historically available material was changed to fit an already existing faith which thus creates its own sources. The influence of the popular faith may also be seen from the fact that St. Jerome, when translating the Vulgata, kept as closely as possible to the widely read Itala as "numerous and far-going changes in the generally known wording would have only created resentment" (*Letter to Damasus* as paraphrased in Wikenhaeuser, p. 75). "The criticism which Luther applied to the received canon is (still) bolder and much more radical. It is not a historical criticism, but is dogmatically, or religiously, oriented. Luther made his interpretation of Paulus the measure by which everything allegedly divine or holy would have to be tested. The 'true and certain main books' of the New Testament are, according to him, Romans and Galatians and of the gospels the Gospel according to John: next come the other gospels, the synoptics, because they contain so few genuine words of Jesus; in addition he mentions a third group which he reprimands severely 'as it does not advance Christianity'" (Wikenhaeuser, p. 44).
    The early history of the canon is described in great detail by Adolf von Harnack in his *History of Dogma*, trans. N. Buchanan (New York, 1961), ii, 43ff. I quote a few excerpts. "The canon emerges quite suddenly in an allusion of Melito of Sardis preserved by Eusebius ... in the works of Irenaeus and Tertullian; and in the socalled Muratorian fragment. There is no direct account of its origin, and scarcely any indirect; yet it already appears as something to all intents and purposes finished and complete. Moreover it emerges in the same ecclesiastical district where we first were able to show the existence of the apostolic *regula fidei*." The principle of selection used by the Church "was to reject as spurious all writings, bearing the names of the Apostles, that contained anything contrary to Christian common sense, that is, to the rule of faith – hence admission was refused to all books in which the God of the old Testament, his creation, etc. appeared to be deprecated – and to exclude all recensions of apostolic writings that seemed to endanger the Old Testament and the Monarchy of God." Again already existing views are made the measure of the alleged basis.
    The origin of the rule of faith itself is even more interesting. From the very beginning, but especially after the rise of Gnosticism, the Church tried to bring about a synthesis of the elements of Christianity (scripture, sacraments, organization, baptismal symbol) that would separate it from the flood of contemporary speculation and would preserve and emphasize its unique character. It was necessary, for this purpose, both to deny the

The circle is closed, the "chosen children of God" – as a follower of Calvin (Beza) calls the faithful – are separated from the "castaways," are made aware of their mission, and are encouraged in their faith.

main tenets of Gnosticism (and of later heresies); and to show that this denial was not *ad hoc*, but was implied by the very essence of the Christian faith. With this aim in mind, Gnosticism was declared to be obviously inconsistent with the content of the simple and quite untheoretical prayers in which the believers expressed their faith (for an example of such a prayer see Bettenson, pp. 90ff). There is no doubt that the spiritual content of the prayers was thereby drastically changed. Very soon the form began to change also; terms of speculative philosophy intruded so that the prayers which originally had expressed the faith of the faithful in a very immediate way finally became summaries of a steadily growing body of doctrine. As an example one should consider the creed of Nicaea (Bettenson, p. 36) and compare it with the simpler early formulations: "We believe in *one* God the Father All-Sovereign, Maker of all things *visible* [against the demiurge of the Gnostics] and invisible; and in one Lord Jesus Christ, the Son of God, *begotten of the Father* [against adoptianism], *only* begotten [against the Gnostic hierarchy], that is, of the *substance* of the Father [against Arianism], God of God, Light of Light, true God of true God, *begotten, not made.* ..." The whole process is described by Harnack, II, 26ff, in the following words: "What was needed [in order to refute the Gnostics who recognized the creed of the old Church 'since they already possessed the art of explaining a given text in whatever way they choose'] was an apostolic creed *definitely interpreted* [italics mine]; for it was only by the aid of a definite interpretation that the creed could be used to repel the Gnostic speculations and the Marcionite conception of Christianity."

"In this state of matters the Church of Rome, the proceedings of which are known to us through Irenaeus and Tertullian, took, with regard to the fixed Roman baptismal confession ascribed to the apostles, the following step: the anti-Gnostic interpretation required by the necessities of the times was proclaimed as its self-evident content; the confession, thus explained, was designated as the 'Catholic Faith' (*fides catholica*), that is the rule of truth for the faith; and its acceptance was made the test of adherence to the Roman Church as well as to the general confederation of Christendom. ... What the Roman community accomplished practically was theoretically established by Irenaeus and Tertullian. The former proclaimed the baptismal confession, definitely interpreted and expressed in an anti-gnostic form, to be the apostolic rule of truth (*regula veritatis*), and tried to prove it so. He based his demonstration on the theory that this series of doctrines embodied the faith of the churches founded by the Apostles, and that these communities had alway preserved the apostolic teaching unchanged." For Irenaeus see *Adversus Haereses* III/iii.1 as well as IV/xxvi.2. For Tertullian see *De Praescriptione Haereticorum* xx.

I mention these parallels in church history mainly as an aid to the better understanding of those features of science in which we are here interested. In religion such features are clearly visible for they are regarded as being of paramount importance. A study of religion will therefore school our eyes and make them prepared for the darkness we are about to encounter. The reasons for the better visibility are to be sought in the wider interests of the churchman and of the church historian. Scientists and scientific historians are specialists and their interests are rather narrowly defined. They will therefore be inclined either to overlook, or consciously to abstract from, phenomena which exhibit certain general tendencies of man. Theologians are specialists too, but as their subject-matter is the whole of man they will be much more sensitive towards the changes of doctrine with which we are here concerned. This sensitivity is clearly exhibited by St. Jerome (see above) who in this way makes us understand similar phenomena in the sciences.

For a more detailed examination of the effect of Protestantism on science, see S. F.

It is clear that this marvellous method that turns an obvious weakness (irrational character of the rule of faith) into overpowering strength can work only if the rule does not introduce new and unknown elements. The logical vacuity of the rule is precisely what is needed if it is to fulfil its most important practical function: *to reinforce an already existing faith* (cf. n. 2 (a)). The results of historical research, to mention but one point on which the Romans differed from the Protestants, cannot be foreseen. They may contradict the doctrine and endanger the loyalty of its adherents. It is therefore the wish to preserve party lines that makes it so essential to use a vacuous rule and, to mention another feature of Protestantism that will not be discussed in the present paper, to keep different subjects apart.

Now this process, this use of a vacuous rule of faith in the practical defence of ideas one wants to preserve, is also one of the most characteristic features of classical empiricism. That devils, gods, witches, have all been defended on empirical grounds is well known. However, for the present purpose a brief discussion of Newton's theory of colours is more appropriate.[6]

VI

When speaking of Newton's theory of colours I am referring to what one might call the *ray theory of light*, according to which light consists of rays of different refrangibility and different colour whose inherent properties are not changed, either by refraction, or by reflection, or by any other process, and which produce colours either singly, or by mixture. This theory is to be distinguished from the *corpuscle hypothesis* which Newton also held, and

Mason, "The Scientific Revolution and the Protestant Reformation," *Annals of Science* IX (1953), 64–87, 154–75.
6 In what follows I shall use the text to give an abbreviated and somewhat dramatic account of Newton's philosophy, while I shall use the notes for bringing in details, sources, and for establishing connexions. Up till now the historical literature concerning Newton has been full of the kind of dogmatism he himself tried to put over on his contemporaries and successors. (There were a few exceptions, such as Goethe, but they were mostly regarded as cranks. However, German scientists were put in a difficult position by their joint veneration of their chief poetic father figure and of what they thought was proper scientific method.) For example, it has been taken for granted, almost universally, that Newton established the nature of white light. This situation is now at last changed by the appearance of Dr. Sabra's *Theories of Light from Descartes to Newton* (London, 1967). This, as far as I can see, is the first consistently critical analysis of Newton's optics and the first account that explicitly considers his methodology and its role in the theory of colours. The dominance of Newton over the historians has at last come to an end; in physics this dominance was terminated over a century ago, though there are still some textbooks for which these developments are practically non-existent.

from the further hypothesis that light is a substance, which he occasionally presented as a direct and unique consequence of phenomena.[7]

7 For the ray theory see Newton's first paper on light and colours, *Philosophical Transactions*, no. 80 (1671/72), 3085. This paper and other papers of Newton are quoted from I. B. Cohen, ed., *Isaac Newton's Papers and Letters on Natural Philosophy* (Cambridge, 1958). For the idea that light is a substance see R. S. Westfall, "The Development of Newton's Theory of Colour," *Isis*, LIII (1962), 352. The remainder of Westfall's paper is somewhat too uncritical of Newton's achievements.

Newton's methodological beliefs and prescriptions may be summarized as follows. It is assumed that general propositions, also called *theories*, can be derived from phenomena (see below) "concluding positively and directly," and not only "from a confutation of contrary suppositions" (*Phil. Trans.* [8 July 1672], 4004; Cohen, p. 93); and that they can be "proved" in this manner. This implies a distinction between phenomena (or facts) and theories on the one side, and hypotheses on the other. Theories are related to facts and phenomena in the unique way just described. Hypotheses are invented (if at all) only afterwards, for "*explaining* the properties of things"; they are not "assumed in determining them" (reply to Pardies' second letter, Cohen, p. 106). They must never contradict phenomena or theories. The nature of things, insofar as it shows itself in experiment, and their behaviour, is settled first, and in a unique way. Reasons for this behaviour and this nature are given later, and with the help of hypotheses. (Note how little this last feature differs from the much more "modern" expositions of, say, Nagel, where high-level theories must agree with low-level theories which have been "established in some area of inquiry" [Ernest Nagel, *The Structure of Science* (New York, 1961) p. 338].) See also my exposition and criticism of this book in the *British Journal for the Philosophy of Science* (1966) 237–49. The only difference is one of length. (Newton expressed himself briefly, and to the point.) No hypotheses are needed if the problem is to establish a theory, or a phenomenon – "to dispute about *hypotheses* ... is [then] beside the business at hand" (Cohen, p. 123). It is also implied that while hypotheses are to be judged by theories and phenomena "and those [are] to be rejected which cannot be reconciled with the phenomena" (Cohen, p. 108; cf. Newton's second paper where he asserts that he "gave a reason why all allowable hypotheses [on light] should be conformable to [his] theories" [Cohen, p. 178]), theories can be criticized only by "showing the insufficiency of [the] experiment used ... or by assigning the flaws and defects in [the] conclusions drawn from them" (Cohen, p. 94). (In effect this is again identical with the method entailed by the present theories of reduction and explanation now presented, e.g. by Nagel.) Newton is very emphatic about this *asymmetry* between experimental results and theories on the one side, hypotheses and associated speculation on the other; he finds it "necessary" to start the labour of science by "lay[ing] aside all hypotheses" (Cohen, p. 106) and he emphasizes that even later on considerations of truth and reality must be related to experiment and theories deduced from them and must not be made dependent on the consideration of alternative hypotheses. "For if the possibility of hypotheses is to be the test of truth and reality of things I see not how certainty can be obtained in any science; since numerous hypotheses may be devised which shall seem to overcome new difficulties" (reply to Pardies' second letter, Cohen, p. 106; note that in his reply to Huygens Newton takes the devising of numerous hypotheses "to be no difficult matter" [Cohen, p. 144]).

All these ideas find concise expression in Rule IV of the *Principia*. Newton rewrote this rule various times. Some formulations make clear the connexion with his earlier point of view: "In experimental philosophy one is not to argue from hypotheses against propositions drawn by induction from phenomena. For if arguments from hypotheses are admitted against inductions, then the argument of inductions on which all experimental philosophy is founded could always be overthrown by contrary

The problems of the ray theory as well as the later history of that theory (and of the logically quite different theory of gravitation) have much in common with contemporary argument in microphysics. So great is the similarity that for each relevant feature that needs discussion in the one case a corresponding feature can be found in the other. One might almost say that Newton had anticipated all the arguments which are used today for the defence of the Copenhagen Interpretation. Three things are at issue: the value of a theory; the value of the methodology (of the "rule of faith") on which the theory is allegedly based; the relevance of the methodology and the question whether it leads to a unique determination of the theory. The interest of the debates at the Royal Society and of the later discussions lies in the way in which these three separate items are made to support each other, so that a solid and almost irrefutable bastion of doctrine arises. One soon agrees that Newton's theory is more detailed than the available alternatives and gives a better account of almost everything that is known about light. The possibility of alternatives is still emphasized, but no one is able to go beyond general suggestions. This considerably reduces the psychological weight of the alternatives. Newton's ability to illustrate the basic principles of his theory by simple and ingenious experiments works in the same direction. But Newton goes one step further and regards the illustrations as an experimental basis.

VII

Two identifications are involved in this step. First, the experimental result is identified with what Newton calls a phenomenon, which is an idealized and

hypotheses. If a certain proposition drawn by induction is not yet sufficiently precise, it must be corrected not by hypotheses, but by the phenomena of nature more fully and more accurately observed." See Alexandre Koyré, *Newtonian Studies* (London, 1966), p. 269; for the final formulation see the text to sec. ix. The final version of this rule has influenced the development of modern science down to our own day.

Let us now examine the effect of the combined use of this rule, of a general proposition, and of the assumption that the proposition has been inferred from phenomena, "concluding positively and directly."

The rule and the philosophy on which it rests allow for two modifications of "propositions inferred by general induction from phenomena," or of *theories*, as Newton calls such propositions. They may be made more precise; and they may be made liable to exceptions. In the first case one adds to their informative content; in the second case one subtracts from it by restricting the domain of application. It is assumed that this domain will not shrink to zero. Such a shrinkage would indicate that there are no phenomena from which to derive the theory – a supposition that is at once refuted by a repetition of the relevant experiments. The concepts of the theory which express these phenomena will therefore remain in use forever, and so will all those principles which have been "established in some area of inquiry." For further details see Sabra, ch. ii.

generalized description of the result that *uses the terms of the theory under review*.[8] The idealizations are again of two kinds. First, the peculiarities of

8 In the optical papers and also in the *Opticks* the reference to colours is neither to sensations, nor to properties of everyday objects. It is true that difference of sensation is sometimes taken to indicate difference of physical colours: "Certainly it is much better to believe our senses informing us, that red and yellow are diverse colours" (answer to Hooke, *Phil. Trans.* no. 80, 5088; Cohen, p. 126). But this is not always the case. A distinction is drawn between subjective and objective colours: "I speak here of colours insofar as they arise from light; for they appear sometimes from other causes, as when by the power of phantasy we see colours in a dream" (Sir Isaac Newton, *Opticks* [New York, 1952], p. 160ff; cf. the explicit specification in Prop. vii, Th. v, *Opticks*, p. 1587). Objective colours remain unchanged whereas subjective colours change as a result of mixture: "... when several sorts of rays are mixed, and in crossing pass through the same space, they do not act on one another so as to change each other's colorific qualities ... but in mixing their actions in the sensorium beget a sensation differing from what either would do apart" (*Opticks*, p. 159). It is also emphasized in Newton's answer to Hooke (Cohen, p. 127) and in his reply to Huygens (Cohen, p. 139), that visual colours may have "a double origin, the same colours to sense being in some case compounded, and in others uncompounded." The possibility of "a new kind of white" is considered which, though giving the same impression to the eye as normal sunlight, would yet "have different properties from it" when examined with the prism. Furthermore "there are as many simple ... colours as degrees of refrangibility" (Cohen, p. 140) that is, Aleph One, whereas the number of visible colours is finite, and a small number at that. (The *SCC-NBS Method of Designing Colours*, National Bureau of Standards Circular 553 [Washington, 1955] uses 266 categories with not more than 100 and sometimes as few as one item in each category. Meanings and translations are given for 7500 individual colour names.) We can even give a quite interesting *physical* reason for this disparity between visual colours and physical colours. It lies in the fact that it is impossible to separate perfectly the "primary" or "homogeneal" colours by experiment. This proof, which makes use of the wave theory of light and of the fact that the simple harmonic waves which represent the primary colours in this theory, are of infinite duration, consists in pointing out that any spectrum, however detailed, appears only when the light source is turned on and disappears with it. See R. W. Ditchburn, *Light* (New York, 1963), I, 102. It is obvious then that Newton, when referring to colours, does not and cannot possibly refer to *sensations*.

Nor are the colours properties of everyday objects: "... colours are the quality of light, having its rays for their entire and immediate subject. ... Besides, whoever thought any quality to be a heterogeneous aggregate, such as light is supposed to be...." (Cohen, p. 57) "Colours of objects are nothing but a disposition to reflect this or that sort of ray more copiously than the rest; in the rays they are nothing but their dispositions to propagate this or that motion into the sensorium, and in the sensorium they are sensations of those motions under the form of colours" (*Opticks*, p. 125).

The "simple" or "homogeneal" colours which Newton thought are the ultimate constituents of all fields of radiation are therefore strictly speaking *unobservable*: it is not possible to produce them in a physically pure form (cf. Newton's own *caveat* in Cohen, p. 59, as well as Sir David Brewster's discussion in his *Memoir of the Life, Writings, and Discoveries of Sir Isaac Newton*, I [Edinburgh, 1855], p. 116; cf. also the general proof at the end of the last paragraph but one). Nor would it be possible to distinguish these colours experimentally from an infinite variety of weak mixtures, or disturbances centring around a prominent peak. To present the results of concrete experiments with all their imperfections in a unique form and as *supporting* (and not merely *illustrating*) the ray theory, therefore involves idealizing assumptions which bend the concrete and very complex experimental result in the direction of Newton's each single experiment and those features of it which do not allow for an immediate description in terms of the theory are omitted. This is how the "pyramids" reported by Linus and confirmed by von Helmholtz disappear from sight.[9] (They leave their traces, though, as is seen from the relevant drawings in the *Opticks*, p. 29.) This is also the reason why Brewster (I, 116) thought it necessary to assert that the "homogeneal colours" always contain *all* colours though in vastly different amounts. Newton was well aware of these matters. He gave detailed instructions for the approximate realization ("exhaustion" as Dingler would have said) of what he considered to be the elementary process of colour separation and he pointed out that success could never be complete.[10] At the same time he described the approxi-

theory. "The effect of this 'demonstration,'" writes Sabra (p. 249), "is, it must be admitted, almost hypnotic. Nevertheless it is certainly inconclusive." See also Westfall, pp. 351ff, as well as T. S. Kuhn in Cohen, pp. 34ff: "Newton combined a precise and detailed description of his experimental apparatus with an imaginative idealization of his experimental results." Cf. also the next two footnotes. The soporific influence which this method still exerts upon contemporary historians can be seen from some of the reviews of Dr. Sabra's book (such as Westfall's).

9 Linus pointed out in criticizing Newton that the spectrum was never capped by "semi-circular" ends but rather terminated in a "sharp cone or pyramis" (Cohen, p. 151). Kuhn remarks, quite correctly, that Newton never replied to this criticism. Newton could well afford to do so as he was never quite definite about the semicircularity. In his first paper he writes as follows: "... the decay of light was so gradual, that it was difficult to determine justly what was their figure; yet they seemed semi-circular" (Cohen, p. 48). Even in the later *Opticks* he still writes that "at its sides [the spectrum] was bounded pretty distinctly, but on its ends very confusedly and indistinctly, the light there decaying and vanishing by degrees" (*Opticks*, p. 29). His description of what is seen, including the drawings, is therefore unexceptionable. But if this description were regarded as the description of a *phenomenon*, that is, as a description of what the *physical light* does under certain circumstances, then Newton's theory would have to be regarded as refuted. The transition from what is seen to the phenomenon in Newton's sense (see below, n. 11) is therefore completely unaccounted for. We know today the reason why pyramids are *seen* even if the *physical light* should happen to terminate in a semi-circle (see H. L. F. von Helmholtz, *Physiological Optics*, ed. and trans. J. P. C. Southall [Rochester, 1924], I, 173). We may suspect that Newton, who also dealt with the physiology of sight, had an explanation of this kind in mind. However, he did not give the explanation but simply redescribed what he saw in order to turn it into a physically useful phenomenon. And in this redescription he introduced the machinery of the very same theory he wanted to prove. Goethe's question, "for how should it be possible to hope for progress if what is inferred, guessed, or merely believed to be the case, can be put over on us as a fact?" addresses itself to this feature of the theory. See Ipsen, ed., *Farbenlehre* (Leipzig, 1927), p. 393. Dr. Sabra (and, of course, Professor Ronchi) apart, I do not know of a single historian of science whose critical sense matches Goethe's in this connection. For Ronchi's view see the quotation at the end of n. 11. Sabra's critical attitude may be explained as a result of his interest in "pure philosophy" (among other things he attended Sir Karl Popper's seminar at the London School of Economics in 1952, where I first had the pleasure of meeting him).

10 Each experiment which Newton produces in order to demonstrate the value, and even the uniqueness of his theory (see note 7 for a brief outline of this feature of Newton's

mations in a manner suggesting that complete separation had been achieved, thus greatly diminishing the distance between "nature" and his theory.

Secondly, not all experiments are given equal weight. Those whose distance from the theory is minimal and which seem to be a visible expression of its basic principles are preferred to others which do not allow us to read the theory in them at one glance. Thus the different refrangibility of rays of light is demonstrated in the most convicing fashion by the *experimentum crucis*. "Now if this demonstration be good, *there needs no further examination of the thing* ... and seeing I am well assured of the truth and exactness of my own observations, I shall be unwilling to be diverted by any other experiment from having a fair end of this made in the first place" (Cohen, p. 174). Phenomena, then, are *selected* and *idealized* experiments whose features correspond point for point to the peculiarities of the theory to be proved.[11]

methodology) is to be regarded as a more or less effective "realization of an elementary process" in the sense of Hugo Dingler. See the latter's *Methode der Physik* (München, 1938), esp. p. 146 where the realization of the "elementary process" of gravitation is discussed. Newton himself has described the manner in which "the elementary process of colour separation" might be realized and has indicated the obstacles lying in the way of such realization: p. 3087 of no. 80 of the *Phil. Trans.* (1671/72). Dingler's investigations, which unfortunately are not very popular today, deserve detailed study especially in connection with Galileo's and Newton's use of experiment. See also his interesting and challenging book *Das Experiment* (München, 1928).

That the experiments of Galileo are illustrations rather than evidence has been shown most convincingly by the late Professor N. R. Hanson. See his "Galileo's Discoveries in Dynamics," *Science*, CXLVII (1965), 471–78.

That the same is true of Newton's experiments becomes evident from the fact, to be mentioned presently, that Newton did not ascribe equal importance to all experiments involving colour, no matter how carefully they were devised. "As others had tailored the experiment to their needs, so also Newton tailored it to his" (Westfall, p. 351). This becomes especially clear from his reply to Lucas, quoted in the text below. Lucas had provided what Newton had invited everyone to do, viz., "other experiments which directly contradict[ed him]" (Queries, Cohen, p. 94). He was thanked for that as the "first who has sent me an experimental examination" (reply to Lucas, Cohen, p. 173). But he was also advised to "change a little the method which he has propounded, and instead of a multitude of things try only the *experimentum crucis*. For it is not the number of [in the present case, different] experiments but weight to be regarded; and where one will do, what need many? ... The main thing he goes about to examine is, *the different refrangibility* of Light. And this I demonstrated in the *experimentum crucis*. Now if this demonstration be good, there needs no further examination of the thing ... Let that experiment therefore be examined in the first place." (Cohen, p. 174) The point of the quotation is that there are experiments which clearly exhibit the basic principles under dispute whereas others are only remotely connected with them. It is interesting to consider that Newton seems to have been led to this classification of experiments by the very same mechanical philosophy he tried to replace later by his own point of view (Westfall, p. 351).

11 It follows that phenomena have the logical status of *laws*. This conjecture is confirmed by a look at the *Principia* where all of Kepler's laws are found among the phenomena. And the optical "phenomena" too do not merely express what occurs in a single

It is clear that one should rather regard them as illustrations of special consequences of that theory.[12]

experiment, but what emerges in all experiments of a certain kind. This feature enables Newton to make good his promise (cf. n. 7) to derive (other) laws from them. For although the derivation of laws from singular statements is a problematic affair (Hume's problem!), the derivation of laws from general statements is not. (Hume's arguments are therefore irrelevant for a criticism of Newton.)

Now what we have said so far, while essentially correct, gives only a rough account of Newton's procedure. The next step would consist in pointing out that not only theories but also the so-called phenomena themselves are "made liable to exceptions" (cf. n. 7, reference Rule IV as well as the formulation of this rule in the text, sec. ix).

These exceptions are mentioned in the very beginning. Thus in stating Phenomenon VI of Book III of the *Principia*: "that the moon, by a radius drawn to the earth's center, describes an area proportional to the time of description" Newton comments: "It is true that the motion of the moon is a little disturbed by the actions of the sun; but in laying down these phenomena, I shall neglect those small and inconsiderable errors" (*Principia*, p. 405). For this and other references to Newton's *Principia* see Sir Isaac Newton, *Mathematical Principles of Natural Philosophy*, trans. A. Motte, ed. and rev. by Florian Cajori (Berkeley, 1960). Phenomenon V reads that "the areas which the primary planets describe by radii drawn to the sun are proportional to the times of description" (*Principia*, p. 405), while a few pages later we are informed "that the action of Jupiter upon Saturn is not to be neglected ... and hence arises a perturbation of the orbit of Saturn in every conjunction of this planet with Jupiter, that astronomers are puzzled with it" (*Principia*, p. 421). This separation of phenomenon and actual *fact* and the definition of phenomena with the help of theory completely reverses the position expressed in Newton's methodology as outlined in n. 7. For the exceptions which are observed are now accounted for by the very same theory that is derived from the phenomena as stated without the exceptions (Hegel seems to have been the only thinker to appreciate correctly this feature of Newton's procedure; see his *Encyclopaedie der Philosophischen Wissenschaften*, ed. C. von Lasson [Leipzig, 1920], pp. 235ff). Used in this way phenomena are no longer a basis of knowledge but they are *conjectures* put forth in accordance either with some rule of simplicity or with the theory to be demonstrated (this difference between basic methodology and procedure corresponds to the difference between critical practice and dogmatic ideology outlined in sec. I).

We get here a very clear insight into the function of phenomena in actual research. Originally (Kepler) they formed theoretical conclusions of an elaborate analysis of observational data. In the *Principia* they form part of an argument leading back and forth between the actual observations, which now contain the deviations from Kepler's laws, and the new point of view of Newton. However, they are arbitrarily separated from the remainder of the argument and given special importance so that a vacuous rule of faith may with their help lend additional support to this point of view. It is a marvellous accident, worthy of an equally marvellous explanation, that this way of building up the theory of gravitation did not create a miserable patchwork but instead a coherent system that astounds us by its simplicity and its effectiveness in the mastery of concrete phenomena. We shall see very soon (text below) that light did not submit to this procedure quite as readily. What we obtain here is a system that has been called, and not without justification, "an incoherent and uncertain theory, a theory so full of contradictions and lacunae that one is surprised to see to what extent it could convince the majority of the physicists of the 18th century" (V. Ronchi, *Histoire de la Lumière*, trans. from the Italian by J. Taton [Paris, 1956], p. 191).

12 This and other features to be given presently make it clear that Newton's method must be described as a *conventionalism* with illustrations. The selective attitude towards experiments also establishes a relation to Einstein who refused to let his appraisal of a

VIII

The second identification is between phenomena and what the empirical rule of faith regards as the foundation of all empirical knowledge, that is experience. We see here again how necessary is the vacuity of the experimental philosophy whose support is enlisted by the two identifications (cf. above, secs. IV, V). All that is known about experience is that it is something that springs to the eye, that it is a "divine illumination," this time not by God, and not through the mind, but by Nature, and through the senses; but which guarantees success. It is therefore again quite easy to turn part of the new theory into its own foundation by first presenting selected phenomena in its terms and by then pronouncing these phenomena, these well-illustrated pieces of the theory, to be the experience that has proved the theory "positively and directly [and not only] from the confutation of contrary suppositions" (queries of 8 July 1672, Cohen, p. 93).

IX

Both identifications go almost unnoticed. Hooke, for example, Newton's main opponent, "regards the phenomena described as facts which leads to much silent advantage for Newton." And now the development is as follows: Those interested in light familiarize themselves with the phenomena, that is with the basic principles of the theory. The detailed manner in which Newton develops this theory allows them to apply it to natural processes also. Everything is now being seen in terms of rays being separated, reunited, absorbed, reflected, but never changed in their intrinsic quality. The theory, then, is very successful. Considering the general attitude of the Royal Society it is quite natural to relate this success to the empirical rule of faith: the theory is successful because the rule has been obeyed.[13] Conversely, obeying the rule gives results and advances knowledge. Attacks upon the theory are soon answered by pointing out how firmly it rests on experimental fact. Attacks upon empiricism are answered by quoting the successes of the empirical rule of faith such as the theory of colours and the theory of gravitation. A little later one altogether ceases to discuss attacks of this kind,

theory be influenced by "verification through little effect[s]." See G. Holton, "Influences on Einstein's Early Work," *Organon*, III (1966), 242.

13 Ipsen, p. 614. "The Society," writes Goethe, "had hardly come into existence as Newton was received into it, in his thirtieth year of age. Yet how he was able to introduce his theory into a circle of men who were most definitely averse to theories, this is an investigation well worthy of a historian."

one simply shrugs them off as further examples of the paradoxes created by armchair philosophers. And so the delicate collaboration between a vague rule of faith and an increasingly popular doctrine has again created a bastion that can withstand the strongest attack.

But Newton is still not content. The bastion must be defended even more strongly by making outside attacks impossible in principle. This is done with the help of the famous Rule IV of the *Principia*: "In experimental philosophy we are to look upon propositions inferred by general induction from phenomena as accurate, or very nearly true *notwithstanding any contrary hypothesis that may be imagined* [italics mine] till such time as other phenomena occur by which they may either be made more accurate, or liable to exceptions" (*Principia*, p. 400). The importance of the italicized clause becomes clear when we now compare the ray theory with the only developed alternative which existed in Newton's life time, *Huygens' wave theory*.

X

According to Newton the wave theory is unacceptable because it cannot explain the rectilinear propagation of light: "For me the fundamental supposition [of the wave theory] in itself seems impossible; namely, that the *waves* or vibrations of a fluid can, like the rays of light, be propagated in straight lines, without a continual and very extraordinary spreading and bending every way into the quiescent medium, when they are terminated by it."[14] This attitude is retained despite the phenomena of diffraction that Newton has described in detail. The rationale that in these cases the "bending is not towards, but from the shadow" (*Opticks*, Query XXVIII) is strange seeing that Newton himself reports a bending into the shadow, in his communication of 1675, quarrelling here with Hooke about the peculiar explanation he proposes (the light is refracted by the aether which surrounds the obstacle in a thin layer). The same quarrel appears in the *Opticks* (pp. 325–27). However, the method to let basic principles be decided not indiscriminately, by every and any experiment, but by paradigmatic cases which visibly demonstrate the truth of the theory, helps us over this difficulty. Having established, both by the *experimentum crucis* and by the swift disappearance

14 Reply to Hooke. The waves which Newton uses to explain interference and which some authors have regarded as evidence that he held a wave theory also are never identified with light but are explicitly regarded as *separate entities* which interact with light. Cf. the paper of 1675.

of fixed stars behind the moon (*Opticks*, Query XXVIII) that light consists of rays, he now accounts for diffraction by additional assumptions, adding "new original properties ... besides those already described" (Query XXV).

This procedure is indistinguishable from the framing of *ad hoc* hypotheses. It is especially helpful in the case of mirror images which the ray theory, taken by itself, fails to explain: "If light were reflected by impinging upon the solid parts of the glass it would be scattered as much by the most polished glass as by the roughest" (*Opticks*, p. 266; also Query XXXI). In the paper of 1675 we read the hypothesis that the aether leaking beyond the roughly aligned atoms of the mirror provides a smooth surface – which fits ill the aversion to hypotheses shown on other occasions (cf. n. 7). In the *Opticks* "the reflection of a ray is effected, not by a single point of the body, but by some power ... which is evenly diffused all over the surface and by which it acts upon the ray without immediate contact" (cf. above) – which is just a description ("soporific power"!) of the fact of mirror images in terms of the ray theory. We see here very clearly how Newton preserves basic assumptions that readily lend themselves to illustrative demonstration with the help of "new original properties", that is, *ad hoc* hypotheses.

A method like this, which starts from a paradigmatic case and adds new assumptions as soon as it appears that the theory expressing the paradigm is in difficulty, will not easily discover "other phenomena by which [the theory] ... may be made ... liable to exceptions" (Rule IV, *Principia*, p. 400) *unless* one is allowed to do what Rule IV explicitly forbids, namely, to "imagine contrary hypotheses" (for example, the wave theory).

XI

A simple look at this theory suffices to replace the success story of the ray theory by a very different tale. The wave theory, too, has its paradigmatic experiments which exhibit its principles at once, and with only a minimum of abstraction and generalization: the phenomena of refraction and reflection follow from this theory as swiftly and as naturally as the *experimentum crucis* follows from Newton's account. Applying the method of modification by addition, suggested by Newton, we can explain rectilinear propagation in a way that involves no new idea and is much more satisfactory than is Newton's account of mirror images and diffraction: the partial waves which spread outside the cone of propagation "do not concur at the same time to compose a wave"; these parts are therefore "too feeble to produce light; "whence one sees the reason why light ... spreads only in straight lines, so that it illuminates no object except when the path from its source to that object is open along such lines."[15] Polarization needs no "new original properties" but is a feature of the basic (transversal) process itself. Moreover, this basic process also suffices for explaining diffraction. It therefore already contains three fundamental properties of light (reflection, refraction, and polarization) and provides means for calculating the others. Looking back from this success (which occurred much later, in the nineteenth century) to the original paradigm (mirror images) as well as to some more recondite phenomena such as diffraction we now realize that these phenomena not merely add "new original properties" to the ray theory but also refute it while the rectilinear propagation of light, if taken together with diffraction, lends support to the wave theory. This story is very different from Newton's claim to have finally established the basic assumption of the ray theory. (Note that we do not proceed here beyond the facts which were known to Newton himself.)

XII

Now it is exactly this kind of criticism that is excluded by the italicized clause of Rule IV. The criticism can be articulated only if we are allowed to view the success of Newton's theory in the light of "contrary hypotheses," and if we are permitted to elaborate and entertain such hypotheses despite their *prima facie* implausibility. If, on the other hand, we follow Rule IV to the letter, then contrary hypotheses will not be used and the criticism cannot arise.[16] Quite the contrary, one will be able to point to the magnificent success of the theories which have been developed with the help of the rule. One will be able to point out that Rule IV does not lead to stagnation. The scientists who adopt it heap discovery upon discovery and continually expand the domain of knowledge. This is a strong argument in favour of the rule and in favour of all the theories supported by it.

This argument, of course, cannot really satisfy us, for just as in the case of Protestantism the success of the chosen theories is entirely man-made. It is due to the fact that the psychological result of a complex process of indoctrination was turned into a basis. In the case of Protestantism the basis supports a faith. Here it supports a scientific theory which is constantly

15 Huygens, *Treatise on light*, trans. S. Thompson (New York, 1962), p. 16.
16 Rule IV therefore corresponds to condition (2), sec. III.

being expanded by the addition of *ad hoc* hypotheses (this is what the "success" of the theory really amounts to). In both cases we are dealing with nothing but a party line.

XIII

Let us reconsider what we have discovered so far. We have discovered that the rejection of authority, of tradition, of the results of speculation, which is such a characteristic explicit feature both of Protestantism and of the empiricism of Bacon, does not lead to a more critical attitude. It leads to the enthroning of new authorities which demand slavish attention – scripture on the one side, experience on the other. We have also discovered that the rules of faith which introduce the new authorities are vacuous. We have seen how the very vacuity of the rules makes them excellent allies in the defence of partisan ideas. Following the demand for an authoritative foundation such ideas are first made plausible. They are then based upon their own most plausible parts and are justified thereby. In the case of Protestantism the plausible parts are the intuitions resulting from a strict and merciless education. In the case of empiricism the plausible parts are those elements of a theory which can be readily illustrated by experiment. The physical stability of those experiments is then seen as proof of the stability of the experience recommended by the rule of faith. This is the main feature of the classical empiricism that forms the subject of the present note. But illustrations are not evidence. Intuition is no objective guarantee. Physical stability of a piece of matter must not be confounded with epistemological certainty. A method that first makes an idea familiar, either by frequent repetition, or by illustration, and that later on uses this plausibility as if it were an additional source of support, is not different from political propaganda, and ideas thus defended are, as we have said, indistinguishable from *party lines*.

XIV

Now this situation, apparently quite deplorable, actually constitutes a tremendous step ahead of the preceding philosophical views. For while the vacuity of the new rules of faith allows circular defence of ideas which have achieved a certain notoriety, it also guarantees that no particular idea is preferred. Any idea can now be presented in a manner that makes it acceptable and capable of winning followers. Of course, there will always be some views which are in the foreground and which try to demonstrate their uniqueness, while others are not yet sufficiently developed and familiar to attract attention. This, however, is only a psychological disadvantage. Given time, colourful and persistent defenders, surprising successes or sham-successes, and satisfaction of special interests, the support of the rules of faith may be enlisted for a quite different philosophy. This very neutrality shows that they are but an ornament, surrounding whatever convictions we possess and presenting these convictions, our own fallible products, in an objective manner, as if they had their origin in and derived their importance from an independent and not human source. The fact that we are dealing with party lines is therefore not really a drawback. Quite the contrary – party lines play a most important role in many civilized institutions, such as in the democratic process, in the process of trial by a competition of opposing opinions which allows examination of the most fundamental assumption and the most convincing expert testimony, and so on. In the last case, the creation of additional party lines, of "contrary hypotheses," is even *demanded* by the law as a means of seeing in the proper perspective a theory or some expert testimony which, taken by itself, would seem to be totally invincible (remember the ray theory!). Party lines are not the problem. Problems arise only when the attempt is made to turn the *subjective* conviction that makes a particular party line stand out into an infallible *objective* judge who withstands criticism and demands that his dictum be obeyed. Classical empiricism which adopts this procedure has not yet completely overcome its even more restricted ancestry. But the democratic way in which praise, blame, and dogmaticism are now distributed, and the humanitarian way in which the word of a clever man is taken seriously, even *too* seriously, allow us to greet it as the dawn of an even more enlightened future.